Lean Guide

How successful Entrepreneurs improve Productivity, Quality and Profits applying 3 lean methods: Six Sigma, Startup, Enterprise to get Competitive Advantages and Continuous Innovations.

Jack Lead

This guide is divided into 3 sections:

- Lean Startup
- Lean Enterprise
- Lean Six Sigma

Each of these will deal in depth with the Lean methodology and how to apply it effectively in corporate management.

Jack Lead

Section 1: Lean Startup............8

Chapter 1.   What Is Lean Start Up?.......................15

Chapter 2.   Lean Startup Models.........................25

Chapter 3.   The 5 Principles of Lean Startup Method. 38

Chapter 4.   Why Do Most Startup Fail?...................45

Chapter 5.   Create a Useful Lean Startup Experiment
....50

Chapter 6.   Introducing The Lean Startup Method
Foreword..56

Chapter 7.   Difference Between Lean Startup and
Traditional Startup..............................70

Chapter 8.   The Lean Startup Technology in Action...84

Chapter 9.   What Is Lean Analytics?.....................90

Chapter 10. Lean Analytics to Succeed...................95

Chapter 11. Benefits and Criticisms....................102

Chapter 12. The Lean Analytics Stages.................107

Chapter 13. Types of Metrics...........................110

Chapter 14. How to Recognize a Good Metric.........115

Chapter 15. Automatize the Company Thanks to the
Analytics..119

Chapter 16. Case Studies of the Lean Startup
            Method..124

Chapter 17. Lean Startup Advantages...................129

Chapter 18. Whom The Lean Method Is Not Made
            For 135

Chapter 19. Managing The Threat of Competition ...139

Conclusions 144

Section 2: Lean Enterprise..........148

Charter 20. What is Lean Enterprise?....................153

Chapter 21. What are the Advantages?..................161

Chapter 22. Why Lean Matters............................175

Chapter 23. Creating A Lean System....................184

Chapter 24. The 5 Principles of Lean Manufacturing..189

Chapter 25. The Types of Waste..........................194

Chapter 26. What Are the 5S's and How They Work. 200

Chapter 27. Applying The Lean Method..................210

Chapter 28. Lean Thinking................................226

Chapter 29. The 7 Principles of Lean Thinking........232

Chapter 30. Kaizen..238

Chapter 31. Six Sigma....................................242

Chapter 32. Deciding If Six Sigma Is Right For Your
Company..251

Chapter 33. Methodology of Lean and Six Sigma......263

Chapter 34. The Motorola Case...........................277

Chapter 35. How to Harness Lean to Foster Innovation
and Develop New Ideas......................278

Chapter 36. How to Foster Learning and
Experimentation through Lean............284

Conclusions 291

Section 3: Lean Six Sigma............292

Chapter 37. What is the Lean Six Sigma Method?....298

Chapter 38. Introducing Lean Production................307

Chapter 39. Introducing Six Sigma......................313

Chapter 40. Why You Should Use the Lean Six Sigma
Method..315

Chapter 41. Benefits of Six Sigma........................322

Chapter 42. The Lean Six Sigma Method................328

Chapter 43. Improving Customer Satisfaction..........338

Chapter 44. The 5 DMAIC Phases........................345

Chapter 45. Lean Six Sigma Implementation
Method..352

Chapter 46. Tools to Use with Six Sigma.................363

Chapter 47. Lean Six Sigma Certification.................372

Chapter 48. Lean Six Sigma Certification Levels.......384

Chapter 49. Criticality of the Lean Six Sigma
            Method..396

Chapter 50. Why Companies Are Not Taking
            Advantage of Lean Six Sigma..............401

Chapter 51. How to Embark on Implementing Lean
            Six Sigma......................................408

Chapter 52. Why Use Lean Six Sigma Systems For
            Your Small Business?......................415

Chapter 53. The Six Sigma Infrastructure.............425

Conclusion 436

Section 1: Lean Startup

The Lean Startup vision presents a strategy for building a tech product. Simply speaking, a little Startup is really a low-burn technology venture that unites the customer advancement plan along with an agile software development program.

Eric Ries and his site 'Lessons Learned' offer insights about how best to construct a Lean Startup. A recent demonstration in Eric Ries' on Lean start-ups at the Stanford University's Entrepreneurship Corner explains his way to creating a tech product. In his pragmatic perspective about just how best to incorporate customer development with agile software development, " he recommends a method using two teams. The cross-functional problem team always validates the situation theory and upgrades the item theory, whereas the clear answer team utilizes an agile software development methodology to construct the item from the product or service idea.

The Pivot

A key facet to almost any startup is defining exactly the situation it attempts to address. Customer growth urges a cross-functional problem team which invisibly functions together with clients and always defines and adjusts the situation theory.

The systematic method of consumer development produces a string of invalidated problem hypotheses. At every iteration, the team adapts one particular part of this hypothesis which comprises, among others, customer segments, feature group and placement. Each switch builds up on the lessons learned in supporting the prior problem hypotheses. The pivot indicates the change of strategy of a startup in relation for example to the positioning of its product or service on the market or changes to the product itself to make it more interesting to customers. The vision of this start-up guarantees a coherent management despite lots of incremental alterations to this item idea. From the lack of a solid vision, incremental changes can direct the product theory to some random direction.

A pivot is really a structured path correction built to try a fresh basic concept about this item, strategy, and engine of growth. A prominent illustration of a business utilizing the pivot is Group on; once the business started, it had been an online activism stage known as the Point. After receiving nearly no grasp, the founders started a WordPress site and started their own very first voucher promotion to get a pizzeria situated inside their construction lobby. Even though they just received 20 redemptions, the creators realized that their idea had been significant, and had empowered visitors to organize team actions. Three decades later, Group on would grow to a billion-dollar enterprise.

Steve Blank defines pivot as "changing (and sometimes even shooting) the master plan rather than the executive (the earnings exec, promotion or maybe the CEO).

The Minimum Viable Product

Deciding when and what to send to clients is an integral part of a venture. As a result of very limited funds, startups are made to discover the minimum feature set needed to participate.

Eric asserts that startup teams regularly violate the minimum feature determined by a significant margin and also that the ideal strategy is to split that initial pair down a few times. Shipping the minimum group of features can create unexpected results from the buyer base.

Despite a restricted feature set, customer could actually be contented with the sent features. Visionary clients are extremely forgiving since they do not just buy in to the present product but also the vision of this startup. What's more, the opinion of the team on required features might not be exactly matched with the consumer's needs. While in the worst instance, clients provide their feedback regarding which features are overlooking to supply a value proposition for them.

By focusing to the minimal workable solution, start-ups avoid the error to build something that no one wants. By engaging with the aim area in early stages, the Client Growth methodology offers more information on building an item for some engaged clients rather than attempting to create an item from the beginning for everybody.

A Minimum viable product (MVP) is the "variant of a brand new product that permits a team to amass the most level of confirmed learning about clients together with minimum attempt" (like a pilot experimentation). The objective of an MVP will be always to examine fundamental business enterprise hypotheses (or even Leap-of-faith assumptions) also to help entrepreneurs begin the educational process as swiftly as achievable.

As for instance, Ries noticed that Zappos creator Nick Swinmurn desired to examine the hypothesis that clients were willing and ready to purchase shoes on line. Rather than building a site and also a massive database of apparel, Swinmurn approached local shoe stores, shot images of their inventory, published the images on the web, bought the shoes out of the stores at top dollar after he had made them available online, then shipped them directly to the costumers.

Swinmurn warned that customer demand was present and continuos, and that's how Zappos grew to become a billion dollar industry even thanks to online shoe sales.

Split Testing

A Split or A/B evaluation is a test by which different variants of something are provided to clients at precisely the exact same moment. The objective of a split up test is always to detect differences in behavior between the two classes and also to assess the effects of each variation in an incremental metric. A/B testing is occasionally erroneously achieved in consecutive mode, in which a set of user's week can see 1 variation of this product whilst the in a few days users view still another. (a set of users can see variation A and then some time later another set can see variation B). This undermines the statistical validity of their results, since external events can influence user behavior. For example, a split evaluation of 2 flavors of ice cream performed consecutively during the hot and cold seasons could observe a marked reduction in popularity (mainly due to the season and not to the taste).

Actionable metrics

All these have been compared to dressing table metrics—dimensions that offer the rosiest picture possible but don't accurately reflect the essential drivers of a business enterprise. Vanity metrics for a single company could be actionable metrics to get the next. By way of instance, an organization focusing on creating online dashboards for financial markets could view the amount of internet page views per person for a vanity as their revenue isn't predicated on amount of page views. But, an internet magazine with advertisements will view webpage viewpoints because site perspectives are directly linked to earnings.

A Normal instance of a vanity is that the amount of users that are new gained each day. While a large amount of users gained daily looks favorable for almost any organization, in the event the price of acquiring each user through costly advertising campaigns is somewhat higher compared to the revenue gained each user (generated by each new user), subsequently gaining more users can quickly cause bankruptcy.

Build-Measure-Learn

The Build-Measure-Learn loop highlights rate as a crucial element to merchandise development. A team or company's potency is dependent on its capacity to ideate, fast build a minimal workable product of this idea, quantify its own efficacy on the current market, and also study out of this experimentation. To put it differently, it's really a learning practice of turning ideas into products, measuring clients' responses and behaviors contrary to assembled services and products, and deciding whether to persevere or throw the idea; this technique repeats as often as required. The stages of this loop are: Suggestions → Construct → Merchandise → Quantify → Data → Learn.

This rapid iteration makes it possible for teams to detect a viable path towards product/market fit, and also to keep on maximizing and optimizing the company version after attaining product/market fit.

Lean Canvas

The Lean Canvas can be really a version of this Company Model Canvas accommodated by Ash Maurya in 2010 designed for startups. The Lean Canvas is targeted on fixing broad customer issues and solutions and bringing them into customer sections through an exceptional value proposition. "Problem" and "solution" cubes replace the "key partners" and also "key tasks" cubes in the Company Model Canvas, whereas "key metrics" and "unfair advantage" cubes replace the "key tools" and "customer relationships" cubes, respectively.

The Lean Concept

Lean startup principle are employed to certain competencies within average startups and larger businesses:

- Lean Analytics
- Lean Brand Management
- Lean Hardware
- Lean Events
- Lean Manufacturing
- Lean Marketing
- Lean Product Management
- Lean Sales
- Lean Software Development
- Lean UX
- Lean Information

Chapter 1. What Is Lean Start Up?

While the idea of the Lean Startup has been around since 2011, many companies are still coming to grips with everything the system has to offer. This is despite the fact that most of the ideas presented in this system were hardly new. This is largely due to the fact that the system actually offers more value to established organizations than it does to startups. However, startups can still be able to build a Lean system from the ground up if they choose to.

Lean Startup Methodology

Build, measure, and learn: Perhaps more than anything else in recent history, the application of the scientific method to demolish uncertainty, where innovation is concerned, has transformed the way breakthroughs happen. Broken down, this includes the process of defining a hypothesis, creating a prototype to test the hypothesis, testing the prototype (and thus the hypothesis) and then adjusting as needed. While this may seem simple, it has the potential to generate massive results by enabling companies to take risks on smaller ideas without breaking the bank in the process.

It can be used to test things like customer service ideas, the process of managerial review, or even a new feature for an existing product or service. As long as you can perform a test that clearly validates or disproves the initial hypothesis, then you will be good to go because you must be able to gather enough data to justify approving or vetoing the idea.

The goal, then, is to do everything possible in order to ensure that build, measure, and learn process proceeds from start to finish as quickly as possible. This will make it feasible to run the process multiple times if needed, while also making it clear when such additional runs are needed. As such, it is important to have a very specific idea for each test because as more variables are added, the more difficult it will be to determine results with any real degree of accuracy. When it comes to products and services, this means determining if they are either wanted or needed by the target audience.

Minimal viable product: Generally speaking, most product development involves an extreme amount of work up front. The process involves working through the full specifications of the product, as well as a significant initial investment when it comes to capital in order to build and test multiple iterations of the product. The Lean Startup process thus encourages building only enough of the product in question to make it through a single round of the build, measure, and learn process at a time. This is what is known as the minimal variable product.

The minimal variation of the product is what enables a full cycle of the build, measure, and learn loop to be completed with the least amount of required time and effort on the part of the team. This may not be something as simple as writing a new line of code, it could be an elaborate process that outlines the customer journey, or a complete set of mockups made out of a cheaper substitute. As long as it is enough to test the hypothesis, then it is good to go.

Validated Learning: An important part of the Lean Startup process is ensuring that you are testing your hypothesis with an eye towards the right metrics. Failing to do so can make it easy to focus on vanity metrics instead. Focusing on vanity metrics may make you feel as though you are making progress while not actually telling you all that much about the value of the product. For example, for Facebook, the vanity metrics are the things like the total number of "Likes" that have been received or the number of total accounts created. The real meat and potatoes are in metrics such as the amount of time the average user spends on the service per week. Early on, the metric that validated the company's initial hypothesis was the fact that more than half its user base came back to the service every single day.

Innovation accounting: Innovation accounting is what makes it possible for startups of all sizes to prove, in an objective way, that they are creating a sustainable business. The process includes three steps, starting with determining the baseline. This involves taking the minimum viable product and doing what you can to determine relevant datapoints that can be referred back to the fact. This could involve things like a pure marketing test to determine if there is actually interest from customers. This, in turn, will make it possible for you to determine a baseline with which to compare the initial cycle of the build, measure, and learn process, too. While better numbers are always desired, poor numbers at this stage aren't terribly important, it only means that the team will have more work to do in the build, measure, and learn cycle.

After the baseline has been determined, the next step is going to be to make the first change to determine what can actually be improved upon. While this certainly makes the entire process take longer than it usually does, making too many changes at once makes it difficult to determine which one of the changes led to the biggest improvement. However, if you have a lot of potential changes to test, you can then test them in groups so when something pops, you will only have to retest a specific range in order to see what caused the inspiration to strike.

Once several build, measure, and learn cycles have been completed, the product should be well on its way from moving from the initial starting point to the final, ideal phase. At some point, however, if things don't seem to be proceeding according to plan, then the question becomes whether it is better to pivot to something new or to stick with the current baseline a while longer to see what improves. The choice between the two should be relatively obvious at this point based on the data provided up to this point.

If the decision is ultimately made to pivot at this point, then it can be quite demoralizing for the team because this means going back to square one, albeit with additional data to draw on in the future. Nevertheless, issues such as vanity metrics or a flawed hypothesis can lead teams down a path that is ultimately not viable. This scenario leaves them no choice but to tear it all down and start again with an alternate hypothesis and a clean slate. It is important to try and reframe the idea of a pivot from a failure to a success because it saved the startup from potentially taking a flawed product to market and paying in a big way further down the line.

There are a few additional types of pivots as well. A Pivot that zooms in is one that takes a signal successful feature of a failed prototype and turns it into its entirely own product. A zoom out pivot, on the other hand, is when a failed prototype is useful enough to become a feature on something larger and more complicated.

The customer segment pivot occurs when the prototype proves solid, but the target audience proves to be different than anticipated. A customer need pivot occurs when it becomes clear that a more pressing problem for the customer exists, so a new product needs to be created to handle it.

A platform pivot occurs when a single application becomes so successful that it spawns an entire related ecosystem. A business architecture pivot occurs when a business switches from having low volume and high margins to high volume and low margins. A value capture pivot is one of the most extreme as it involves restructuring the entire business to generate value in a new way. The engine of growth pivot occurs when the profit structure of the startup changes to keep pace with demand.

Small batches: When given the option to fill a large number of envelopes with newsletters before sending them out, the common approach is to do each step in batches, fold the newsletters, place them in the envelopes, etc. However, this is actually less efficient than doing each piece by itself first, thanks to a concept known as single piece flow, a tenant of Lean manufacturing. In this instance, individual performance is not as important as the overall performance of the system. Time is said to be wasted between each step because things need to be reorganized. If the entire process is looking at a single batch, then efficiency is improved.

Yet another benefit to smaller batches is that it is easier to spot an error in the midst of them. For example, if an error was found in the way the envelopes were folded once all the newsletters had been folded, then that entire step would need to be repeated, adding even more time to the process. On the contrary, a small batch approach would determine this error the first time all the steps were completed.

Andon cord: The Andon Cord was used by Toyota to allow any employee on the production line to halt the entire system if a defect was discovered at any point. While this is a lot of power to give to every team member on the floor, it makes sense as the longer a defect continues through the process, the more difficult and costlier it will eventually be to remove. As such, spotting and calling attention to the problem as quickly as possible is the more efficient choice, even if it means stopping the entire production line until the issue is fixed.

Continuous deployment: Continuous deployment is one of the most difficult Lean Startup processes for many companies to deal with as it means constantly updating live production systems each and every day until they reach an ideal state. The ability to learn directly from customers is essential in this scenario as it is one of the primary competitive advantages that startups possess.

Kanban: This is another part of the process that is taken directly from Lean manufacturing. Kanban has four different states. The first of which is the backlog which includes the items that are ready to be worked on but have not yet been actively started on. Next is in progress, which is all of the items that were currently under development. From there, things move to build after development has finished and all the major work has been done so that it is essentially ready for the customer. Finally, the item is validated by a positive review from the customer.

A good rule of thumb is that each of the four stages, also known as buckets, should contain more than three different projects at a time. If a project has been built, for example, it cannot then move into the validation stage until there is room for it. Likewise, work cannot start on items in the backlog until the progress bucket has been cleaned out enough to free up the space. One outcome that many Lean Startups don't anticipate is that this method also makes it easier for teams to measure their productivity based on the validated learning from the customer as opposed to the number of new features being produced.

Five whys: Many technical issues still have a root at a human cause at some point in the process. The five whys technique makes it possible to get close to that root cause from the beginning. It is a deceptively simple plan, but one that is extremely powerful when used by the right hands. The Lean Startup system posits that most problems that are discovered tend to be the result of a lack of personal training, which on the surface can either look like a simple technical issue or even one person's mistake.

For example, with a software company, they may see a negative response from their customers regarding their most recent update. Looking more closely at the issue, it was discovered that this was due to the fact that the update accidentally disabled a popular feature. Looking closer still, this was discovered to be due to a faulty service which failed because a subsystem was used incorrectly due to an engineer that wasn't trained correctly. Looking closer still, you will find that this is due to a fact that a specific manager doesn't believe in giving new engineers the full breadth of training they need because his team is overworked and everybody is needed in one capacity or another.

This type of technique can be especially useful for startups as it gives them the opportunity to determine the true optimum speed needed to make quality improvements. You could invest a huge amount in training, for example, but that doesn't mean this is always going to be the right choice at the given stage of development. However, by looking closely at the root causes of the problems in question, you can more easily determine where there are core areas that require immediate attention as opposed to solely focusing on surface issues.

Another related issue is connected to the fact that many team members are likely prone to overreacting to things at the moment, which is why the 5 Whys are useful when it comes to taking a closer look at what's really happening. There can be a tendency to use the Five Whys to point blame, at first, but the real goal of the Five Whys is to find any chronic problems caused by bad process, not bad people. This is also important to ensure that everyone is in the room together when the analysis takes place because it involves all of the people impacted by the issue, including both customer service and management. If blame has to be taken, it is important that management falls on the sword for not having a team-wide system in place to prevent the issue in the first place.

When it comes to getting started with the Five Whys, the first thing that should be focused on is instilling a feeling of trust and empowerment in the team as a whole. This means being tolerant of all mistakes the first time they happen, while at the same time making it clear that the same mistake should not happen twice. Next, it is important to focus on the system level as most mistakes are made due to a flaw in the system which means it is important to put the focus on this level when it comes to solving problems.

From there, it is important to face the truth, no matter how pleasant or unpleasant it might be. This method may bring up some unpleasantness about the company as a whole but the goal is to fix these issues, after all, and you can't fix what hasn't been brought to light. This is why it is easy to turn it into the Five Blames if you aren't careful which is why the blame should flow up in this instance. Start small and be specific. You want to get the process embedded, so start with small issues with small solutions.

Finally, it is important to designate one person on the team as the Five Whys Master. This person will be the one who is primarily in charge of seeing that change actually comes to the team. This, in turn, means they will need a fair amount of authority in order to ensure things get finished. This person will then be the one accountable for any related follow-up, determining if the system is ultimately paying off, or if it is better to cut your losses now and move on. While it can ultimately be a great way to create a more adaptive startup, it can also be harder to get into the groove of than it first appears, so it is important to look at it as a long-term investment rather than something that will be completed in the short-term.

Chapter 2. Lean Startup Models

The lean startup model was introduced in the year 2011, and its impact on the economy has been enormous. The book written by Eric Ries gained immense publicity, and many companies use the information in the book to develop their startups.

However, the ideas in the book are not new; these ideas have been forgotten by most entrepreneurs since success is always measured in numbers in the business world. The methods and ideas in the book are valuable to startups as well as well-established organizations.

In his book, Eric Ries has defined a startup as a human institution whose goal is to create a new service or product under uncertain conditions.

Build-Measure-Learn

The way different companies pursue innovation in today's market has been affected by the idea of using certain scientific or statistical methods to handle or calculate uncertainty.

This means that the company must define a hypothesis, build a product or service to test that hypothesis, use that product or service and learn what happens and finally adjust the attributes of the product or service to increase the value for customers.

The Build-Measure-Learn methodology can be applied to almost anything. You do not have to use this methodology to test new products alone. You can also test a management review process, customer service idea, new features to existing products or website offers and tests. You have to carry out a test and validate the initial hypothesis to ensure that you have enough data to assess the value of the product to the customer.

The aim of every company should be to move through this methodology quickly. You have to identify if the product or service developed is worth going through another cycle or if you should come up with a new idea. This means that you must define a specific idea that you want to test with minimum criteria that can be used for measurement.

Minimal Viable Product (MVP)

A traditional company will first have to define the specifications of every product it wants to produce or manufacture and then assess the significant cost and time that will be invested to produce that product. The lean startup methodology encourages every startup to build the required amount of product through one loop of the Build-Measure-Learn Loop.

If the company can identify such a product, it becomes the minimal viable product. This product is manufactured or developed using minimal effort and less development time.

Every startup does not necessarily have to write a code to automate processes to create an MVP. An MVP could be as simple as a slide deck or design mockups. You have to ensure that you run these products by your customers to get enough validation to pass this product through the next cycle.

Validated Learning

Every startup must test or validate a hypothesis with the right idea in mind – learn from what is observed. There are times when startups have focused on vanity metrics that made them believe that they were indeed making progress. This is not the right approach since you must always look at metrics that will give you some insight on the product and how it can be changed to increase its value to the customers.

For example, the number of accounts opened on Instagram is a vanity metric for that platform. The actual metric would be the number of hours spent scrolling through Instagram by each account holder. This will give the developers the true value of the product.

In the book Lean Startup, Eric Ries has provided an example of his own. A company called IMVU always showed a chart that painted a good picture to its management and investors. Many registrations were being made every single day.

However, this graph did not show if the customers or users value the service. The graph did not show the costs that went into marketing to acquire new users. This chart only looked at vanity metrics and was not designed to test a hypothesis.

Innovation Accounting

Through innovation accounting, a startup can prove that it is learning to grow and sustain as a business. A company can do this in the following ways.

Establish a baseline

The startup can run an MVP test and collect data that will enable it to set some benchmark points. You can use a smoke test where you can market the product or service you want to offer and assess your customers' interests.

This includes a sign-up form to understand if the customers want to purchase the product or service. Using that information, you can set the baseline for the first iteration of the Build-Measure-Learn Cycle. It is alright to make mistakes or have low numbers since that will help you improve.

Tuning the Product

Once the baseline has been established, you should identify one change that must be made to the product and test that improvement. Do not make all the changes at once, as it can lead to chaos.

You can try to see how a change in the design of the form attracts more customers when compared to the earlier design. This step must be carried out slowly to ensure that every hypothesis is tested out carefully.

Persevere or Pivot

When you have made several iterations through the cycle, you have to move up from the initial baseline towards the goal that was set out in the business plan. If you are unable to reach that goal, you must learn why using the data collected at every step.

Pivot

A successful entrepreneur is one who has the foresight, the tools and the ability to identify which parts of the business plan are indeed working for the company. They also learn to adapt to changes in the market and their strategies according to the data collected during the iterations.

One of the hardest aspects of the lean startup method is to make the decision to pivot since every entrepreneur and founder is emotionally attached to the product they have created. They spend a lot of money and energy to get to where they are. If a team uses vanity metrics to test its products and hypothesis, it can go down the wrong path.

If the hypothesis selected is not defined clearly, then it is possible that the company may fail since the management does not know that the endeavor is not working. If you, as the management, decide to launch the product fully in the market and then assess the outcome, you will see what happens, and there is a higher probability that you may fail.

If you choose to pivot, it does not mean that you have failed. It means that you will change the hypothesis that you started out with. The following variations are often used when a startup chooses to pivot.

- Zoom-in Pivot: A single feature in the product that sets it apart from other products becomes the actual product.
- Zoom-out pivot: This is the opposite of the above definition where an entire product is used as a new feature in a larger product.
- Customer segment pivot: The product designed was correct. However, the customers that were selected were wrong for the product. The startup can change the customer segment and sell the same product.
- Customer need pivot: When the startup follows the principles of validated learning, it will identify the problem that needs to be solved for the customer who was initially selected.
- Platform pivot: most platforms start off as applications. When the platform becomes a success, it transforms into a platform ecosystem.
- Business Architecture Pivot: Based on Geoffrey Moore's idea, the startup can choose to switch to low margin and high-volume products from high margin and low-value products.
- Value Capture Pivot: When you decide to measure the value differently, you will be able to change everything about the business right from the cost structure to the final product.
- The engine of Growth Pivot: According to Ries, most startups follow a paid, viral or sticky growth model. It

would be more prudent for the company to switch from one model to the other to grow faster.

- Channel Pivot: In today's world, advertising channels and complex sales have reduced since the Internet provides a huge platform for a company to advertise its products.
- Technology Pivot: Technological advancements are being made every day, and any new technology can help to reduce the cost and increase performance and efficiency.

Small Batches

There is a story where a father had asked his daughters to help him stuff newsletters into a document. The children suggested that they fold every newsletter, put a stamp on the envelope and write the address on the envelope. They wanted to do every task one step at a time.

The father wanted to do it differently – he suggested that they finish every envelope fully before they moved on to the next envelope. The father and daughters competed with each other to see which the better method was.

The father's method won since he used an approach called "single-piece flow" which is common in lean manufacturing. It is better to repeat a task over and over again to ensure that you master that task. You will also learn to do the task faster and better.

You have to remember that an individual's performance is not as important as the performance of the system. You lose time when you should go back to the first task and restack the envelopes. If you consider the process as a unit, you will be able to improve your efficiency.

Another benefit of using small batches is that you will be able to spot the error immediately. If you fold all the newsletters and then find out that that newsletter does not fit into the envelope, you will need to fold all the newsletters again. This approach will help you identify the error at the beginning and improve your process.

The advantage of working with small batches is that you will be able to identify the problems soon.

Andon Cord

The Andon Cord is a method that was used by Taiichi Ohno in Toyota, which allowed an employee to stop the process if he or she identified a defect in the process. If the defect continues longer in the process, it is harder to remove that defect, and there is a higher cost involved.

It is highly efficient to spot the defect at an early stage even if it means that the process will need to stop to address the defect. This method has helped Toyota maintain high quality.

Eric Ries mentioned in his book that the company IMVU used a set of checks that ran every day to check if the site worked accurately. This meant that they were able to identify and address any production error quickly and automatically.

There were no changes made to the production until the defect was addressed. This was an automated Andon Cord.

Continuous Deployment

Continuous deployment is a scenario that is unimaginable and scary for most startups. The idea of this method is that the startup must update the production systems regularly.

IMVU was regularly updating its production system by running close to fifty updates. This was made possible since they made an investment in test scripts.

Over 14000 test scripts would run at least 60 times a day and simulate everything from a click on the browser to running the code in the database.

Eric Ries also talks about Wealthfront, which is a company that operates in an environment regulated by the SEC. However, this company practices continuous deployment and has more than ten production releases a day.

Kanban

Kanban is a technique that was borrowed from the world of lean manufacturing. It was developed by Taiichi Ohno in the late 1980s to improve the manufacturing unit of Toyota automobiles. Eric Ries mentions the company Grockit, which is an online tool that helps one build skills for standardized tests.

This tool creates a story in the development process, which is then used to develop a feature. They also mention to the user what the outcome or benefit of the tool is. These stories are validated to see how they work for different users. A test is conducted to see how this tool benefits the customer. There are four states:

- Backlog: The tasks that can be worked on but have not yet been started
- In Progress: The tasks that are currently being developed
- Built: The tasks that have been completed and are ready for the customer
- Validated: Products that have been released and have been validated by the customers.

If the story fails the validation test, then it will be removed from the product and produced again. A good practice would be to ensure that none of the buckets mentioned above have more than two projects at a given time. If there is a project or task that is in the built bucket, it cannot move to the validated stage until there is enough room for it. The same goes for the processes that are in the backlog bucket. These tasks cannot move to the "In Progress" bucket until it is free.

A valuable outcome of this method is that the team can start measuring its productivity based on the validated learning and feedback from the customer. The team will then stop measuring its productivity based on the number of new features developed.

The Five Whys

Every technical defect or issue has a human cause at its root. The five whys technique will allow the startup to get closer to the root cause. This is a deceptively simple technique but is powerful. Eric Ries has mentioned in his book that most problems or issues that are identified in a process are caused due to lack of training. These problems may look like an individual's mistake or a technical issue. Ries uses IMVU as an example to explain this technique.

- A new product feature or release was disabled for customers. Why? The feature tanked because of a failed server.
- Why did this server fail? There was a subsystem that was used incorrectly.
- Why was that server used incorrectly? The engineer using the server was not trained to use it properly.
- Why did he not know how to use the server? He was never trained.
- Why was he not trained? His manager did not believe that new engineers needed to be trained since he believed that he and his team were too busy.

This technique is extremely useful for startups since it helps them make improvements within a short period. A huge amount can be invested in training, but this may not be the optimal thing to do when the startup is still at its development stage.

If the startup takes a look at the root cause of every problem, it can identify the core areas that need to be worked on and not focus only on the issues at the surface.

Most people tend to overreact to issues that happen at the moment, and the Five Whys help them understand what they need to look at to understand what is happening.

There is a possibility that the Five Whys can be used as a way to blame people in the team to see whose fault it was. The goal of this method is to identify problems that are caused not by bad people but by bad processes. It is essential that every member of the team be in the same room when this analysis is made.

When blame needs to be taken, it is important that the management should take the hit for not having a solution at system-level. Good practices to follow to get started with this methodology are:

- Mutual empowerment and trust. If a mistake is made for the first time, you should be tolerant of them. Ensure that you do not make the same mistake twice.
- Maintain focus on the system since most mistakes happen due to a flaw in the system and ensure that people always solve problems at the system level.
- The company should always face some unpleasant truths. This method will bring out some unpleasant truths to the surface, and the management should ensure that these issues are taken care of at the initial stage. If this method is not conducted in the right manner, it will change into the Five Blames.

- Always start small and be specific. You have to look at the process in detail and always start with small issues. When you understand the issues, you must identify the solutions. Always run the process regularly and involve as many people from the team as you can.
- Appoint someone who is a master at Five Whys. This person must be the primary change agent and should have a good degree of authority to ensure that things get done. This person will be accountable for judging whether the costs were made to prevent or work on those problems are paying off or not.

The Five Whys methodology is used to transform the startup into a more organized and adaptive organization, which can be hard.

Chapter 3. The 5 Principles of Lean Startup Method

Believe it or not, the lean startup methodology has had its fair share of criticisms, both constructive and destructive. For instance, some people said it's already an easy enough process; thus, oversimplifying it seemed redundant. So many blogs have been written about the subject claiming the lean startup is already simple – all of its basic elements are there to explore – so why make it simpler?

Well, dissatisfaction is, perhaps, human nature. It's impossible to please everybody. Here's the thing, though: inasmuch as the lean startup may seem simple, it's one heck of a complex system. You think you know what to do with it, but once you're actually doing it, you'll realize its intricacy.

Moreover, just as it is with any other system, you can't just window-shop for the parts you "like", choose those, and leave the rest behind. No. It's impossible to make a system work without tapping on all its parts to work seamlessly together. And that's what makes the lean startup multifaceted.

Like I have said earlier, it's a research-intensive process. You can't downplay the importance of research since it will gauge whether or not you're up for the challenge. If, during the course of research, you realize you're not cut out for the lean startup method, you're free to consider a different approach. At least, you haven't expended much time, effort, energy, and money yet since you're still on the research phase. On the other hand, if you think you can take on the challenge, by all means, go!

Perhaps understanding the five principles on which the lean startup is hinged will help you see if it's something you can work with. That's what I did, and that's why I can freely talk about the methodology in this book. I'm not saying I'm an expert at this method, but I try to apply what I learn (after all, it's a continuous process). And that's what I want you to do, too.

The Lean Startup Principles

Principle is defined as a fundamental truth serving as the cornerstone of a particular system of belief or reasoning. With that said, it's only right to assume that the lean startup methodology is founded on a set of fundamental truths that govern how it works. In this part of the book, I will try to expound on those five principles that are behind the lean startup methodology (The Lean Startup, n.d.).

Entrepreneurs are everywhere. Unlike regular employees who are cooped up in their offices from nine to five, entrepreneurs (self-made people, if you will) are found just about everywhere. You can create a startup from your garage or your bedroom (or dorm room like Mark Zuckerberg). That's the beauty of entrepreneurship: it, in itself, is a human institution from which innovative products and services can be created regardless if conditions are uncertain. With entrepreneurs being everywhere, it goes without saying that the lean startup method will work anywhere, regardless of the size of a business or which sector of the industry it belongs to.

Entrepreneurship is management. Just because it's a self-made business doesn't mean management practices can't be applied. Like I have discussed in the early goings of this book, there is such a thing as entrepreneurial management. It's a type of management specifically geared towards entrepreneurship. Keep in mind that entrepreneurship is a human institution, not a product or service, and an institution cannot function fully unless capable hands are managing it.

 Validated learning. You don't create a business with the sole purpose of making money or being at your customers' beck and call. Heck, you don't even create it, so you'll have an excuse to make products or formulate services. You start a business with the aim of learning how to make it

sustainable. Remember how I said the six parts of the scientific method applies to the lean startup method? Well, the experiment part applies when you need to validate your learnings scientifically to see whether these work. It's a continuous process.

Build-Measure-Learn. Ah, if it isn't our favorite concept. Seriously, though, this three-step concept is basically what makes the lean startup methodology tick. Overall, the primary activity of a startup business, is to formulate ideas, turn these ideas into viable products (build), see how customers react to the products (measure), and use customers' feedbacl to see whether you need to go to a new direction or continue until the product becomes marketable (learn). It's an on-going loop intended to accelerate the growth of a business.

Innovation accounting. In the lean startup method, it's important to measure certain metrics like how much progress you're making, how milestones should be set up, and which task should be prioritized. Implementing entrepreneurial management whole making sure these metrics are met can be difficult. Hence, innovation accounting is necessary. This novel type of accounting is specifically designed for startup businesses. Its use is the only way you can figure out if you are, indeed, making progress or if your efforts are for naught. This particular principle of the lean startup focuses on numbers that are pivotal for the growth of your business like engagement and customer acquisition cost.

Are you now fully convinced that you should try the lean startup methodology for your business? If you're still having second thoughts, then perhaps this next segment will tickle your fancy even more.

Is Adapting the Lean Startup Methodology Necessary?

I have been giving you the 411 about the lean startup methodology almost from the get-go, but I am quite sure you're still adamant about giving it a try. After all, it's the fate of your business at stake here. One wrong move and everything you have worked and been working hard for can go down the drain.

Of course, I can always convince you that it did work for me. However, what works for one will not always work for another, right? That's why I still want to share some reasons why I think you should adapt the lean startup in your business. In fact, these reasons will work whether yours is a new business or already an established organization.

Regardless if you're a startup or an existing business, you are bound to create new products or services. Hence, you will potentially be reaching new markets. Adapting the lean startup methodology will help your business decrease cycle time, gather customer feedback faster, and reduce waste.

There will be new processes you will want to employ in your business, processes that will certainly have a bearing on your customer base. So you want to ensure the best results by deploying a customer-validated process. Through the lean startup, you will get continuous feedback and validation.

You may already have a five-year projection in place. In a volatile environment, that five-year plan may not succeed. Nevertheless, adapting the lean startup will bring in the agility and speed you need so you can adapt in an ever-changing environment. It will certainly help you go a long way.

Adapting the lean startup methodology will help you foster innovation in your business minus the wasted money.

With the lean startup backing you up every step of the way, you will not be overly concerned about the success and adaption rates of the new digitized system you are planning to deploy.

Keep in mind that two of the main purposes of this methodology are: to make your business competitive in such a cutthroat environment and drive growth. In a nutshell, here are some benefits of adapting the method:

Throughout the course of adapting the process, you stay focused on your goals and you get clear visibility of which direction you plan on going.

The process gives you a heads up when it's time to make necessary changes to the strategies you are currently using. As a result, you spend less time, effort, and money.

By the time your product or service is deemed marketable, you will have already established a customer base. This includes the test customers you reached out to during the build-measure-learn phase.

The process/es you will create using the lean startup will already have been tried and tested.

The lean startup method is focused on five key points:

- Speed
- Flexibility
- Innovation
- Customer focus
- Elimination of uncertainties

Chapter 4. Why Do Most Startup Fail?

Marketing is considered by many as one of the most important investments for any small business. Without it, your target customers may never know about you, your products or services offered, or why buying from you is a better decision than buying from your competition. As a result, your products or services go unnoticed. Marketing is a broad discipline and entrepreneurs must be able to overcome the pitfalls of small business marketing in order for your business to succeed.

Consider this a bonus section that will outline and discuss some of the most common pitfalls of small business marketing. This particular section will definitely provide you with useful insights that can help improve your marketing strategies and methods. That way, whether you're starting a small business or you're more likely to brave your way into a startup, you will know what you should and shouldn't do if you want a successful business that follows the lean startup methodology.

Defining Target Markets

Who do you plan to target? Where can you find them? This thing may seem like a very basic matter, but the groundwork of your marketing efforts actually starts here. If you want to achieve marketing success, you need to have a clear concept of who your target market will be. Create a brief narrative or profile of your target customer. Jot it down and polish it; collaborate with your team; figure out what your target client uses as its buying criteria. Defining who your ideal customer is will help you put everything in order and customize your marketing efforts based on their needs and wants.

Creating a Marketing Plan

Every small-scale entrepreneur must have a marketing plan to support their business goals. If developing a marketing plan is a challenge, there are plenty of resources on the Internet that can provide you with marketing plan templates. Download some of these templates and use them as a guide. Be sure to keep it short and limit it to three pages if you can. If you can afford it, get a marketing specialist who can help you develop the plan.

Finding Resources for Marketing

One of the most common pitfalls of small business marketing is the cost of advertising, but small businesses cannot afford not to invest the time and money into this thing. Buying a full-page Saturday newspaper ad or NBA TV commercials is usually not a financial dilemma for large-scale businesses. However, such costs are obviously a predicament for many small businesses. To overcome this, spend some time studying and exploring what you can achieve with the low-cost marketing methods that are now available to small businesses.

Getting Referrals

Most small business entrepreneurs will probably agree that referrals are an important asset to their business. Even so, many remain cautious when openly asking for referrals. If you want to grow your business, be sure to let your existing customers, as well as your network of contacts, come to the realization that their referrals are a great help to your business. Try to make referrals an integral part of your marketing strategies so you can expand your reach and widen your customer base.

Increasing Sales Conversions

If you are faced with this common pitfall of small business marketing, try to look again at your marketing message. Deal with this challenge by making sure that you make a relevant and attractive offer to your intended customers. Before running a marketing campaign, test it first and then refine it. Small businesses cannot afford to only invest on advertisements that build image or brand. You can develop and promote your company image while causing increased sales by providing an offer to motivate your target customers to take action within a specific period of time. In general, your promotional campaign should focus on eliciting a response from your target customers that translates into sales while building your brand at the same time.

Whatever industry you are in, it is very likely that you would encounter one or more of the common pitfalls of small business marketing. Fortunately, there are ways to overcome this dilemma. All you have to do is explore your options and be creative in your marketing methods.

Now that you know the difference between the two, as well as the common pitfalls associated with marketing a small business, let's go back to the discussion on hand – the lean startup methodology. As the name of this innovative method implies, it was founded with startup entrepreneurs at the forefront of Ries' mind. Why do I say so?

We've mentioned earlier that a startup is riskier to create than a small business. Risk is the epitome of a startup because you are practically venturing into the unknown. Some of you have probably done it. I have done it. I have left a stable job just so I can start my own business without even considering what will become of me in case things don't go according to plan.

The risk factor of startup businesses is what prompted the idea of the lean startup. Its founder wanted to lend companies of all sizes a hand, so to speak, to help them navigate through rough waters and lower the risk factors through three things – minimum viable products or MVPs, painstaking experimentation, and full commitment to learning (McGowan, 2017). In a nutshell, the lean startup methodology centers on the creation of a sustainable business where minimal time and money is wasted.

Think of it this way: you spend an obscene amount of money trying to come up with products that you think the consuming public will love, "you think" being the operative words. Did you even stop to think if the products you're creating can solve a particular problem or address a pressing situation? You probably didn't, and guess what? You're more than likely to fail. Scratch that. YOU WILL FAIL.

Harsh words, right? However, I'm speaking the truth, and that is something that Ries' realized as well.

Earlier, I said that Ries' concept of the lean startup method was developed because of two Japanese men who worked for Toyota – Taiichi Ohno and Shigeo Shingo. Observing how these two worked, Ries' saw how the entire process of building Japanese cars worked – waste is reduced and eliminated, if at all, in order to release the cars at the lowest cost and without sacrificing the high value of the cars. Through his observation, Ries' was able to visualize a system that can likewise be applied by entrepreneurs.

Chapter 5. Create a Useful Lean Startup Experiment

Qualitative or Quantitative: While many people assume that their startup experiment needs to be either quantitative or qualitative, the fact of the matter is that one is not inherently superior to the other. Instead, it is better to think of the two as if one was a hammer and the other was a screwdriver. While a hammer is better at putting nails in wood, that doesn't mean it is inherently superior on all fronts. Any tool can be used for good or evil, which is why it is important to focus more on validating the right metrics than it is to worry about which of these two processes is superior. In fact, using qualitative research and then validating it with quantitative research is likely going to do the most good anyway.

Generative or Evaluative: A generative research technique is one that doesn't start with a hypothesis per se but can still result in a wide variety of different ideas. Things like Customer Discovery Interviews fall under this type of technique. Evaluative, on the other hand, is all about testing a very specific hypothesis in order to determine a very specific result. The popular smoke test falls under this type of testing. It is perhaps this distinction, more than any other, that explains why some people end up with poor results from their experiments.

For example, a smoke test could be run to test the hypothesis that some percentage of the market will be interested in shoes that are compostable. To test this hypothesis, you would then put up a fake coming soon landing page explaining that compostable shoes are totally going to be a thing and see who signs up for the newsletter. After the work was done and the results were in, it turns out that there was about a 1 percent conversion rate when it comes to the shoes. The good news is that the hypothesis was confirmed, the bad news is that it wasn't particularly useful.

What's more, the results are unclear because it still isn't clear if the interest isn't there, if the advertising was poor, or if there is a third variable that you aren't yet aware of. This can be broadly defined as the difference between people not being interested in the value proposition and people not understanding it. The truth of the matter is that there are hundreds of reasons out there why someone might get a false negative result from a given test, just as there are a number of reasons why a false positive might be generated.

To get started, you will need to determine if the hypothesis is flawed or simply vague and, in this case, it is both. Some people are too vague when it comes to a target audience, some are a poor qualifier. As such, first, you would need to focus on a more specific demographic, and second, you would need to do research to determine how big the audience for compostable shoes would ultimately be. Only once the hypothesis is falsifiable and specific can it benefit from an evaluative experiment like the smoke test. If you can't clear up your hypothesis then you will want to start with Generative Research and work back from there.

Market or product: When it comes to the distinction between methods and tools, the biggest is perhaps the distinction between Product and Market. Some methods are useful when it comes to helping startups learn about their customers, their problems, and their best lines of communication. As an example, startups can listen to their potential customers to make it easier for them to understand their specific situations and what their day to day problems are like.

Other methods make it possible to learn about the product or a potential solution that will help to solve a specific problem. One good place to start is with a set of wireframes as a means of determining if the interface is as usable as it seems at face value. Unfortunately, this still won't make it clear if anyone is going to buy anything in the first place.

As these methods don't typically overlap all that well, it is important to choose one and stick with it throughout its cycle. If you combine evaluative research and generative research with Product and Market, you will end up with four different means of determining the best path forward.

Generative Market research asks questions like:

- Who is our customer?
- What are their pains?
- Is our customer segment too broad?
- What job needs to be done?
- How do we find them?

If you can't answer these questions clearly and easily, then your startup is in what is known as the Customer Discovery phase. During this phase, it is important to get to the basis of the problem prior to testing out any potential solutions to ensure that you are actually solving the right problem in the end. If you don't have a clear hypothesis to start, then you will need to generate ideas.

To do so, you may want to talk to customers to see what is bothering them or you could use a data mining approach to determine the problem, assuming you have access to enough data. You may even want to use a survey with open-ended questions if you are really fishing for ideas. Some of these methods will be qualitative and some will be quantitative, but this distinction is ultimately irrelevant in the long run. Data mining is a quantitative approach, but it helps identify problems, most famously the existence of food deserts which would have been difficult to determine in virtually any other way.

Generative Market Research Methods include:

- Surveys
- Focus groups
- Data mining
- Contextual inquiry / ethnography
- Customer Discovery Interviews

Evaluative Market experiment questions include things like:

- How much will they pay?
- How do we convince them to buy?

- How much will it cost to sell?
- Can we use scale marketing?

In order to properly evaluate a specific hypothesis, you may want to start with a landing page to determine if there is likely to be a demand. You may want to put together a basic sales pitch if you are working on a B2B enterprise type product. You could even go so far as to run a conjoint analysis as a means of further understanding the relative positioning of a few value propositions.

Evaluative market experiments that are useful if you have a clear hypothesis include:

- High bar
- Fake door
- Event
- Pocket test
- Flyers
- Pre-sales
- Sales pitch
- Landing page
- Video
- Smoke tests
- Surveys
- Data mining/market research
- Conjoint Analysis
- Comprehension – link to the tool
- 5-second tests

While this sort of research can provide lots of interesting data, it is important to keep in mind that much of it still has the potential to be wrong as signing up for a landing page is very different than actually putting money down on a product. In any situation where the customer doesn't have to commit anything more than an email address, then they don't signify an actual customer demand.

It is important to keep in mind that the value proposition and the product are not the same things. The value proposition is the benefit that your product will deliver to your target audience. As such, you cannot have a validated value proposition if you don't have a validated customer segment.

Chapter 6. Introducing The Lean Startup Method Foreword

When you build a startup, you have to know where to start which means that you will need to create a team that oversees the management of the startup.

You will also need to learn to define your product and startup to help customers understand why your product is different from the other products in the market.

Ensure that your learning is incorporated into the product and experiment with different ideas before you launch your product in the market.

How to Start

When you build a startup, you build an institution, which needs to be managed.

This may come as a surprise to some entrepreneurs since they believe that there is no correlation between management and startup. It is good that most entrepreneurs are wary of setting up a traditional management system since it can stifle creativity and invite bureaucracy.

Entrepreneurs in different industries have been trying to look for solutions to their problems in traditional management for quite some time which leads to the "just do it" attitude. These entrepreneurs avoid all forms of discipline, management and process.

What they forget is that this attitude leads to failure more often than it does success. It must be remembered that the principles of general management are not well suited to handle failure or chaos that every startup must face.

Every startup must have some level of managerial discipline to ensure that the company can harness all the opportunities it has been given. There are many entrepreneurs today when compared to any other time in history, which has been made possible due to globalization.

For example, most news channels and radio stations have commented about how people are losing jobs in the manufacturing industry. However, the manufacturing output of every company has increased over the last decade, which means that modern technology and management have helped to improve productivity.

If you wish to build a lean startup, you should consider entrepreneurial management since it encourages employees to expand their horizons and knowledge. Consider the following situation – there is an established company with a team that has not made any sales in over a year. This department has not roped in new customers either.

However, the employees in that department have identified a new industry or line of business the company can diversify its assets into. In an established organization, the department would be dissolved since the company is always looking for ways to make a profit.

However, in entrepreneurial management, these employees are considered entrepreneurs since they are looking for ways to improve the business.

Define

If you ever go for an entrepreneur meet, you will notice that many people have no idea what is expected of them. You will find a group of traditional entrepreneurs and managers from well-established companies who are expected to create product innovations or ventures.

These managers are good at organizational politics and know how the company can be divided into groups and how the profit and loss for each department can be separated.

The surprising thing is that these individuals are visionaries since they can see the future of their company and are prepared to take risks to find innovative and new solutions to any problem the company faces.

Entrepreneurs who work in an organization are called intrapreneurs since they work on products or build a startup within the organization. Intrapreneurs have a lot in common with entrepreneurs.

The lean startup method is a set of principles and practices that every entrepreneur can use to build a successful startup.

It was mentioned earlier that Eric Ries defined a startup as a human institution that is designed to develop a new product or service under uncertain conditions. This definition omits the industry, sector of the economy and the size of the business.

Most people lose sight of the fact that a startup is a brilliant idea, product or a breakthrough apart from being a human institution. Additionally, it is a product or service defined as an innovation.

It is important that the word innovation is understood in a broad sense. Every startup uses a different kind of innovation to increase value to its customer.

It is also important for the startup to understand the conditions under which innovation happens. Startups enter an industry where there is an established organization that already sells the same product.

They must find a new attribute to the product that has not been sold to the customers before developing it. The development stage is uncertain since the product could either be accepted or rejected by the customer.

Learn

Every entrepreneur must make an effort to learn and understand whether the company was indeed making progress. Many entrepreneurs develop a product using their creativity, and they launch that product in the market. If the product fails at the market, they believe they have learned why and they go ahead and develop a better product. Unfortunately, this is the oldest excuse for failure.

These entrepreneurs become wildly creative about what they have learned from their failure. However, this is not comforting for employees or investors since the former are giving the startup their time while the latter have allotted their money to the startup.

An entrepreneur cannot go to a bank and tell them that he or she has learned what needs to be done to sell the product in the market. It is no wonder the word learning has a bad name in the market.

It is important that every startup learns how a product can be improved and also understands what needs to be done better to succeed.

Experiment

When an entrepreneur has an idea in mind, he or she will want to find a way to execute that idea. Every startup is built in the hopes that the entrepreneur has identified a product or service that does not exist in the market and will increase value to its customers.

A mistake that most entrepreneurs make is that they launch the product on the market before they test it. There is a high probability that this product or service may not appeal to the customers.

Therefore, it becomes important that the startup launches the product to a smaller audience and gathers feedback before launching the product in the market. This gives the entrepreneur the chance to tweak the product to increase value to the customer.

How To Steer

When you have identified your product and developed it, you will launch it in the market and ask your customers to use it. You must remember that there is a possibility of a failure. But, do not worry too much since you can learn from that failure and develop a better product.

Leap

Every entrepreneur must have the ability to take a leap of faith and make a risky decision about his or her idea. There are two types of assumptions that can be made – Value Hypothesis and Growth Hypothesis.

Value Hypothesis

How can you as an entrepreneur validate every assumption you have made about your product's value? It depends on how quickly you can develop a prototype and give your customers the chance to use that prototype and give you feedback. You do not necessarily have to give the main product to the customers.

You can do what Zomato did. Deepinder Goyal saw that people had trouble waiting in a queue for food. Instead, they launched a website that had scanned copies of menus which enabled people to decide their order before they stepped into the line.

When this became a success, they developed Zomato and roped in more restaurants and cafes.

Growth Hypothesis

You must focus on the growth of your company only when you have an established product. You have to ask yourself how customers will use your product constantly.

The best way to do this would be to ask the customers for feedback. Facebook and WhatsApp are great examples.

Test

When you use the minimum viable product (MVP) approach, you will learn more about how the product can be improved. An MVP is not a small product, and it is simply a faster way to complete one iteration of the build-measure-learn cycle.

You have to remember that your first product does not have to be perfect. It should be a rough idea of what you had in mind and then test that idea with your customers and gather feedback. You must ensure that through this test, you can validate your initial hypothesis.

There are different tests that can be conducted to understand how the customers received the product.

Quantitative versus qualitative

There is a constant debate to understand which is superior. It is a good approach to first use qualitative research and assesses the feedback before validating a hypothesis using the quantitative approach.

Generative versus Evaluative

The former can be used to test the product if there is no hypothesis in place. The latter is where a hypothesis is tested to understand whether or not the product is a success or failure. If you do not have a clear hypothesis, you should use the generative approach to either obtain new ideas or to develop a particular hypothesis.

Market versus Product

There are some situations where the market will give you an idea of what the customers want. All you need to do is listen to the customers and understand what problems they face. There are other situations where a product or service must be developed to solve a problem.

Measure

Every startup is a more than just a piece of paper. The initial business plan will list out the number of customers the company expects to have, the cost it will incur and the revenue or profit it will make.

This plan is usually far from where the startup is in the early days. Therefore, it is important that a startup works on the following:

- It must identify where the startup is right now by accepting the truth that is revealed through constant assessment.

- Devise new experiments to understand how the startup can move towards the numbers mentioned in the business plan.

Most products, including the ones that fail, have some growth, positive results and customers. As an entrepreneur, you will be optimistic and will trust the ideas that you have. This does not mean that you can bumble around and be happy with the little traction that you have. You should ensure that you do not persevere when things do not go your way.

Persevere or Pivot

When one says pivot, it does not mean that they should give up on their ideas.

There are different ways that an entrepreneur can still make his or her product work. Try the methods mentioned above to help you when you reach the pivot stage.

If every test and experiment conducted gives you the best results, you should develop the product fully and launch it in the market. Ensure that you do not trick yourself by using vanity measures to test your hypothesis.

Always use criteria that will affect your company to assess the products that you are developing. You must also ensure that you listen to your customers and understand their wants and needs better.

You have to remember that a startup's productivity is not measured by adding more features to a product.

It is about how the startup aligns its efforts with a product or business to drive growth and create value. If you learn how to pivot successfully, you can reach the path of sustainable business growth.

How to Accelerate

Most decisions that need to be made by a startup are not clear or straightforward. They have to constantly question their product and assess when it can be launched in the market. They have to also look at how the product should be released and the cost that they will incur.

Batch

The issues mentioned in that example are found in every process in an organization, and they are of greater consequence in the work of small or large companies.

Some companies use a large-batch approach where they develop and deliver all the products at the end of the process and at once. Other companies use a small-batch approach where it produces and delivers a finished product every few minutes.

A big advantage of working in small batches is that problems in the product can be identified faster. Lean manufacturing discovered small-batch processing a few decades ago when Taiichi Ohno and Shigeo Shingo worked to enhance the productivity of Toyota Automobiles.

They started to manufacture products one at a time and stopped any activity if there was a defect in the process.

Once the defect was removed, the product was manufactured in small batches. This gave Toyota the ability to produce diverse products.

They gathered that every product can be different and does not have to be produced in bulk. This allowed them to serve smaller customer segments and give the customers products that they needed.

Grow

There are times when a startup can have customers at early stages and good revenue at that stage. However, the company may stop growing in the sense that it continues to make the same revenue and has the same number of customers now that it had at its start. So, where does growth stem from? A company can only grow if new customers are brought into it, which can only be done by the action of all its past customers. There are four ways to obtain new customers:

- A startup can use the Internet to advertise its products and services. Most businesses do this to encourage new customers to buy their products. If you want this to be a successful venture, you should pay for advertising through your revenue and not out of the initial capital.
- New customers can be brought through the use of products. For example, if a customer sees someone wearing new clothes, he or she may want to purchase similar clothing. The same can be said about cars and

bikes. This is also true for products like PayPal and Instagram.

- If a customer is satisfied with the product or service provided by the company, he or she will spread the word and encourage more people to purchase that product.
- There are some products that need to be repeatedly purchased. If you develop such a product, you can create a subscription plan that ensures that customers keep coming back to you.

Adapt

It is important for a startup to adapt for change. Every employee in the startup should constantly be trained. Some people working in traditional organizations may tell you that you should not spend too much money on training when you are a startup.

This is bad advice since it is important to train every employee in the organization to help them develop new ideas. It has become evident that technology is going to take over many jobs in the near future. This does not mean that someone should sit tight and continue with their work and not develop their skills.

It is important that they learn new skills or programming languages that will give them an edge. New jobs can be created to cater to these new skills. The same can be said for a startup. It must constantly evolve its products and develop new products or services that will appeal to the customers.

As an entrepreneur, you should be strong and deal with negative comments or feedback. You must learn from that feedback and develop products that will add value to the customers.

Use the Five Whys technique to help you understand what your customers want and why the initial prototype of your product failed in the market. You also have to learn to start small. Do not begin with four or five hypotheses. Start off with one hypothesis and test that with the data collected from the customers.

You must ensure that you do not blame an individual or a team for failure since that brings the morale of the employees down. Accept that mistakes do happen and learn from them.

Innovate

Innovation is the key to a bright future for any company. It is believed that when companies become large, they lose the ability to innovate. However, this is a myth that has been bringing many companies and employees down.

When a startup is growing, it will test its products in the market and find ways to make the product better to appeal to its customers. It will also need to find new attributes to add to the existing product to generate new customers. This is innovation since the company is looking for ways to enhance the existing product.

If a well-established organization is willing to change its management, it can also start innovating. Innovation teams must be built to ensure that a company succeeds. This is what keeps Apple apart from all other companies.

Apple is one company that has always developed new versions of its devices to meet customer demands. The developers include new features into the code every few months to generate a new product. Apple has also ensured that its products are user-friendly and can sustain bad handling.

Most customers have confirmed that an Apple laptop has a firewall that makes it difficult for any virus to penetrate. This is the kind of product that you should develop. Ensure that you constantly innovate and make your products better to meet your customers' demands.

Remember to listen to the customers and make informed decisions about what the customers need. Customers are not sure of what they want or need on most occasions.

They believe that they know what they want, but in reality, they use the products that have great reviews. It is important that you pay attention to what your customers want before you develop a product or make changes to an existing product.

Chapter7. Difference Between Lean Startup and Traditional Startup

Are you aware that business-plans arrive rather than just one, but 2 categories? More frequently than not, once we think about a business plan we think about a conventional format. This usually means a hefty record, roughly 30 to 40 pages in total, written three to four years outside which summarizes every detail which may result in the results of the small business.

A Lean start-up program, alternatively, requires less detail and time to put together, however should have the ability to convey the ongoing future of the company within an understated fashion. Which sort of business program if you draft for the own startup? If you are uncertain whether one format is more preferable on the other, then keep reading.

Traditional Business-plan

A traditional plan skewers towards becoming more extended and detailed than people at thin start-up arrangement; it's essentially a blue print that provides you a glimpse in to the near future of your own startup. In each Conventional company plan, You Will Need to pay for these regions:

Executive Overview—Here you ought to have the ability to explain, no longer than two pages, that you and your organization really are, what exactly your company does, exactly what industry it's in, where you are located (or are located), once you'll start conducting business when you have not begun already, the way the enterprise will earn money, and also consumers will probably require items and/ or services provided by the company.

Business Description, strategy, and concept—This section contains extra info about your services and products, for example what they're doing, making them distinctive and unique, where in fact the concept of the organization originated out, where you are in the evolution stages, and also over all objectives and plans to your business, together with its projected deadline.

Industry Analysis—Who's the competition? Here you will examine competitions of your own brand and touch in their own offerings, company background, and also exactly why consumers may choose your services within theirs.

Marketplace Analysis—given you know that your rivals, that can be the target market? This section defines your marketplace, their requirements, and the way your company should have the ability to draw, capture, and maintain that particular audience.

Organization and Management—when you have staff or management engaged, this section enables you to share with you their biographies, wallpapers, and heart responsibilities.

Financial Projections—this provides readers a glimpse into the income of your business enterprise. It's really a table-heavy region which features projected profit and loss, a 12-month revenue announcement, expenses funding, sales prediction, and also a breakeven investigation with the revenue necessary for the primary investment. And talking about investment...

Financial Request—In case you're trying to get financing from investors, then this really is the place to summarize the sum of money asked, how it's going to be spent, and also the way it has been spent.

Appendix—Your appendix will incorporate business research, letters of incorporation, trade mark registrations, and venture arrangements, simply to list a couple records.

Lean Startup Plan

In case you have to compose a business plan fast or if your company is rather straightforward and straightforward to spell out, your arrangement of choice will be probable a lean startup program. This is not as much a rigorous layout and more of a fast overview—some times no further than 1 page! However sweet and short that your arrangement is, a more lean start-up Program must include the following components:

Value Proposition—the worth your small business brings to its market, summed up at a transparent statement.

Key Partnerships, activities, and resources—extra info about the spouses working together alongside your small business, plans for gaining a competitive advantage, and tools, such as intellectual property or funding, used to make value for the intended audience.

Customer segments, channels, as well as relationships. Who's the audience? Where are you able to accomplish them? How are you going to build an enduring relationship together? Define your intended audience, options for having the ability to keep in touch with them, and tips to establishing the client experience.

Revenue streams—Explain and list the sales flows your organization gets for earning profits. Be certain that you include a fast section that defines your own cost structure plan too.

which format does your business need?

The good news about writing a business plan? There is room for editing. If you are displeased with the structure or will need to make adjustments, then you always have the option to update the file. Additionally, there is the choice to modify formats if you start with a slender plan, however, wish to shift to a more conventional plan, and vice versa.

No matter the arrangement, the main issue is always to be both succinct and critical regarding your business from the start. Your small business plan works to align with your team towards a frequent vision to your own organization and evaluate its feasibility as quickly and seriously as you possibly can. With this type of document leads to the results of the company and places you as being a certain CEO.

Startup Approach

A lean Startup approach is actually a style of business development which appreciates a small business's ability to improve quickly with very little waste of funds. The purpose is to use a set management arrangement (i.e. eliminating of central management) and tools in a manner that is flexible in order for the company runs economically. This means the evolution cycle of a startup gets briefer and much more predicated on iteration (repetition and revision) using three stages: build, quantify, learn.

The thought of the lean startup technique is that should start-ups invest their time in construction services or products to fit the requirements of premature clients (through iteration) they are able to cut the demand to get considerable quantities of initial financing and pricey product launches/tests. By way of instance, a technology startup utilizing the lean startup procedure will assemble a prototype fast (build platform) and launch it in the current market and measure the achievements of this item through data investigation in ancient market testing (step stage), then utilize this data to iterate and further develop the procedure to your next construction of this goods (learn period). This method will not only simply connect with technology startups and may be utilized across all kinds of start ups.

Solving Challenges at Your Site Using a Lean Approach

Adopting Lean techniques to address issues in medical settings is burdensome for just about any company. The transformation in to a small organization demands significant cultural modifications. I believe that the change could be like moving to some other country and never have to learn about new habits and a new vocabulary. You've got to learn how to behave in fresh ways and also think otherwise. The changes involve the adoption of fresh tactics to finding answers to issues, implementing the solutions, and sustaining the services. Lots of you could know such while the Plan, Do, Study, Act (PDSA) cycle.

One attitude that must be embraced could be the "continuous excellent improvement" mindset. If you embrace this mentality, then you definitely feel that procedures and outcomes on your website can always be improved. It's like the notion you could do more to increase your own personal wellbeing. Too frequently managers and physicians feel that just how things work is just nice and their website is quite efficient. Then there are people that think outcomes might possibly be better but merely pay attention to clinical impacts and those associated with clinical procedures. Practitioners of Lean recognize that all procedures in a site are interconnected-clinical and administrative staff also there is always room for advancement.

Still another switch for the majority of sites is how one discovers solutions to issues. Too frequently it's 1 person or even a small set of individuals who show up with methods to issues. Often times a physician or boss in a clinic determines how things will be carried out. One other health practitioners do not want to get bothered; they only desire to operate with patients and also become paid. If you would like to earn substantial improvements afterward you definitely want to feel that teams may solve problems better compared to 1 individual and everyone on the team could subscribe to answers to issues. I am not saying that for every prospect for advancement that the whole team needs to be engaged.

Rather, a wide representation of this team should help solve issues; a representative from each area afflicted with means of a procedure needs to really be involved. You may desire to involve some that do not appear to get involved in an activity you're improving. They may get a notion which features their participation also that boosts the approach. The vital attitude with this preparation area is that almost all issues might be solved by tapping on the ability, invention and understanding of their employees.

A compliment to the adoption of teams to address problems is really a big change in direction style. In the place of one individual dictating changes, the pioneer in Lean should be in a position to effortlessly direct classes. A pioneer of a problem-solving group has to have the ability to have answers from all of the team members, so get set members to work together effortlessly, and bring close at the right moment. The best choice of work groups shouldn't be exactly the exact same person every and every time; but an organization formerly formed should last to own exactly the exact same leader before an answer to a marked advancement problem can be available. If the other class is formed to get another problem, then it's okay to own a fresh pioneer.

Only as the practice of creating methods to process or quality issues will call for substantial changes for most health websites, the execution will probably necessitate changes too. Suppose you've produced a policy for a brand new process that you imagine will significantly enhance a few consequences and eradicate some waste in your website. Perhaps, for example, you've created a fresh means to handoff patients in 1 shift to another at a hospital ward. What exactly are several of the situations you want to accomplish in order to really make the roster from this master plan effective? You need to be certain all who'll participate from the master plan know the new procedure and are familiar with it. The participants at the new process must not just know their role but additionally the job to be played by other people. Once participants are correctly informed the various tools required for the newest process should maintain place. As an example, a brand new checkoff sheet for off patient hand may possibly have to get distributed and printed. Once the supplies and training are all in position, a startup period has to become designated.

Only as a brand fresh type of leadership is essential for team leadership and also the growth of methods to healthcare process issues, a brand new method of direction is needed for the execution of this answer. The first choice for the roster out must take note that the roster and execution is greatly influenced by people engaging; all too often at sites at which leaders do not count on teams, execution failures turned into a blame game.

A Leader that works well with teams may observe a nurse at off our hand problem may possibly have one concept of the appropriate approach to make use of the test off sheet developed to the method where as your doctor who additionally uses the sheet may possibly possess a slightly different perspective. The purpose is that the best choice of this roster outside should be conscious that since various folks may take place the onset of the clear answer could occur otherwise than intended. A fantastic leader will closely monitor the problem and also solve the bugs. A pioneer may even watch out to people that might desire to interrupt the newest process as a result of an awareness of loss in power or influence.

To ensure a powerful installation of a fresh process lasts and more buy to its own effectiveness, somebody will have to get data demonstrating favorable outcomes-improved clinical effects, positive perspectives of the involved from the procedure and the removal of waste (increased income). As an example, I know of a single hospital which used data to demonstrate they had paid down the time of Set for payables by more than 50%. This enhanced income because less attempt Was required for set to get a single thing as well as the cashflow improved.

The documentation of these outcome insured the continuation of this brand new strategy and additionally pointed into help paths for advancement. Thus, it's very important that you specify measures to track the outcomes of a brand new procedure and also to figure out strategies to finetune it. The demo of favorable outcomes may even contradict the commitment of these involved and also convert individuals who could have already been reluctant to connect. Obviously, it might be the data illustrates that the new process is not worse. Rarely are the situation.

At This stage you may possibly believe continuous excellent improvement (PDSA for a) is extremely tough and perhaps not worth every penny. New methods for working in teams, fresh styles of direction, complications in implementing new procedures and keeping up the fluctuations simply do not look worth every penny. The inertia you need to overcome to triumph is similar to obtaining an individual with newly diagnosed hypertension to adjust their life. Some will change instantly; a few may change gradually; plus a few may not change at all and certainly will build up more complications. Exactly like individuals who triumph in managing their hyper tension, you are going to realize this new method of problem-solving at the medical environment is worth. The data will probably establish it.

Funding A Startup

Funding a Startup is among the most challenging facets of establishing a brand new small business. If it boils down to it, you need to navigate investment capital firms, angel investors, angel investors, and consider what the funding will be worth in lack in control of one's own firm. Most start ups fail because while in early stages of the firm that they were underfunded from the evolution stages. Other folks neglect right after launching despite the fact that they've got an remarkable solution, however they ran out of capital to mark the business and gain the critical mass required to sustain operations. This is just a painful situation to know about as you will find simple ways to have Startup Funding and Business Credit to turn your Startup to a grown up. We've three questions which we'd suggest any Startup inquire before seeking financing from outside sources.

1. The amount of money would you NEED to receive your startup from the bottom? There's not any doubt you're shaking your head at the close absurdity with this question nevertheless you'd be amazed what you should figure out about your organization if you glance at just how thin you can conduct the business at first. Thus many businesses believe they want an enormous store front, higher end furnishings, and the complete staff the afternoon that they start their doors for the business. For this is an excellent 5-year-old goal however in the start you could well be in a position to complete so Apple failed and start having a notion and also a couple of talented employees. For those who haven't read re work it'd not be advisable to test it out since there are lots of fundamentals which may save your self-start-ups a significant little bit of hassle in the future.

2. Are you prepared to become a member of staff in your company? This too can seem as an unusual question but should you opt to assist a VC business in lots of instances you'll be in charge of the shareholders in ways you might not have initially hoped. There are reports out of Silicon Valley into

Dubai that begin with a keen entrepreneur and also ending with a burnt out "employee-owner" who is made to simply take their startup at a fresh leadership due to the effect of their own investors. Entrepreneurs beware.

3. What's going to happen over the first ninety days to getting the financing you require. There are businesses available which have minimum $50,000 financing warranty which ensures qualified organizations can obtain access to this financing they desire; nonetheless it's remarkably important you get a very clear vision of exactly what your priorities will probably soon be later becoming financed. It sounds really straightforward but lots of times organizations get financed with no contingency collection of essentials; and after becoming ample funds they end up without essentials they should've procured from one.

Lean Startup - Startup Incubator

There are zillions of smart ideas that occur to people. Several of those individuals are extremely courageous to carry it forwards and put in an entrepreneurial journey. Because nearly all of these have previously read and comprehended that the characteristics clarified by 37Signals inside their publication Getting Real - entrepreneurs begin to create the very first minimal version in these product focusing only on the crux of the undertaking.

As a web consulting firm, we assembled those minimal versions quite inexpensively. This original variant is known as the Minimal Viable Product. And we found the wonder of the beasts, simply to appreciate it isn't bringing some clients and even though they perform, that the churn rate is high. Clients decide to try it rather than return. This fizzles off the driveway and we build greater enhancement to the goods and finally after losing time and money, we provide up departing the entrepreneurs disheartened.

Realization: It will take more than MVP to build a sustainable business enterprise.

Complementing the teachings of 37 signs could be the Startup moment. It discusses early adopters, supported learning, linking to this development engine and construction sustainable business enterprise. Entrepreneurship is all about going into the anonymous and although you fully grasp that the Lean startup approaches it becomes difficult to map those on you to your enterprise version. It's really a tough beginning, but undoubtedly a one. Returning into the failed startups, it's more surprising to observe that a day or two after, somebody managed to get by means of a comparable idea. What exactly did the MVP shortage could be that the question we frequently needed a thousand replies but none who have been funny.

Additionally, it boils down to how the majority of entrepreneurs possess certain expertise. They may be designers, programmers, marketer, business programmers or real visionaries. But before you started building the MVP, then you failed to answer the vital question - Which are the clients? Assembling an MVP is insufficient. The target ought to be to generate an MVC - Minimal Viable firm. To accomplish that you'll need pros in the branding, promotion, fund raising, web development, business construction and a lot more things. Solopreneurs could have one or even at the three of the aforementioned skills. Deficiency of mathematical abilities could be the key source of failure for the majority of startups. Seeing that, a fresh strain of incubators is forming which offers a more" Startup in a box" services with expertise in each of the elements required to make success. They truly are construction pros in each one of the four principal areas from business construction, promotion, financing and web development. Each one these services are extended in a structure that could permit cover while you grow version that's the vital requirement of almost any startup.

Chapter 8. The Lean Startup Technology in Action

One specific area I will talk about in relation to lean startup is how you can efficiently manage your employees using the methodology (Sheth, 2019). It's a vital approach that ensures continuous progress for your business.

Nevertheless, you need to anticipate that trials and errors will be part of the process since you will need to continue experimenting, testing, and investigating whatever it is your offering, whether products or services, repeatedly as these develop.

You will notice the stark difference between a business that follows the lean startup methodology and a traditional startup. A traditional startup follows a methodological process that is built on long-term vision, strategy, and plans. On the other hand, a business following the lean startup will expedite the processes by going through the steps. Another difference is that information about the products or services will be kept to a minimum few – employees, investors, and test customers – until such time that the offerings are deemed marketable, keeping in mind that the entire process is done in stealth mode.

By now you're probably wondering, "What do all these have to do with effective employee management?" The answer is quite simple, actually. The more streamlined process offers managers a chance to discern whether or not there are some inefficiencies with the current processes. Thus, they can correct or change whatever needs correction and only deliver to customers what they deserve – value for money.

Bonds Strengthened Because of Lean

Another example of the lean startup technology in action is the development of a strong A-team. Because the build-measure-learn process is put in effect, the right people are hired and put in the right place. As a result, each one is given tasks based on the skills they possess, as well as their adaptability to the lean startup methodology. As your business grows, you can transition your first batch of employees, you're A-team, as brand marketers. This time, their job will be to talk about your business to others. This will result in a chain reaction of sorts in which brand awareness is raised without you having to invest money. In turn, this awareness will start raking in revenue and improve the confidence of your employees.

Once their confidence level is improved, they can go ahead and train a fresh group of employees with the same vision they had when they started with you. This unified faith in the vision and mission of your business is crucial because as much as possible, you want to have people working collectively for you to help you reach your main goal.

How to Get Started with an Effective Lean Startup A-Team

Here's the thing: a business' A-team doesn't just fall automatically down from the sky. In fact, one of the key elements in forming an A-team for your business using the lean startup approach is to hire people based only on the open positions. If there are no open positions in the business, then don't hire people. That is the best way to keep the business efficient. Moreover, because the lean startup methodology is somewhat of an unorthodox approach to starting a business, another vital element to forming your A-team is to choose people who will fit ideally to the lean startup culture you are trying to cultivate.

Then, you will want to entice these employees comprising your A-team to stay with your company by offering them something tangible. Knowing what an employee can bring to the table to add a unique value to your business can help you determine what sort of "incentive" you'll offer them.

Some businesses that follow the lean startup methodology offer employee stock ownership plan (ESOP) to their employees. An ESOP is a benefit plan, an equity, in which employees are given ownership interest in a business (Ganti, 2019). The ESOP, will be based on a distinctive skill that an employee can offer to make the business better.

Why should you, the business owner, go through such great lengths to keep your current roster of employees that comprise your business' A-team? Well, most of those employees left the security that corporate jobs offer just to join a new business. It is such a huge leap of faith, one that requires you to make them see that the big risk they took was not for nothing. They will have something to gain out of their big move. On the flipside, you need to make sure the incentives you will offer the employees will not, in any way, impede with business activities. You need to ensure the company stays protected and that every business activity is always carried out in a professional manner.

If you decide to give your employees ESOP, you need to ensure you're doing it properly. There needs to be a structure you will follow to make sure the process flows smoothly. Perhaps a good way to decide how much an employee will get is to have a pre-determined range of equity stake. This percentage will be paid over and above the salary that an employee receives. Here's a model you can follow:

- Rank-and-File Employees and Junior Managers – 0.2 to 0.33%
- Managers and Senior Lead Managers – 0.33 to 0.66%
- Directors – 0.4 to 1.25%
- Product Development Leads and Engineers – 0.5 to 1%
- Independent Board Members – 1%
- Vice Presidents – 1 to 2%
- Chief Operating Officer (COO) – 2 to 5%
- Chief Executive Officer (CEO) – 5 to 10%

As you can see, the bracket range above includes everyone, from the rank-and-file employees to the business founder(s). Keep in mind that the above is just a model you can use in your own business. There is no hard and fast rule as far as range brackets go. You will decide on the best compensation; thus, it's vital that you fully understand the types of ESOPs you can offer to employees.

A flexible schedule is yet another thing you can offer employees. Believe it or not, there are people who work best during daytime and there are those who work best after the sun has set. If that is the case with your current roster of employees, then by all means, yield to the schedule that allows them to function in their fullest potential and efficiency.

Really now, if you want to keep your top employees happy, you need to learn how to be flexible especially when it comes to their work hours. Applying the lean startup methodology in your business will allow your employees to either work together in teams following a rotational schedule or anytime that is convenient to them. If you will opt for the flexible schedule, then you may want to consider allowing some of your employees to work from home, too.

Another way to allow for flexibility in a lean startup "environment" is to veer away from setting hours for team members. Try giving project-based work that follows a specific timeline. This means there is only a set number of hours they have to get the job done.

Indeed, the lean startup methodology can do wonders to improve the efficiency of employees. Nevertheless, it will all depend on how "understanding" of their circumstances you are as an employer. If you're unyielding, then the growth of the business will be stunted no matter how hard you try to implement the lean startup approach.

The whole idea of adopting a lean startup culture in a business is to help it improve continuously. If you will not be open to changes, continuous improvements in your business, no matter if these are big or small, will be impossible. Remember, a business that applies the lean startup approach revolves around change.

Just make sure everyone of your employees, from the lowest to highest rung of the ladder, is aware when changes are implemented. It doesn't matter what the changes are about. The changes are meant to benefit not only the business as a whole but also each and every one of your employees. Hence, you need to make them aware of the changes if you want them to be on the same page as you are during the implementation period.

Every one of the people comprising a "lean startup team" must be moving in the same direction. That is the key to the successful implementation of the lean startup methodology. Employee's commitment, whether you're the CEO or a rank-and-filer, is necessary since the whole idea of the lean startup is everyone having a shared purpose to foster a culture of improvement in a business.

Chapter 9. What Is Lean Analytics?

Lean Analytics is part of Lean Startup methodology that is made up of 3 elements—Construction, Assessing and Learning. These three elements sort a lean analytics cycle of product creation. This highlights that fast assembles an MVP (Minimum Viable Product). You may create more intelligent decisions with accurate dimensions of lean Analytics.

The main aim of these lean analytics businesses needs to make the most of the educational at a quick time period. The end result of using lean analytics will probably be much more successful and nimble firm.

Lean Analytics that's a sub category of Lean Startup methodology insures the step and also learn section of this cycle. What this means is without proper dimensions you can't take any choice. Before employing this methodology that the businesses should definitely understand what ought to be monitored, for why it needs to be monitored and which would be the ways for use for tracking. The lean stats cycle is displayed at the picture underneath.

Recognizing An Excellent Metric

As we know more about the lean analytics cycle may be that the dimension of movement towards your specified aims. Thus as soon as you've defined your small business aims then you want to be aware of the dimensions to get progress towards your aims. There aren't many faculties of metrics that are good. It's recorded below

1. Comparable—A fantastic metric ought to have the ability to compare. You Can answer these questions together with your metric
- How was the metric the last season or even the preceding month?
- Is your conversion speed rising?
- The conversion rates could be monitored most useful with Cohort Analysis.
2. Understandable—Metrics ought to perhaps not be complicated or complex. It ought to be readily understandable by everybody else in order they are able to be aware of exactly what the metric measures.
3. A rate or ratio—Total numbers must not be utilized in Metrics. If whatever is expressed concerning percent it'll be far superior to compare and make conclusions based on this.
- Adaptability—Great metrics should alter the way your business varies. In case the metric is proceeding and you also don't understand for that which then it is perhaps not really a fantastic metric. It will always proceed alongside you personally.

Correlation and Causation in Lead Analytics

To get any company, it's extremely crucial to differentiate between your co-relational and also causational romance.

To get example, consumption of ice-cream can be associated with fever. The more folks eat up ice-cream you will find greater odds to obtaining a fever. We can't even arrive at the end that ice cream induces distress. That is only because fever may also occur as a result of times of year, that correlates with ice-cream ingestion. Fever mostly does occur through the summertime that's the growing season where folks eat more ice cream. This really is a spot in which significance and casualty match.

When we state two things are connected, then this usually means two factors affect just as ice-cream and congestion at the above mentioned example. An informal variable here's that the summer weeks since they directly impact both dependent factors, ice-cream, as well as congestion. The reason being the summertime are somewhat more vulnerable to ice cream consumption and congestion.

Correlation helps to forecast the near future and it's going to let you know what goes to happen

Casualty is a super power that will allow one change the upcoming

The process goes like this

- Locate the significance on your data
- Evaluation for casualty
- After locating the casualty factor optimize it

Lean Analytics Framework

The Lean analytics framework can allow one find out the business enterprise you're in and also the stages of one's small business. Your enterprise design should think about the clients and their buying procedure. You need to ask yourself a few questions before forming a company model such as

- How clients purchase your product or service?
- The reason why they purchase from you?
- At what point of one's company they're in?

What is the budget of your own customers?

Do not replicate the others business version. Frame your own personal company version. Your enterprise version needs to perform best for your own customers. Listed below is your picture symbolizing the company version.

Lean Analytics Stages

In Lean Analytics stages, you will find gates that the company have to maneuver to make it into the next point.

In the very first lean analytics phases, you want to discover a challenge where the folks are looking for an answer. This phase is more essential for B2B enterprise. For those who are finding this kind of issue then you are able to move ahead into this next point.

In the 2nd lean analytics phases stickiness, you should produce an MVP product to early adopter clients. Within this phase, you ought to target for user participation and preservation. It is possible to figure out that when folks begin to use your goods. It is possible to even be conscious of user participation and retention out of the moment that they stick to your own website. In the event the users remain quite a while then it demonstrates you have given what they wanted. Next, you could spread into this future stage Virality.

In 3rd lean analytics phases, you want to secure more clients in a cost-efficient way. Once you receive the clients it is possible to move ahead into the following stage Revenue.

In this 4th lean analytics phases, you're able to concentrate on the calculation of one's earnings and also do the economics work. You're able to pay attention to optimizing the revenue. LTV means that the revenue expected from an individual and CAC usually means that the fee required to find the client. The ratio is also seen out by dividing the LTV from CAC. You are able to assume your gross profits are good if the LTV is just three times in your CAC. After calculating your revenue you're able to go on into the previous point, Scale.

In this lean analytics phases, you could take crucial actions to cultivate your company. You're able to create plans at which to concentrate longer as a way to grow the development of the small business and enlarge it.

Chapter 10. Lean Analytics to Succeed

Implementing the Lean Analytics envisages the use of change in the thinking at the workplace. The first step to achieve this is to make a pivotal point in the hierarchy. When we use this, the clarity in the workplace remains enhanced. In most normal cases, this occurs by implementing the agent for change. This person remains responsible for all changes brought into force through Lean.

By choosing one leader, it becomes possible to revert any changes that do not work. This happens by streamlining the work through this central point. Also, we make the responsible person take action for all the work-related activity. So, if there is no action from the responsible person, the downstream activity ceases. Only when the leader agrees and approves of the changes, the rest of the work undergoes implementation.

The work then proceeds forward and the same condition gets applied to further activity. The change remains regulated by streamlining it through the central point of activity. And when any change gets detected that is not normal or expected, all the further downstream activity ceases. Once this flow path has come into force, it is easy to govern the natural evolutionary process for downstream activity.

Use the Services of a Lean Consultant

Learning the Lean Path is essential. It is easy to govern the workers once the process has begun. But, only the people who are conversant with the method of Lean will know when to make the needed changes. The knowledge is needed for the parallel working types in Lean that control each other. All the decisions and management principles remain data-driven and systemized through actual use.

For instance, you have two or three HR situations, which do not yield, direct answers in a normal analysis. One is the case where the turnover is low and the number of employees leaving the firm is rising. Next, the budget for training is big, but there is no clear-cut region where employee deployment will be profitable. And third, the hiring expense rises all the time due to attrition among the employees at the workplace.

To arrive at the solution, get a snapshot of the metrics. This will give a view of the nature of the problem. Check the metrics in related areas and see if there is any correlation. Use of KPI gives you the answers needed to make the changes. You can make use of pre-designed KPI software to do the analysis. It helps you to centralize the data related to the business and simplify real-time reporting. Actionable work gets broken into smaller pieces and removed until only those relevant to the work remain.

Use a Lever to Begin the Transformation

Most of the hardships one faces are situations begging for alternatives. And, every business undergoes these situations often. Rather than wait for a crisis to begin to make the change, begin the movement towards Lean by initiating the change yourself.

When you face a troublesome situation, one must change. The Lean philosophy anticipates changes and makes provisions for each. By preparing for the change, it is possible to overcome the negativity and create the positivity that will take the business to a profitable end. This situation applies to the client, the business owner, and the suppliers involved in transacting business.

The other alternative is to change the focus so that the problem does not seem as large. The Lean expert waits until the crisis has passed before he seeks the solution. In doing so, he gets a solution with ease.

Do Not Aim for Grand Solutions

The idea is avoidance of the key issues that precipitate the issue and look for solutions away from the hotspot. Many business problems solve themselves if you give it enough time. With this in mind, the Lean expert tries to figure out how to keep the mechanism of the business moving without overlapping in the key problem areas.

The first thing to do is to stop thinking of grand solutions. You will not get anything that will heal the situation instantly. And if you continue to think along those lines, you will only become disillusioned. It is better to think of small actionable solutions that have a better chance of working.

If you consider applying growth metrics in the workplace, you need to apply the Lean Analytics related to this metric. This includes the acquisition to growth employee life cycle and the lifecycle during retention. You must then consider the cycle after attrition to reacquisition.

One may improve the bottom line impact in the HR department by using better resource application. Also, use cross-training across all departments. Using Lean, you can improve the sensitivity of the training program by a huge amount.

Make a Map with the Implementation Timetable

The scientific approach to the problem of making the map involves the use of the positivist perspective on one hand. And, you use the hermeneutic perspective on the other. In the first, the user remains distanced from the aim and the research problem.

The problem gets divided into smaller pieces so that there is the possibility of refining the process and cutting out the waste. In the second method, the researcher remains central to the problem. All the flow processes get importance relative to him and those processes that lose their importance get eliminated.

The creation of the timetable helps to improve the flow value and the perspective. Each work function becomes more important or less important because they have to meet the time check. When the tasks fail to meet the time check, we check for alternative solutions that have a better possibility of meeting the timetable.

Take the First Step Immediately

It is important for progress in any business to begin activity immediately. This means that one uses any one of the scientific approaches existing between theory and reality to come through with an action plan. In the most normal case, one uses the induction-deduction method. These are opposing methods of analysis and find applicability to any kind of work situation.

If you have the reality worked out, then there is no need for any deep analysis. One may put into action the plan in a step by step approach. Inductive reasoning finds a use for most of the cases where there are no real results and the opinion remains needed to take the next step.

In the deductive or scientific method, there is an existing theory. This means that the reality is apparent. So, you can use it to proceed to the next step. The main focus is to show visible activity. This will set off the process and the chain reaction will continue until there is no more productivity. To see the result, one must begin the first step immediately.

Check for the Results Immediately

It is important to check the results fast and see the amount of progress one has made. Changes to the amount of working capital show in a clear way to all. But, the deeper metrics such as the Return on Equity and Vendor Expenses may not come to light as fast. Yet, these will impact the business in a big way.

You need to set the benchmarks and targets for the vendors in the first place. By checking the results immediately, you will know if you made the right decision and if so, how much profit is accruing from this.

You make use of Lean thinking and methods to improve profitability through timely action. You also cut the redundant processes. By concentrating on the processes that have more value, you improve the efficiency and lower the labor overheads.

Use Progressive Results into Value Stream Building

One side of the Lean method is where one cuts the unneeded processes. The other side is where one builds the processes that show positive results. When implementing qualitative processes, there is a lesser amount of control. You can improve the formalization and grade of control by the use of quantitative structures.

Use of real-time targets will cut the amount of uncertainty and bring more cohesiveness into play. For the practical values, one must use tests and questions. Then, one must study documents and information registers before using the suggested values. But, once you do this, you have a viable working system that you can depend on.

Tips for Using Lean Analytics to the Fullest

They're simple and to the point, so you can get down to brass tacks and generate movement within your company!

- If you're considering A/B testing, you need a large user base to give you an accurate picture.
- Make big changes so your A and B look different enough to matter.
- Take great pains to ensure you're measuring test results properly.
- Cut out the tools that don't work and hold onto the best one like your company's life depends on it because it does.
- Always be willing to reevaluate where your business stands in the present moment and make changes accordingly.
- Make sure you fully understand your metrics before doing anything with them.
- Focus on the main problem before the minutia.
- Cut back on waste wherever you find it. It is toxic to your business.

Chapter 11. Benefits and Criticisms

It portrays another methodology for new businesses and endorses practices they ought to adjust to improve the probability that they will succeed. While the idea is most appropriate in an innovation or Internet setting, it has a more extensive application for all startups.

So what are the key precepts of the approach?

In numerous regards, the idea begins with a redefinition of what a startup is. For Steve Blank – a startup is basically 'an association shaped to scan for a repeatable and adaptable plan of action.'

I have reverberated this subject that depicts how a startup needs to concentrate on finding a feasible plan of action while working in a climate of 'extreme vulnerability.' Framing a startup along these lines causes move the concentration to a progressively logical methodology where activities attempted are seen as tests that rapidly assist you with approving presumptions (or something else).

Scanning for a suitable business model

Given that you are in examine mode, it is imperative to grasp some straightforward procedures to guarantee the quest for an adaptable business model is a productive one. From numerous points of view, these are lessons in hyper – proficiency, where time and money are valuable, and the reason for basic educated leadership is essentially on the rear of building what they call a Minimum Viable Product

(MVP). An MVP is an essential rendition of the product that can be sent to certain clients (in a perfect world early adopters) who will give you input, which will enable you to choose what to do straightaway.

The accompanying example perfectly delineates the concept: As opposed to building the service and giving it a shot on clients, make a sign-up page that vows to convey this weighty ability. At that point, present it to some forthcoming customers. Contrast their enlistment rate and that of a benchmark group given the standard indication-up page. The outcomes will give the group the certainty either to continue or toss the thought into the round record. Nobody would get the new element yet, obviously, because it hasn't been manufactured.

As a result it has been proposed that you search for 'proof of interest' before building the total product, and a simple method to test for this is to watch genuine client conduct on the state, a web page. Each snap-on a catch signals plan, paying little heed to whether the product in the back end is there or not, and this information causes you to survey likely request.

Additional Lean Startup Concepts

The accompanying speaks to a short portrayal of a portion of the fundamental ideas related to the L.S. approach.

Test Frequently and Learn Quickly

As the above case of the MVP approach illustrated, they prompt that you don't assemble a detailed product before you have embraced various tests along the way (They are large supporters of A/B testing).

Watch and Measure Real Customer Behavior

Eschew focus group and watch how genuine clients carry on. Getting the MVP under the control of genuine clients right off the bat and rapidly gaining from what they do supports their entire methodology.

Concentrate Exclusively on Capturing Actionable Metrics

Maintain a strategic distance from metrics, for example, measurements that make an ideal impression about execution when they are fanciful. For instance: what great is 1 million page impressions if none of them convert? Rather business people need to concentrate on noteworthy measurements, for example, genuine measurements that can advise choices.

Be Comfortable Pivoting dependent on Key Learnings

The suggested you turn or stop what you are doing if the underlying arrangement isn't working (and your discoveries support the view that changing tack is bound to be effective than proceeding with the first arrangement). This view is especially steady with the perspectives on business arranging Guru John Mullins as portrayed in his book, getting to Plan B.

Grasp New Accounting Methods

Generally Accepted Accounting Principles (GAAP) have supported financial representing numerous years. In any case, it is contended that L.S needs to grasp 'innovation accounting' before they arrive at where traditional accounting kicks in. With this technique, he recommends that progress is best followed by watching things like client movement, commitment, maintenance, and virality. As it were, if client numbers are expanding, and they are being held with the end goal that Life Time Value (LTV) is developing fundamentally, this is a superior pointer of 'progress' than traditional accounting strategies.

Stay Lean

The word 'lean' alludes to speed and agility and not 'cost savings' as certain per-users confound (although that stated, they are against misuse 'all things considered'). Again it is prescribed that new businesses exploit the disclosure mode to rapidly realize what isn't working so they can make changes right away.

Some Criticism

Like every single 'new concept,' the methodology has a lot of critics too. A few people refer to the absence of fruitful examples as problematic, and others center on author's generally disappointing profession before composing the book. Others center on the risks of putting up a substandard product to market (MVP). In the meantime, Ben Horowitz has contended the case for the fat-startup:

"Quite a bit of what has been composed and said about lean beginning up's bodies well. In any case, that exhortation is regularly inadequate, and a portion of the things left inferred the least instinctive. There are just two needs for a beginning up: Winning the market and not coming up short on money. Running lean isn't an end. So far as that is concerned, nor is running fat. Both are strategies that you use to win the market and not come up short on money before you do as such. By making "running lean" an end, you may lose your chance to win the market, either because you neglect to support the R&D important to discover item/advertise fit or you let a contender out-execute you in taking the market. Some of the time, running fat is the correct activity. Thin is in, yet once in a while, you gotta eat."

For me, It feels that paying little mind to the idea; individuals will consistently discover defects and have solid counter contentions to specific components of the methodology. The consciousness of these contentions assists business visionaries with settling on progressively educated decisions in regards to whether they grasp elective methodologies. They are simply assessments of all things considered.

Chapter 12. The Lean Analytics Stages

There are several different stages that you will need to follow in order to have success when using Lean Analytics. You will find that you will not be able to proceed with a later stage until one is completed.

The stages are:

Stage 1

This is the finding and fixing stage. This is the stage at which you identify or find the problem that is causing difficulty on the lines of production or in your business. If your business specializes in Business to Business (B2B) selling, you will find this stage to be one with a great deal of impact for your business and your operations.

Once the problem is found, you will need to decide on and carry out the steps to get is resolved. Get the problems you found completely remedied with whatever methodology (consider Six Sigma) works best for you and your business), then proceed to the next stage.

Stage 2

In this stage, you're going to create a Minimal Viable Product (MVP) that can be used by early adopter customers. This stage is the point at which you're aiming to retain the users or customers that you acquire. This stage may take some time, as you'll want to nail down your product, nail down the methods of retention, and to learn about the current habits of the customers or users that you do have.

You may find that you need to cycle through a few different products before hitting the one that will get you the results that you need.

Stage 3

Once you have an idea of how the early adopter customers will respond to a product or a service that you offer, it's time to find the most cost-effective way to reach more customers that will want your product. Once you have a plan ready to obtain those customers, you can start to draw in more of them, get them purchasing your product, and move onto stage 4.

You don't want to get a product that your customers love, but which you can't sell at a decent profit. Such products can make growth dodgy and difficult and should be avoided.

Stage 4

This stage involves a bit of an exercise in economics. You will want to optimize your revenue, which will mean calculating the ratio of Lifetime Value (LTV) to Customer Acquisition Cost (CAC). LTV is the revenue that you anticipate getting from each customer you've acquired for your business. CAC is the cost you've put into acquiring those customers. By simply dividing the LTV by the CAC, you will have an accurate picture of how viable the ratio is. If the result is three or higher, you're in great shape.

LeadCrunch advises that you get $2.50 back for every $1 you spend on lead acquisition. You want a 250% return on your investment into those leads on potential customers.

If you find that your LTV: CAC ratio is lower than 3:1, then you need to reevaluate the leads that you've chosen and find some with demographics or specifics that fit your target market more appropriately.

Stage 5

The final stage will require you to take the actions necessary to grow your business. You are welcome, to begin with, your current plan if that is making enough from the efforts of the previous steps to satisfy your margins or you might find that you need to make some changes in order to keep your business growing and thriving.

It is also at this stage that you can make plans for later execution that will help your business to grow if you're content to continue using a certain plan for now, but you would like to work on another one in the future!

The main goal is to keep your business moving and growing at all times. The speed at which this happens is completely up to you and what your team can reasonably handle. Laying out plans for this and carrying them out over a reasonable and digestible timeline is a valid approach to that end.

Chapter 13. Types of Metrics

Learning to use Lean resources and principles is half the battle. Also, you will come across questions such as, "Is Lean better than Six Sigma?" Or, "Is it better to use the Theory of Constraints?" When you use more than one method, you will get lost. One may get over the arguments over philosophical or even technical differences with ease. You only have to stick to the basic Lean principle of avoiding excess and getting rid of waste.

Overview of Over-Production

The production cycle has in-built questions to start the next cycle. The first one is to please only the customer and stop when you reach the target. Have I achieved today's quota? If the answer is yes, then stop production. Until the customer places a new order, do not make anything.

This principle applies to all departments in the organization. The idea is to achieve the perfect value stream. Other than this, there is nothing you need to worry about. In Lean, we reduce the steps we use to help cut waste, while the Six Sigma principle checks for variation. The more variations there are in the process, the more chances there are for waste to accumulate. You need to follow only Lean principles of keeping the number of steps down.

Use of Lean Principle at Work

To separate technicality from the working, it is important the workers understand and use Lean principles. Often, there are problems that seem technical in nature but involve real people. You begin to use Lean principle at the core, the place where the problem arises with only one man. Then, expand the core team to as many as you need, until the problem gets resolved.

It takes some time for the principles to go into operation because there is a learning curve involved. If you do not have the Lean thinking, then there will not be much progress. Also, the team must know if the circumstances are right. If they are not, they must identify the cause and size of the problem. It may be due to one or more of the following:

Lack of commitment: The worker does not feel there is a need for Lean methods. He uses traditional principles but gets foxed when others seem to feel something is extraneous. Shift the focus and reexamine the problem.

Performance not aligned with commitment: This is more serious because work is ongoing and the value is not reaching the expected level. We need a change in the attitude because the worker wants to get measured according to the performance parameter. He is not worried about the process parameter.

Lack of training: The workers get deployed before they have got trained. So, they keep looking at the others when the work proceeds. Change the worker to another place and keep the work going. Wait until the person addresses the problem by confronting it.

We see that the Lean working method is not a toolbox we can pick from to achieve our ends. It is a total perspective that involves the entirety of the work process. When you see a segmentation of the workforce, say the people on the shop floor working at a different pace from the rest of the workers, you face a problem. Here the plant manager has to hit the stop button. Slow down the process, check where overproduction occurs.

He has a target to meet and must keep the workforce occupied. But, he can do other work and still meet the target. This is the Lean principle. Any extraneous work gets eliminated first. By moving the focus of the work to a new place, any kind of waste, in material or labor, is got rid of. The people need to have a Lean eye to develop the perspective they can depend on. This helps them understand how the factory works with each component getting linked to the next. They learn to recognize the elements that are important and work with these first.

Choose to Operate the Pull

You have many aspects affecting how to operate the Pull. The Pull is important because there will be instances where the workflow gets interrupted. One of the ways to use it is to address the question or problem from two or more perspectives. Pull exists at the nodes or joints of the structure in the organization.

The workflow question is, "Have you finished this work?" The problem question is, "Where is the box of material I am supposed to deliver?" And the Pull question becomes, "Who is the driver delivering the box to the work spot?" You can change the Pull in many ways until you have got rid of the externality existing in the structure.

So, you see the work proceeding, but there is a lag due to the lack of the box. The Lean principle tells you to cut the waste. Here you are wasting time. To cut this, you must address the issue by finding out who is bringing the box. The truck needed to deliver the box must undergo preparation. And then the box must get loaded onto the truck. But, since there is a problem, you shift the focus of the problem by diverting the loaders to a new place to do new work.

The problem is now resolved at two or three levels. One is the basic worker level where you give new work to the worker. The second is at the management level where you identify what caused the lack of the box. The third is at the deployment level where you keep alternatives ready to prevent any further occurrence of this event. Lean, thus, operates at many levels.

Make Comparison of the Steps

As the value stream progresses, the number of options keep on adding up. Many businesses keep these options open in the hope that some good will come of it. But, it ends up as a waste of space and effort. So, it is wise to get rid of all but one working option. When you have more than one option, it will end up in confusion.

If you have to make a choice, list out the options. Then, compare the merits and demerits of each one. Try reducing the steps in each and see, which one gets done first. This will prove to be the best choice.

Chapter 14. How to Recognize a Good Metric

One of the first conclusions that will help you to learn what your business really needs is that most businesses are using the wrong data or doing the wrong things with the data that they've gathered. When you don't make appropriate use of your data, you will be getting just about the same results that you would be getting if you had no data at all.

The Biggest False Metrics to Watch Out For

Any business that is working on eliminating waste and on delivering the best and most effective customer service will find that false metrics are a big risk. Many people don't understand how data works, what it means, and what to do with it. When one doesn't quite know what to do with the data in front of them, it can be easy to think you know what you're looking at, and it can be easy to be enticed by the incorrect metrics for your business. Some of the most common false metrics are:

The number of hits. I blame the movies for this one. This metric tells you next to nothing about who is looking at your site or why. This metric doesn't tell you where those people heard about your site, why they're there, what they want, and how you can get them to come back in the future. This might initially feel great and get you excited about the number of people seeing what you've put online, but you ultimately need more focused data than this.

Page views. This metric refers to how many pages on your site are clicked on during a given time period. This is a

115

slightly better metric than hits, as it does give you a bit more information than the previous metric. You typically will find that this metric won't bring about a lot of impact. In many cases, you will find that your business won't benefit very much from page views unless your business is in advertising. You want to count people visiting your site and this is typically measured over the course of a month so you know how many people you're getting on your page.

Number of visitors. This metric is better, but since there aren't any specifics about the people who are visiting the page, it's often too broad for the average company to use unless your business is in something like advertising. This metric doesn't separate out people who are visiting multiple times, so this metric could also be called "Number of visits."

Number of unique visitors. Given what was just said about the number of visitors, you might think that this is the proper metric for you. That is where you see the demonstration of what was said earlier. These metrics can be very deceiving in some ways. You may think by their names that they will tell you what you need to know. This metric tells you how many individuals visited your page in a given timeframe, but it won't tell you anything about what they did once they got to your page, how long they were there, what brought them there, what they wanted if they got what they needed, or how to convert that visitor into a customer.

Number of likes, followers, or friends. With the vast rise in social media popularity and the traction of social media marketing, people will think that a vast number of likes, followers, or friends means that they hold a lot of influence, that they can sell things to all of those people, or that they've cultivated potential customers within those numbers. The fact is that those are very different things and they aren't necessarily synonymous. You can be a follower on a popular Instagram page without ever buying anything advertised on it, right? Having those likes, followers, and friends is a good thing if you know what to do with them, but they're not a good metric by which you can measure success of your company or the programs you're using.

Email addresses. Having a big list of valid email addresses is a great thing, and I won't tell you it's not. What it isn't, however, is a metric of success. It's a marketing tool that you can use to get the word out about your business, your plans, your products, and more. It's something that you can use to help you to bring more people in through your doors, as well as bring back past customers. Email addresses can and should be used for marketing, but they should not be used as a metric of the success of your company.

The number of downloads. If you have downloadable products for the public, you will find that it's easy to get excited over the quantity of people who have simply downloaded your materials. Those are your products in the hands of consumers, and that's what you want for your business. The things you miss out on when you count this include but are not limited to:

- How many people downloaded this multiple times?

- Who liked it?
- What did they use it for?
- Was this item helpful?
- Would they pay for it?
- Did they pay for it?

Time spent by customers on a page or website. Businesses that are directly tied to behavior or engaged time will find this metric helpful. Otherwise, you'll be tempted to make changes to your website to fill this metric, which won't do your business any long-term favors.

By avoiding these common false metrics and by understanding what these are really for, you will have a better shot at picking the metrics that will help you to expand and improve your business.

Chapter15. Automatize the Company Thanks to the Analytics

Lean Analytics help you track the metrics vital to the growth and profitability of your business. The first step involves identifying those that are good. So, what is a good metric? A good metric is one that satisfies the following criteria:

1. You Can Understand A Good Metric

This is important because unless people understand the metric and discuss it, they will not try to get involved. Only when people are involved in the change, the metric has a real impact on the growth of the company.

2. It Is Comparable

The users and people in your company can relate to the change of the metric over time. They remember the time when the metric was not growing so fast or when the growth slowed almost to a standstill. They discuss this aspect with the metric of a different company or competitor. It makes them involved in the growth process.

3. Ratios And Rates Are Good Metrics

The nature of ratios and rates make them good metrics. This is because they already relate to something and so you get the growth aspect straight by reading the number given. If you have this kind of metrics, use them as they will help you develop the true picture of the company and its growth.

4. Metrics Are Adaptable

The changes you have in the business remain reflected by the metric. First, you must be able to read the metric. Then, you must be able to use the metric. An adaptable metric is more useful than one that is not.

Find the stage your business is in

You know what business you deal with and so you can arrive at the metrics involved in the process. To find the stage you are at, check the gating metrics.

- Empathy
- Stickiness
- Virality
- Revenue
- Scale

Starting from the lowest one, you can pass onto the next gate by checking your present position. For instance, if you have found a need in the market that did not have enough suppliers, then you pass through the Empathy Gate.

At the second stage, you find the MVP (Minimum Viable Product) that satisfies the customers in the market now. The MVP has only the bare minimum features but takes care of the need of the customers. This is the Stickiness stage and the early users will find your solution easy to use.

The third analytic stage is Virality. It means that you have the product with all the features that the customer looks for and they like it. You need to make your product more cost efficient and attainable. Once you do this, you can pass on to the next stage. This stage is the Revenue stage where you get involved in the economics of the product.

Find means to optimize the revenue. The calculation involves determining how much of money you expect from the customer and how much money you spend to get the customer. If the first amount is at least three times the second, you have good margins. This brings you to your last stage. This we call Scale.

The Scale is the stage where you grow your business. You can make plans to allow the business to grow. More than getting the metrics and working with it, you should make the wise choice of metrics at all times.

This means that you should work with one metric that matters to you most. This may be Churn. If the Churn is less than 3%, it means your business is stable and growing. But, if the Churn is more than 3%, then it means that your business is in trouble and that you have to take action.

Use Metrics for Your Automation

Automation means letting the machines, here computers, do the work. This will involve three big steps other than the calculation and the setting up of metrics. They are as described below:

Put a Global Strategy based on Lean into Place

To be a global player, the businessman must have the access to the foreign markets. It is easy to build the market through the supply chain network or the sub-network if you invest enough money. This step is crucial and once this is in place, you have the means to merge your gains through Lean.

Every market has its risks and international exposure brings its own share with it. Use Lean methods of testing and placing new footholds in the market. Eliminating wasteful methods and time-consuming processes will be the starting point in the process.

Many companies used low-risk and low-cost strategies for making the market entry. One example of this is export. This proved fruitful for those companies that did not face much competition. Using the Lean strategy of labor reduction and cost optimization proved beneficial to the businessmen.

- Use of mobile app monetization
- Applicability of media sites
- Balance the inventory
- Create website content

You can hire the local delivery services to take care of making deliveries in foreign lands. This is the first basis for expansion. The second is to establish an online presence that helps you become a household name. You need to use mobile-friendly content and ads. This will get you to most of the people in the world because they all use mobile phones.

Completing the Transformation

Create an SEO friendly website that has links to heritage sites. Only this helps you establish your product on the internet. Facebook, Twitter, Tumblr, Instagram, WhatsApp, and the others provide more exposure for your product. Provide the links for all these on your website. Conduct contests that give rewards to the users that link your website to the most number of sites. The publicity is cheap but effective.

Get your customers and suppliers into the Lean chain

Integrating the supply chain and the delivery network through the market and finding the best point of entry and delivery for your product is the first step. Value stream management has lots of interest among Lean users because of the way it gives the best solution. To maintain market viability, you need to have a good delivery system.

The supply chain will succeed if your end users remain satisfied. Value-adding activities for your product will depend on the choice and deployment of the decoupling points. While agile systems are best applied to the downstream side of the decoupling point, the Lean system gets applied to the upstream side.

Use good bookkeeping software to keep track of the inventory and bill management. Also, add good content to your website to attract more visitors. Use well-written content by a professional to add real value to the website.

Chapter 16. Case Studies of the Lean Startup Method

L.S. has numerous points of interest. As indicated by a survey from HBR, the best five advantages of the L.S. approach referenced most much of the time by their corporate respondents were:

- Settling on choices dependent on proof and information instead of executives' instincts;
- A quicker process duration for creating thoughts;
- Better-quality criticism from clients and partners, frequently because you're asking them to purchase something instead of gush sentiments in a center group;
- "Escaping the structure": addressing and watching genuine clients and partners;
- Greater adaptability about gaining changes to thoughts as they ground from idea to least practical product (MVP) to a completed product.

Inspiring Lean Startup Examples

The confirmation is in the pudding. To exhibit the plausibility of the L.S. approach, It will portray three motivating contextual analyses. Note how unique these associations are, while regardless, they profit by a similar technique.

- Votizen

In 2007, David Binetti propelled Votizen, a platform that composes US voters online, as an MVP. The L.S., Binetti's first MVP, was not a major achievement. In the underlying client accomplices, just 5% pursued the service, and just 17% checked their enrolled voter status.

"David went through the following two months and another $5,000 split-testing new product highlights, informing, and improving the product's plan to make it simpler to utilize. Those tests demonstrated sensational upgrades, going from a 5% enrollment rate to 17%, and from a 17% actuation rate to over 90%. Such is the intensity of split testing. This enhancement gave David a minimum amount of clients."

This entire procedure of building, emphasizing, and estimating is the center of L.S. It was the start of an example of overcoming adversity. In September 2010, Votizen reported it had brought $1.5 million up in subsidizing. After three years, Votizen was gained by Causes, an online civic-engagement established via Sean Parker.

- General Electric

As a 125-year-old organization, General Electric is by definition about as far away from being a startup as you could get. Notwithstanding, they are regularly referred to as a fruitful cause of an enormous association utilizing L.S.

L.S principles and other problematic methodologies over its environment to consolidate the speed and agility of a startup with the scale and resources of an enormous endeavor.

In this program, client-centricity is significant. GE starts by asking clients questions about what result they are attempting to accomplish. Hence, the group taking a shot at an issue concocts a theory for an answer, after which the hidden suppositions are tried.

FastWorks has been a triumph for GE. The procedure has brought about shorter item cycles, speedier IT implementation, and quicker client reactions.

- RevelX

At RevelX, we attempt to turn into somewhat better in what we do each day. The L.S. approach is one of our managing lights, explicitly the fabricate measure-learn feedback loop. We have instated our development group, working in 3 weeks sprints, continuously testing.

For example, we explore ceaselessly with our website to acquire further initiation and new acquisitions. The site normally experiences little upgrades dependent on what seems to work.

Another model is that we dispatch huge numbers of our thoughts as a feasible base product. Take, for example, our growth. Directory. A spot where you can locate the best and most recent curated tools for running your growth tests.

- Dropbox

Dropbox is outstanding amongst other known instances of a business that has developed utilizing L.S. principles.

The file transfer service presently has more than 500 million clients worldwide; however, it began life as an insignificant practical product as a 3-minute screencast indicating shoppers what Dropbox could do.

Reaction to the video-enabled Dropbox to test if there was interest for the product and, simultaneously, catch an underlying crowd through a holding up list.

But, above all, remarks on the video gave an approach to Dropbox to increase high--quality feedback from target clients, which the group in this way used to shape item advancement following customer needs.

- Zappos

Another incredible case of the L.S. in real-life originates from Zappos, one of the first online shoe retailers, which currently sells everything from boots to packs.

When Zappos began in 1999, founder Nick Swinmurn didn't have the foggiest idea of whether clients were prepared to purchase shoes online. Presently Swinmurn could have left, purchased stock, developed inventory systems, constructed a system of dissemination focuses, and checked whether the plan of action took off. However, rather Swinmurn needed to test his hypotheses that customers would purchase shoes online. What's more, he did this through a minimum viable product.

Swinmurn moved toward nearby shoe stores, took photos of their stock, and posted the photos online on a basic website. If he got a request, he'd purchase the shoes from the stores at the maximum and afterward sent them straightforwardly to clients. Swinmurn before long demonstrated that client request was available, and Zappos would, in the end, develop into a billion-dollar business dependent on the model of selling shoes online.

Chapter 17. Lean Startup Advantages

As a startup, you have the huge natural advantage of having more straightforward access to enter from your clients, and being able to actualize changes dependent on that info significantly more rapidly and productively.

That is something most huge organizations would slaughter for and painfully miss. Here are a couple of ways you can take advantage of the nearer closeness to your clients.

The most effective method to Fully Exploit this Advantage:

- Uncover the entirety of your workers to your clients
- Build up input circles between deals and the remainder of your groups
- Concentrate your client service interactions
- Screen social interactions
- Jump on the telephone with your clients (or even better, meet they face to face)
- Mine your web analytics
- Consolidate data assembling straight into your product
- Make client feedback and information profoundly unmistakable over the association

You Can Turn on a Dime

Deftness and agility aren't two things enormous organizations are known for. Normally, the bigger an association gets, the more reliant it becomes on built-up structures and procedures.

There's more bureaucracy to manage, lines of communication become less and less immediate, and to top it all off, there are a greater amount of the greatest efficiency enemies of all — groups. Accordingly, arranging skylines will, in general, be in years instead of days, weeks, or months.

On the other hand, you can turn and respond to opportunities in the time it takes them to sort out a phone call.

The most effective method to Fully Exploit this Advantage:

- Pick a product to advertise that is quickly advancing or has dynamic needs or tastes
- Pick a product market that has huge long term advancement potential
- Fabricate your market before huge organizations comprehend what hit them
- Utilize new and creative innovations and plan of model segments
- Quickly advance all parts of your business
- Ensure senior management is getting out in the field however much as could be expected

You Can Develop an Intense Focus on a Target Niche Market

Huge organizations make some troublesome memories with focus. They, for the most part, need to expand their degree to support their development, creating products focused on various client sections utilizing numerous circulation draws near. Even they have more assets, and they need to spread those resources over an assortment of item showcases.

Interestingly, you can commit all that you need to build up a laser center around one quite certain objective section. That gives you a ground-breaking advantage. Not exclusively would you be able to build up a rich and inside and out comprehension of your clients — their agony focuses, needs, needs, and purchasing forms (also how they utilize and acknowledge an incentive from your product) — you can likewise get staggeringly clear and compact with your informing.

Instructions to Fully Exploit this Advantage:

- Pursue a niche
- Get everybody in the organization concentrated on that niche
- Strengthen that concentrate each opportunity you get starting from the top
- Keep your groups as little as could reasonably be expected

You Can Go After Smaller Opportunities

Huge organizations need to follow enormous market openings. They regularly can't legitimize following what they see as little markets (especially if those business sectors have unique needs). That leaves a noteworthy number of chances of getting lost in an outright flood that you can jump on.

The key for startup business people is to recognize and assault markets/socioeconomics that might be little presently yet are in an upward direction and have the potential for development. While this may paint you into a little corner in the first place, the upside is that you ought to have the option to build up yourself and become moderately undisturbed, after which you can hope to extend.

The most effective method to Fully Exploit this Advantage:

- Search for business sectors that are unreasonably little for huge organizations, or basically off their radar
- Search for client portions with extraordinary needs that aren't by and large completely tended to by enormous organizations
- Pinpoint a little or inert market that different new businesses are just starting to attack

You Can Innovate Much More Quickly and Effectively

Change is something any enormous association with built-up frameworks and procedures inalienably battles with. The equivalent goes for grasping risk. Not exclusively would it be able to be incredibly hard to arrange changes and new activities basically from a calculated perspective, there can likewise frequently be critical protection from it from workers and the executives the same.

To finish it off, there's likewise the propensity that Gladwell featured in his keynote at HubSpot's inbound conference.

For officeholders, inventive reasoning and critical thinking are frequently limited to making little changes and cycles to existing procedures and structures. They stall out in a "that is how we've constantly done it" attitude.

As a startup, you don't need to be controlled by those kinds of restrictions. In reality, the more imaginative and problematic you can make your business/arrangement, the harder it will be for greater organizations to duplicate, get up to speed, or compete with what you're doing.

Step by step instructions to Fully Exploit this Advantage:

- Be strong and take risks
- Fabricate innovation that contenders would experience issues incorporating with their present stage
- Execute a methodology that would be troublesome for a bigger organization to reproduce
- Enable individual groups and workers to test, repeat, and receive inventive methodologies

You Can Run on Next to Zero Sales and Marketing Costs

Perhaps the ideal way you can fight your Goliath-sized challenge is to make it your main goal to work as a high productivity benefit machine. The fundamental thought is to make all that you do — your item, evaluating, client support, and so forth — so convincing that you can change over your objective clients with next to zero deals and advertising costs on your part.

Note: The stunt isn't to remove deals and to showcase, by and large, yet to continue pushing for effectiveness by keeping costs as low as conceivable comparative with the gross benefit created.

The most effective method to Fully Exploit this Advantage:

- Concentrate on UX
- Construct social sharing highlights legitimately into your product
- Make your sign up and buy process as straightforward and erosion free as would be prudent
- Always improve your item and join client input with fast advancement cycles
- Influence free beta and preliminary variants of your product, at that point value it intensely
- Keep deals and showcasing costs as low as could reasonably be expected, and put your assets to the past five things.

Chapter 18. Whom The Lean Method Is Not Made For

After the distribution of The L.S. in 2011, the underlying method immediately spread among entrepreneurs, enterprise instructors, incubators, quickening agents, and enormous organizations. The L.S. (L.S.) method has since gotten one of the foundations of enterprise education in business colleges around the globe.

During their investigations, business students overall are probably going to have gotten guidance in probably a few parts of the L.S. method – it's regularly depicted as an important aptitude to be a director in the 21st century. Rather than the more static nature of business arranging, L.S. is more involved, as business people look to approve the suppositions hidden their plan of action utilizing "live" testing.

At the core of the L.S., techniques are the plan of the falsifiable plan of action hypotheses and their resulting tests with potential clients utilizing a minimum viable product (MVP). Generally, entrepreneurs are informed about structuring an arrangement regarding investigations to test and refine their plan of action through direct cooperation with clients from the start of their endeavors.

Until this point in time, L.S.'s ubiquity has generally been unchallenged by any basic bits of knowledge about potential constraints of the technique. In any case, ongoing academic investigations alarm to significant limitations in three areas.

The L.S. Isn't Free

To start with, Contigiani and Levinthal (2019) point to the potential expenses and risks related to utilizing the L.S. method. A portion of these expenses and risks are industry-specific, while others are increasingly conventional. Testing in the market with an MVP requires some serious energy and resources, which can generally be high in industry parts, for example, biotech.

Rather than IT-related sectors, fixed expenses in biotech are considerable, making back to back cycles of testing the item unfeasible. Moreover, business visionaries need to understand that testing items with clients may include the revelation of significant strategic information. Particularly in businesses where IP security is feeble, the potential dangers of data exposure might be huge. Concerning the last mentioned, making changes to at least one part of the plan of action dependent on the criticism got from clients includes costs. Moreover, these expenses can go past unadulterated money related expenses as more than once changing the plan of action conceivably disintegrates the entrepreneurs' motivation.

Utilizing the L.S. technique may likewise include reputational risks. By definition, the L.S. method expects entrepreneurs to show a beginning period, inadequate product to potential clients. It puts the business people in danger of contrary input that may spread to the more extensive objective market.

A Lot Of Testing Can Kill You

Second, Ladd (2016) finds that more approval isn't better. While enterprising groups that detail and test speculations perform superior to anything those that don't, there seems, by all accounts, to be a reducing and negative connection between the number of approved theories and the group's prosperity. As it were, business visionaries need to realize when to quit utilizing the L.S. method since, at one point, the extra time, consideration, and assets of leading an extra investigation may exceed its latent capacity benefits. Business people need to quit testing, lock the key components of the plan of action, and begin to scale the endeavor.

Preparation Is As Yet Significant

Third, De Cock, Bruneel, and Bobelyn (2019) show that the experience of entrepreneurs has obtained likewise assumes a significant job in the degree to which they can get an incentive from applying the L.S. technique. It isn't the involvement in L.S. strategy that confines its latent capacity benefits, yet rather the degree to which the business visionaries have earlier market information. Business visionaries that need earlier market information are less ready to understand the feedback obtained from testing in the market. Accordingly, earlier market information empowers business visionaries to make significant emphases of the plan of action utilizing the L.S. method.

Bearing on the mind these three focuses, maybe it might, in this manner, be progressively helpful to show the L.S. method as a probability instead of a sweeping arrangement. As set forward by Ladd (2016):

"As is valid for any business procedure, the method must be tailored and utilized with reflection and imperatives, not visually impaired devotion."

Acolytes are quick to shun understood methodology devices, for example, SWOT analysis (investigation of inner Strengths and Weaknesses joined with an assessment of Opportunities and Threats that can be found remotely) and conventional market investigation, at the same time, as a general rule, such instruments are as yet applicable.

L.S. bad-to-the-bone clients ensure that flexibility is vital to finding that item showcase fit. We concur with this, by and large, yet, significantly, the enterprising administrator should be versatile to realize when to utilize L.S. and when to utilize other management tools.

Chapter 19. Managing The Threat of Competition

How do you feel about competition? Are you hoping that there isn't anyone else doing what you do, and therefore you will be able to get the whole market to yourself? Give it a minute and think about it.

Now, as you've been thinking for a while, what is your answer? If your answer is "yes", you are most likely wrong. Not having any competitors usually means that there is no market, or maybe just a small market. There is some market for almost anything that you can think of, right? But you aren't going to build a big company for a small market. And investors aren't going to invest in a startup that is targeting only a small market. Of course, investors usually don't want to see that you are entering a crowded market with a lot of competitors, either. So, what do you need to do?

First, you need to do your homework, identify your competitors and show them to the investors. There is nothing worse than saying that you don't have competitors (or only one or two), and the investor immediately names a couple of them that you didn't find. Once you've identified the competitors, you need to understand and show why you are different, and most importantly, why you are better.

Don't try to reinvent the wheel here. You need to show something that investors are used to seeing, because you want them to understand quickly. There are few ways to do that.

The most common is to show the four quadrants describing two benefits. One on the x axis and another on the y axis.

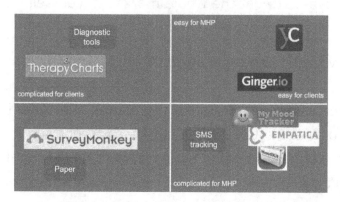

Of course, the top right corner is reserved for your startup and no other is supposed to be anywhere close.

When we were raising the first seed round (we rebranded from Youcognize - or yc - to Mentegram after that), we were pretty confident that our niche wasn't very crowded. As we were growing, we learned that Mentegram overlaps with some other companies we hadn't considered before, as well as some new companies that had emerged in the meantime.

Healthcare is a huge industry, and there may be the cases when it's not easy to differentiate you from your competitors. When we were raising the second seed round, we had to be much more specific with our competitors and be able to show the clear difference. However, the same approach as above would put quite a lot of companies close to Mentegram. That, obviously, leads to a very important question from the investors - "How are you different and better?". You need to have a very clear and sharp answer on that.

If you can't describe your competitive advantage in a few sentences, how do you expect investors to believe that you have the competitive advantage and are better than the competitors? In such a situation, you may want to consider a bit of a different way to show the competitors, listing them in a table with their benefits and features. Set it up just like you see prices being compared in a table on the websites that sell something. Can you imagine how pricing plans are compared? Think of something like that. However, a few minor features that competitors don't have aren't going to get you an investment. What investors like to say, you need to show that you are 10-times better than the existing competition. Clearly, a few minor features won't make it.

	Mentegram	qualifacts	empower	SelfEcho
Patient/Consumer App	✓	✓	✓	✓
Clinical App/Dashboard	✓	✓	✓	✓
Custom Questionnaires	✓			✓
HIPAA Compliant	✓	✓	✓	✓
Software Integration	✓			
Treatment Plan Integration	✓			

Another challenge waiting for you on the big market, especially when there are old and existing solutions, as well as young startups that haven't succeeded yet, is that you can find many overlapping products. The table will not be the best solution, either. That was also our case, so we ended up using the third approach. We listened very carefully to investors' questions about our competitors and used those as a hint to differentiate us. In general, there are three types of software that they knew, and they wanted to see how we were different. So, we took those and showed that we combined the best from all of them and that's what was making us unique.

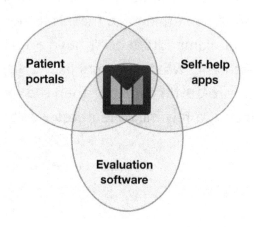

If the market doesn't have clear leaders that everyone knows, it might be better not to list the particular companies/products, but rather to describe the group. You are risking the fact that the one that investors know will be missing there. On the other hand, if there are some strong players, you should definitely show them and be pretty specific about how you are going to be better.

Questions for you

- Who are your competitors?
- Why are you better than your competitors?
- What are the barriers to entry for a new competitor?
- Is any intellectual property required?

Conclusions

The main key for achievement at lean is to know it is actually a journey. There's certainly no "silver bullet" in almost any service or manufacturing industry. When there have been, it will be sold along with every firm might contain it.

Lean starts with the best management of this venture. Best management should have the vision to comprehend both requirements and expected outcome, and devote the funds to achieving these. In the event the expected requirements and tools do not fit, any platform such as lean manufacturing will likely neglect.

The prerequisites depend on the business. If the business enterprise has 5000 employees spread across 1-5 centers in 20 distinct nations, certain requirements will probably be large. A tiny centre with 100 employees will demand less.

Management needs to comprehend that Lean manufacturing is actually a journey. It's something of employed maxims which contributes the organization to a country of "lean". When direction is hoping to reach "head count loss", they have been going for the wrong process. Any head count reduction should happen before applying lean production.

Lean systems demand everybody in the Enterprise to operate faithfully to eliminate all muda (waste) from the computer system. There are just eight common kinds of waste found in lean manufacturing. These wastes are therefore pervasive in associations which everyone else needs to pursue and expel them. People simply aren't likely to work themselves out of work, and so everybody else has to be supportive of their travel.

Lean additionally entails constant advancement through "kaizen". Kaizen in Japanese means "small incremental progress". Kaizens involve employees from all possible purposes to interact to eradicate waste, improve productivity, and enhance the company in every facets. Again, direction should have employees permitted to boost the performance. 1 part flow is just another system employed in lean manufacturing. Hence SMED (single minute exchange of die) approaches to decrease changeover times needs to be employed.

Other lean concepts used include "pull systems", "cell production", "kanban", OEE (overall equipment effectiveness), TPM (total productive maintenance), mistake proofing, real cause removal, and lots of more. Each one these systems need the attempt of a huge mass of employees to become more prosperous. For that reason, employees should not be scared of losing a project or lean manufacturing won't succeed. Once employees believe that they are able to expect direction, the lean journey will begin. The journey begins with lean manufacturing training plus it never ceases.

Lean manufacturing isn't a method which can be managed or employed by some individuals. It could be directed by A couple of individuals, however, the execution will demand everybody else. Every Individual From the company needs to understand the provider is implementing Lean production. Can it be to possess a competitive edge? Can it be to remain in business?

Many company procedures exist in Various forms of organizations from the recovery of garbage into sending the products that are completed towards the waiting customer. Saving time makes everyone else happy by eliminating the requirement to hire workers to fulfill tasks which must not be accomplished. By finding work arounds to your activities which do not have any means to better the creation of goods, each one these goals might be gained. One method is ensuring proper positioning of products whenever they're off loaded. What this means is nothing is setting idle, and distance isn't bought out also it's simpler to obtain what exactly is necessary at time minus needing for those searching for goods as when they're wanted.

Employing technology and machines too helps. This, together with smart programming, lets computers to see when matters aren't moving according to plan. By doing this, no body has to determine where online the error occurred saving the requirement to hunt every part. The opportunity of injuries occurring is lessened when everybody else is given a particular job to maintain . Broadly speaking, these threats are generated when one person isn't fully capable in what they're doing.

Measure Learn loop highlights rate as a crucial element to merchandise development. A team or company's potency is dependent on its capacity to ideate, fast build a minimal workable product of this idea, quantify its own efficacy on the current market, and also study out of this experimentation. To put it differently, it's really a learning practice of turning ideas into products, measuring clients' responses and behaviors contrary to assembled services and products, and deciding whether to persevere or throw the thought; this technique repeats as often as required. The stages of this loop are: Suggestions → Construct → Merchandise → Quantify → Data → Learn.

This rapid iteration makes it possible for teams to detect a viable path towards product/market fit, and also to keep on maximizing and optimizing the company version after attaining product/market fit.

Section 2: Lean Enterprise

The core principle of lean is to minimize waste and maximize customer value. In other words, lean is to provide customers with products and services of greater value while using fewer resources.

Every lean business understands what the customers want and focuses on improving fundamental processes to meet those demands. The goal is to provide the customer with products and services of exceptional value through a process that has minimal or zero waste.

Lean thinking will change the areas that are focused on by management to accomplish this. Instead of focusing on separate technology, vertical departments and assets, the management will focus on how the flow of products and services can be optimized horizontally across assets, technology and departments to its customers.

The management will also need to look at how waste processes can be eliminated along the value stream. It will need to look at how processes can be optimized to reduce human time, human effort, space and capital, which help to reduce the cost incurred to finish the product or service.

Such companies can respond to the changing needs of their customers with high quality, high variety, speed and low cost. Information management will also become more accurate and more straightforward.

Lean Management for Production and Services

Most people believe that lean management works best in manufacturing. This is not true. Lean management can be applied to different businesses and processes and is not a cost reduction program or a tactic. It is a way of acting and thinking for the whole organization.

Businesses in all sectors and industries, including government and healthcare have started to use the lean principle to change the way they work and think. Many organizations choose not to call this type of management lean, but state that it is their system.

You may wonder why organizations do this. It is done to drive home the fact that lean management is not a short or long-term cost reduction program but is the way the company operates.

The term lean transformation is used to define a company that is moving away from old thinking towards a new way or lean way of thinking. This means that the company has started to change the way business is conducted which takes perseverance.

The term lean was coined in the late 1980s by a James Womack, Ph.D., who was leading a research team at an International Motor Vehicle Program at MIT, to describe Toyota's business.

Lean Business Principles

Lean business principles entered the American business market in the early 1990s through the book "Lean Thinking." Lean thinking originated in the manufacturing models in Toyota automotive in the late 1980s after the introduction of Kanban.

Lean models are now used in different industries to reduce time spent on delivering high-quality products and reducing the number of resources used to achieve that goal. Let us take a look at some lean model principles.

Value Identification

It is important to remember that value to a company begins and ends only with the stakeholders or customers. If a customer requires a specific product or service from your company, you must use all the resources you need to deliver the product within the stipulated time. It is essential for every business to identify the products or services that will add value to its customers.

Value Stream Mapping

When a business identifies the products and services that provide value to its customers, it should map every process and procedure that the company must follow to manufacture or produce that product or service. It is during the mapping process that the business can identify the steps that contribute to waste or add no value to the goal. For instance, if the business discovers the process to place orders by employees is complicated, it must either eliminate that process since it is a waste contributor.

Flow

When the business creates the process map, it will identify the steps that are unnecessary or waste contributors. The business must then remove those processes or steps to create a flow. This flow will ensure that there are no obstacles that will hinder the delivery of products or services to customers. For instance, if a gardening service must visit an off-site location to stock up on supplies, it will take a longer time to deliver its services. The business must look at whether it can increase on-site storage space to enhance the flow of the process.

Pull

Lean processes always produce based on the demand from customers, which makes the processes "pull processes." Pull processes are those that call for the production of products and services on an as-wanted or as-needed basis. In service businesses, the delivery is always dependent on the workforce. For example, a pizza delivery service can choose to hire delivery executives based on the demand for pizza. If it is football season, there are bound to be more orders from customers. It is prudent for the business to hire more delivery executives during that period.

Perfection

It is important for a business to continually refine the first four principles to ensure that processes have minimal or no waste in them. The idea behind this principle is that any waste that goes unnoticed in the first four stages is always exposed over time.

It is important to eliminate that waste to help a business adapt to the changing needs of its customers.

Peter Hines has argued that the five principles of lean thinking may be insufficient for some or most contemporary business situations. He stated that businesses need to apply lean thinking only to some processes like order fulfillment without giving any regard to communication, leadership or quality management.

Therefore, it is essential to understand how lean thinking can be applied to help a business develop a holistic approach to the delivery of products and services.

Charter 20. What is Lean Enterprise?

What sets apart the companies that have stood the test of time from those that failed to take off? Well, aside from learning how to polish their branding, they continuously work on improving their human capital and management systems — changing accordingly with the times, and adjusting their strategies as they seem fit.

In contrast, brands that were never heard of again weren't able to plant a firm footing in the industry. It's mainly because each step in their workflow had issues that they weren't able to solve. It most likely didn't occur all at once, though. More often than not, a failed business' downfall started with a seemingly harmless misstep — until the rest of their system followed.

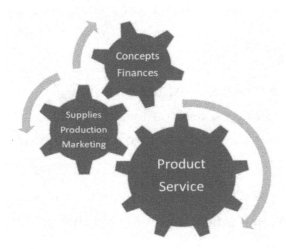

No matter how seemingly good a product or a service may be, it will only remain relevant to the market that it's supposed to serve if the whole work process is meticulously addressed. This is especially necessary during the beginning phases of building a business. The key is to lay down everything such that they will move in sync, so that when one part starts working, the rest will simply go with the right flow

The supposed workflow of any organization can be compared to a group of gears working in unison to move an entire machine. The picture is just an ultra-simplified version of how products and services — or more generally, outputs — are related to all the steps that come before it. So long as the gears are constantly well-oiled and nothing gets caught in them, the machine will move and operate as it should.

However, when faulty components start slowing down the movement of the smaller cogwheels, every part of the process becomes inefficient. Ultimately, the biggest cogwheel will be affected, and no output will be delivered according to the company's set standards — if any had been set at all.

This is why all parts of a process must be constantly assessed and measured. Otherwise, improvement will almost always be impossible, and moving towards the next goals will just remain a pipedream.

Thus, if you don't get your act together within the company, you're bound to offer people a bunch of products that aren't serving any real purpose for them. This may also damage your relationships with investors and suppliers. All it takes is another careless mistake and your reputation will now be forever tainted.

Successful businesses are going to have none of that. They know exactly how to get things done by using the most effective processes that they have applied through the years. Otherwise, they wouldn't be able to keep their gears rolling at the speed they want to. The question is, are they going through their workflow in the most cost-efficient and most resourceful way possible?

Lean Company, Lean Manufacturing, and Lean Enterprise

It's one thing to know how to get the job done. It's another thing to know how to get it done outstandingly. But it's a whole other level to know how to deliver high-quality outputs using the least amount of wastes and resources. Given the complexity of planning and production, it's normal to wonder whether it's possible that simple waste elimination can lead to the best products and services.

This is where the concept of lean thinking comes in. At its core, lean thinking focuses on how to come up with better methods of utilizing financial and human capital. Its ultimate goal is to provide maximum benefits not just to loyal and potential customers, but also to society as a whole.

This system attempts to operate on the idea that if each individual or group in the entire system can identify and eliminate the biggest wastes in their tasks, then all of them — as a whole — will be able to produce more valuable outputs using far less expenses. Not only will this drive an organization to its golden age, but it will also develop its employees' overall competence and confidence in themselves.

Lean thinking is the basis for all efficiency-driven mechanisms that are practiced in companies, manufacturing or productions, and even enterprises. But what does it really mean when every aspect of an organization is "lean"?

The following items illustrate the general idea of how lean enterprises are built:

1. Building a Lean Company

This is a company that follows lean thinking methodologies when it comes to production. Each step of the process has been aligned with the rest of the workflow to give way to a smooth and continuous cycle. Goals are typically addressed by creating a team that is composed of experts from various departments (cross-functional team).

2. Employing Lean Manufacturing

Also called "lean production", this involves a series of systematic methods for eliminating wastes and hurdles within production processes. It carefully assesses the wastes caused by uneven workloads, evens them out, and minimizes the chances of overburdening staff to improve output value and overall costs. A lean company abides by a number of lean manufacturing principles to enhance the workflow — beginning from the conceptualization phase, distribution, and even beyond.

3. Establishing a Lean Enterprise

This can be regarded as the ultimate product of all the offshoots of lean thinking. The lean enterprise is a grand collaboration among a number of companies — all of which are working to perfect a product or service that all of them will benefit from. The caveat, however, is that it can be tough for a lean company to reach its full potential if it's working with companies that aren't following lean methodologies.

Lean Thinking and Lean Behaviors

For lean thinking to make it to the enterprise level, it needs to be perfected on a personal level first. If individuals can make their tasks more efficient, these seemingly minute improvements are bound to translate to enterprise-wide successes.

However, members must also learn how to trade extreme individualism for team effort. It is inevitable that certain members or teams may have legitimate needs that are in conflict with other components of the system. A strong sense of cooperation then becomes necessary, which can only be achieved when all individuals agree to expand their roles in the name of a company or an enterprise's ultimate goal.

Members of cross-functional teams are usually trained to become more well-rounded. For example, full allegiance to their original function (e.g. marketing, financing, engineering, design, production) isn't encouraged in a lean environment. Team-oriented thinking and behaviors are needed to ensure that no phase in the workflow will ever end up being stuck.

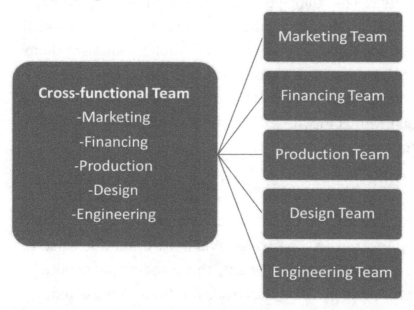

This is why it's necessary for members of cross-functional teams to accept, right from the beginning, that they will need to pursue an offshoot of their original career path to succeed as an employee of a lean company. Instead of performing their original function, they now work together with other experts to establish new value-adding processes or best practices for the roles that people like them play in an organization.

The picture illustrates how the members of a cross-functional team work with each other to develop a grand system that will sync team roles for maximum efficiency. They will look into the various roadblocks that get caught up between tasks performed by different teams. Once they come up with a viable solution, they will then meet with the respective teams so they can start implementing the new and improved system.

Now, when these roles are translated to the lean enterprise, member companies will need to establish new behavioral standards that will help regulate behaviors and activities involved in the enterprise workflow. What's important is that companies focus on what they're really good at to become a reliable member of the enterprise.

Lean as the Key to Productivity

In order for a lean enterprise to succeed, member companies need to refine their existing models to become more adept at doing more tasks using less resources. The problem is, while companies work towards eliminating wastes in their processes, this may cause stress in their employees, who fear that they might eventually be laid off from their jobs due to redundancy. Hence, companies need to explore and exhaust all of their options when it comes to job preservation as they work towards becoming lean.

Becoming a lean company may take years before you notice the fruits of all your efforts. Of course, when you have more wastes to eliminate, you also need more time to straighten out your workflow. This book will give you an overview of what you need to go through, plus the tools that can help you accomplish this huge task.

The lean models of business may be the key to building a company — and eventually an enterprise — that will generate the workflow efficiency that you've always wanted. If you're looking for ways to improve how business is done within your company, gradually shifting to lean thinking will not only help you increase your overall productivity, but also provide your employees with their much-needed career growth.

Chapter 21. What are the Advantages?

Becoming lean as an individual can make a big difference in your tasks as an employee. When you apply its concepts consistently enough, they're bound to affect your life's other aspects positively. Over time, you'll find that you're able to process decisions in a more systematic way. If lean concepts can have such a profound effect on a personal level, you can just imagine the possibilities if you scale the leanness all the way to an enterprise.

Shifting To Lean: What's In It For You?

Lean thinking encourages people to apply doable changes in small increments. The ultimate goal is to speed up all the workflows within a system without compromising product or service quality. Lean is certainly not a quick fix for eliminating company wastes. It involves being in a long-term commitment with continuous growth and improvement.

Even if a particular lean technique has been proven effective by many companies, changes certainly didn't happen within a few months of applying the methods. It usually takes far longer than that for anything significant to be noticeable. Of course, it's also understandable how people may feel discouraged to stick with the new methods if the benefits aren't that obvious. To help you stay lean when you're tempted to think that it doesn't work, here's a list of its short-term to long-term benefits:

Short-term Benefits

- Improved Management: Even though problems will still come up every now and then, lean makes the work environment more convenient to deal with if you're a manager. With better task standards in place, it will be easier for you to pinpoint anything that's disrupting the flow of the value stream. Most of the time, you will be able to figure out that something isn't quite right just by looking at an area's set-up or layout.

- Improved Efficiency and Productivity: As a result of standardizing every piece of the workflow, it becomes automatic for employees to know what exactly they need to do — and when they need to do it. It reduces a lot of redundancy and overlaps that stem from task confusion. It also ensures that they are doing their work correctly every single time. They no longer have to constantly ask whether a particular task is under their responsibility. They can just focus on their own task list without worrying about anything else.

- Safer and More Convenient Layouts: Since literal wastes will be decluttered, turning lean gives your company more space to move around. This will instantly make task movements a lot more convenient. Additionally, it will provide your staff with a safer space for working when the layout is reorganized to eliminate hazards.

- Involvement from the Whole Company: Lean is something that isn't applied only to one team or department. When a company decides to go lean, every level of the hierarchy is involved — from those on the top all the way to the ones on the bottom. After all, lean systems depend on the cooperation of everyone involved.

Medium and Long-term Benefits

- Improved Cash Flow: Once you get rid of DOWNTIME, you can now focus your energy on ensuring that the value-adding steps of your value stream flow as smoothly as possible. In the absence of roadblocks, workflow bottlenecks, and delays, not only will you be able to deliver products in a just-in-time manner, but you'll also improve the cash flow within your company.
- Customer Satisfaction and Loyalty: Customer satisfaction is one of the most immediate results of applying lean, so they become more likely to trust your brand again in the future. If you keep on doing what works, you're bound to gain their loyalty in the long run.
- Employee Satisfaction and Loyalty: While lean systems are mainly focused on the desires of the customer, it also promotes better mood and morale among employees. The changes may be met with resistance at first, but once they see that it takes them far less time to complete tasks compared to before, they'll become more open to the overall idea of lean. Additionally, since lean is all about constant

improvement and collaborations, they tend to feel better about themselves because they're part of a team that actually cares about others. Lean systems give them a safe space to voice out their concerns and provide suggestions for further improvement.

- Marketability for Collaboration: What makes something marketable? In terms of companies, marketable companies are usually unproblematic ones. You need to be that company if you wish to be a part of a lean enterprise. After all, lean is all about efficiency, and you need to be an efficient team player to ensure that you don't disrupt the flow of the entire system.
- Lean is not merely an exercise in cost-cutting. It is more of a long-term opportunity for consistent growth. Once you have smoothed out your lean processes within the company, you will eventually become the preferred suppliers of particular products and services.
- That's because your consistency and standards translate well to your products — something that lets both customers and collaborators know that you're a company that they can trust.

Challenges?

Lean thinking all sounds good in theory, and it can be exciting to continue applying it once you've seen how great it can be in practice. However, as Figure 8 shows, the tasks between teams or entities cannot always be as conveniently executed as getting from Point A to Point B in a clean, straight line. Their involvement with each other goes back and forth, which emphasizes how every component must be free of wastes to ensure a smooth flow.

Of course, shifting to lean has its own set of issues and challenges. Like any other form of change, you should resist hoping that it would do its "magic" in just a few weeks or months.

Technically speaking, when every factor is ironed out right from the beginning, it can be possible to have everything sorted out in just a short time. But that only applies when the scenario is ideal. Experience will tell you that situations are rarely ever ideal, especially when transitions are concerned.

Here are some issues that you might have to deal with on your way to lean:

Cultural Resistance

This may be the biggest hurdle that you have to get through when transitioning from wasteful to lean. When a status quo has already been set, most people are resistant to any change in the company culture. That's usually a result of staying in their comfort zones for long enough. They feel that change is unnecessary since they already like the current workflow.

To gradually ease the workforce into the lean system, training (or retraining) people must be prioritized. Here's what you need to clarify with them:

- What are the changes that you'll be implementing?
- Why are you implementing them?
- How are they going to benefit from these changes?
- How will it benefit the whole company?

Although all four of these are important considerations, they're likely going to be most concerned about the third point, as this involves their role in the company. However, if you can clearly explain the good things about these changes, then people will be more inclined to accept it.

Costs and Upkeep

On a personal level, there are cases in which you'll need to spend money today to be able to profit or save more money in the future.

Going lean requires the same thing. Eliminating wastes will need money because going for the long-term fix requires money. Eventually, however, the money you spent will eventually go back to you in the form of increased profits from minimized defects.

And, just like your home needs yearly maintenance, lean also requires upkeep. Proper planning and execution will ensure that you won't have to worry about running out of certain parts or having outdated systems.

Talent Gaps

Since lean processes may now require updated technologies, companies that are going lean must bridge the talent gap. This means that they may have to let go of general-labor employees in favor of those who have licenses and certifications to operate lean system equipment. These employees are adept not only at handling these systems, but they are also capable of performing maintenance, inspections, repairs, and designs.

Lean principles were first discussed by a MIT student named John Krafcik in his master's thesis. Before joining MIT, Krafcik had already spent time as an engineer at both Toyota and GM, and he used what he had learned from the Japanese manufacturing sector to set a set of standards that he believed companies of all sizes to be more efficient could work.

The basic idea is that, regardless of the type of business in which a business operates, it is still only a group of interconnected processes. These interconnected processes can be categorized such as primary processes and secondary processes. The primary processes are processes that directly create value for the company. In the meantime, secondary processes are needed to ensure that the primary processes run smoothly. Regardless of the type of process you are viewing, you will find that they are all made up of a number of steps that can be performed in a way that ensures that they work as effectively as possible and that they must be viewed as a whole in order to be effective complete the analysis.

As a whole, you can consider the Lean process as a group of useful tools that can be used to identify waste in the current paradigm, either for the company as a whole or for its upcoming projects. Specific attention is also paid to reducing costs and, where possible, improving production. This can be achieved by identifying individual steps and then considering how to complete them more effectively. Some tools that are often used in the process are:

- 5s value flow allocation
- Error resistant
- Elimination of time batching
- Restructuring of working cells
- Control cards
- Rank clustering
- Multi-process handling
- Total productive maintenance
- Mixed model processing
- Planning of one point
- Exchange of a minute of dice or smed
- Pulling systems

In addition to these tools, Lean also consists of a number of principles that are loosely linked around the dual ideas of eliminating waste and reducing costs as much as possible. Among which:

- Flexibility
- Automation
- Visual control
- Production flow
- Continuous improvement
- Load distribution
- Waste minimization

- Reliable quality and pull processing
- Build relationships with suppliers

If used correctly, these principles will ultimately lead to a dramatic increase in profitability. Whenever the opportunity is offered, the Lean process strives to ensure that the required items reach the required space within the required period. More importantly, it also works to ensure that the ideal amount of items are moved as needed to achieve a stable workflow that can be changed as needed without creating excess waste.

This is usually achieved through the tools mentioned above, but still requires extreme buy-in at all levels of your organization if you ever hope it will be effective in both the short and the long term. Ultimately, the Lean system will only be as strong as the tools that your company uses to implement it, and these tools will only be effective in situations where its values are expressed and understood.

Important principles

Although it was originally developed with a focus on production and production, Lean proved to be so effective that it has since been adapted for use in almost any type of business. Before taking over the Lean process, companies have only two primary tenants. The first focuses on the importance of incremental improvement, while the other is respecting both external and internal people.

Incremental improvement: the idea behind the importance of continuous improvement is based on three principles. The first is known as the Genchi Genbutsu and is discussed in detail below. Finally, to be truly effective, it is important to understand that you must lead your business with a clear understanding of the challenges that you are likely to face, as it is the only way to determine how you can effectively can handle.

In addition, it is important to approach every challenge with the right mindset, an approach that supports the idea that each challenge leads to growth, which in turn leads to positive progress. Finally, you also want to ensure that you take the time to regularly challenge your prejudices because you never know when your company could work with an assumption that is no longer true. This is ultimately the best way to find unexpected waste that will really start to improve, not only in the short term, but also in the long term.

Respect for people: this tenant is both internal and external, because it applies to both your own people and your customers. Respecting customers means taking an extra step when it comes to considering their problems and listening to what they have to say. When it comes to respecting your team, a strong internal culture that is committed to the idea of teamwork is a must. This should further express itself in an implicit commitment to improve the team as a means to improve the company as a whole.

Get a head start

Prior to the digital age, companies were able to determine their sales margin by starting with all relevant costs, adding a reasonable profit margin and calling it a day. Unfortunately, the prevalence of screens in today's society means that everyone is a bargain shop, simply because it takes so little effort. This in turn means that you are not only competing with other companies in your city, province or state, you are now also competing with companies around the world. As such, there are only a few options when it comes to overcoming any profit margin. Companies can add extra real or perceived value, or they can reduce the amount of waste they pay as much as possible.

Most companies think it is better to determine their margins by looking at what customers are likely to be willing to pay for specific goods or services and then working backwards. Ideally, you can lower that price by five percent to ensure that you are truly competitive in a cost-conscious world. Although it may not seem like much, this extra five percent is extremely important because customers are constantly looking for the next sale, regardless of how much is actually saved. The mental benefits that together with five percent are better than those around them will be more than enough to remain committed to your product or service.

Add value: no matter what your company does, you will find that there are Lean principles that can be implemented to improve the total amount of value that you offer your customers, while also showing that you value their company and them as individuals respects. In addition, you will be able to address the potential for wastage in your organization, while also maintaining the power and work to achieve perfection.

Often you can manage this by doing something simple, such as listening to the specific wishes and needs of your customers, making it easier for you to determine what they really value most when it comes to the niche of your business habits. Value is usually generated by adding something tangible that improves or alters the most common aspects of the good or service being offered. The goal is that this improvement is something the customer wants to pay for, so if they receive it for free, they see this as a viable reason for your service to cost more out of the door. It is also very important that the added value for the customer is very easy to claim, because otherwise they will feel that you have misled them.

Cost saving: since the Lean system is already quite large in reducing waste in all its forms, it is no surprise that it has some ideas when it comes to cost-saving measures. To begin with, it is important to understand that when it comes to Lean, all different types of waste can be divided into three types.

Muri is the name for the waste that arises when there is too much variation within common processes. Muda is the name given to seven different types of waste, including:

- Transport waste is created when parts, materials, or information for a specific task are not available because the process for allocating resources for active products is not where it should be.

- Waiting waste occurs when a part of the production chain has the ideal time when they are not actively working on a task.
- Waste overproduction is common when demand exceeds supply, and there is no plan to use this situation to the advantage of the company. The Lean systems are designed to ensure that this number reaches zero, so that supply and demand are always in balance.
- Defective waste is known to occur when part of the standard business process generates a problem that must be sorted at a certain point later.
- It is known that inventory waste appears if the production chain remains inactive between runs because it does not have the physical materials required to run constantly.
- Motion wastage is generated when required parts, materials, or information must be successfully moved to complete a specific step in the process.
- Additional processing wastage is generated when work is completed that does not generate value or adds value to the company.
- An often added eighth muda is the waste that is caused by the under-utilization of your team. This can happen when a member of the team is placed in a position that does not fully use them. It can also refer to the waste that occurs when team members have to perform tasks for which they have not been properly trained.

Muda also comes in three categories, the first being muda that does not directly add value, but also cannot be easily removed if the system continues to function properly. When faced with this muda, the goal must be to minimize it slowly as a precursor to remove it completely. The second type of muda is that which has no real value, and you should work to remove it immediately once you become aware of it. Finally, the third type of muda does not directly add value, but it is required for legal purposes of one or the other type. Although it can be annoying, this type of muda is inevitable in most cases, and the best thing to do is make sure you are always aware of relevant policies.

Chapter 22. Why Lean Matters

As a whole, you are able to think about this process of Lean as a group of tools that are useful and can be called up in order to identify if there is any waste in the current system, either for the business overall or for an upcoming project. Lean is all about reducing waste. There are some businesses that will take a look at the Lean process because they want to fix the waste and issues within the whole business. They may see that they have too much time between processes, they see that there are a lot of customer complaints, or they run into other issues along the way. Other businesses may just want to work with just fixing and reducing the waste in just one process within them.

With Lean, there is going to be more focus given to reducing costs, while also improving how the production goes any time that is possible. This can be accomplished by identifying the small steps that are needed and then considering the ways that they can be completed in a manner that is more effective. There are a lot of different steps that will show up in the Lean methodology, and we will talk about some of them. Some that you may want to utilize with Lean includes:

- Pull systems
- Single minute exchange of die, or the SMED.
- Single point of scheduling
- Mixed model processing
- Total productive maintenance
- Multi-process handling

- Rank order clustering
- Control charts
- A restructuring process with the working cells
- The elimination of a process called time batching
- Error proofing
- 5S value stream mapping.

Beyond the tools above, Lean is going to be made up of a few principles that are all loosely connected thanks to the idea of reduction of costs and eliminating wastes as much as possible. These would include load leveling, continuous improvement, production flow, visual control, automation, flexibility, waste minimization, building up good relationships with the suppliers, pull processing, reliable quality and more.

If these principles are used in the proper manner, it will result in a small increase in the amount of profitability. If it is used in the proper way and it is given the opportunity, this kind of process is going to strive in order to ensure that all necessary items get the space they need and at the right periods of time. Most importantly, it is going to work to make sure that the ideal amount of items will move as needed so that your workflow remains stable while still allowing for any alterations that are needed without all the waste.

The Lean method is one that many different businesses are going to try to implement into them. They want to be able to meet a bunch of different goals, and Lean can help them to get there. First, they want to make sure that they are able to provide a high-quality product to their customers. In order to retain these customers, reduce customer complaints, and other things that can waste time and resources in order to solve any problems.

Along with this, the company wants to figure out how to reduce any waste, reduce their costs, and earn more profits in the long run. Many times the waste that the company is able to get rid of with the Lean process will result in the customer receiving more value as well. It may take some time, and you may need to work through the process of Lean for a while, but when Lean is done properly, it can help your business out with all of those issues and can help it to grow more than ever before.

Important Principles to Remember

While the Lean process was originally developed to help with the industry of manufacturing and production, Lean has been so effective that many other businesses and industries have found ways to adapt it to their own needs. Every business wants to increase profits, reduce waste, enhance the customer experience, and just become overall more efficient. The Lean Process can work to make this happen.

Before you adopt any of the Lean processes, you must understand the two primary tenants. The first one is to focus on the importance of incremental improvement. The second is that the company needs to have a high level of respect for people, both those who purchase the product, and for their own employees.

With regard to the businesses' focus on its incremental improvements, the improvements do not have to be done overnight. However, the business needs to strive in order to steadily and effectively improve their processes so that there is less waste present. You must take a good look at the processes that you currently use and see where things can be improved. Is there to much waiting time in one area? Are the suppliers not getting things in on time? Is there a lot of movement for one part, such as a paper needing approval from three different areas before starting? Are some of the departments that should be working together on different sides of the business?

All of these can lead to more waste in your business, and it is important to avoid them as much as possible. When you take a step back and look objectively at the system you have in place, you are likely to see several spots where you are able to make improvements. Even if these are small, or incremental changes, you will be amazed at what they can do to eliminate waste, speed up your process, and even help customers enjoy a better experience.

But when working on the Lean methodology, we can't forget that there needs to be a high level of respect for people. This tenant is meant to be applied not only to your customers but also to your own people, the employees. When we show respect to the customers, it means that we go the extra mile any time there is a problem. We listen to them and then work to make the experience better. We help to fix the problem, and maybe even throw in something extra to help it get solved.

This same idea needs to be applied to your employees when you are working in the Lean process. When a company wants to respect their team, they will work on creating a strong internal culture that is dedicated to teamwork and treating the employees fairly. Employees will learn that they are valued, and that their opinion means something and that they aren't just another number that brings in the money. Any business that wants to implement the Lean process will need to improve employee morale, teamwork and more because they realize that by improving the team, they are able to effectively improve the company as well.

Getting an Edge

Before the digital age we live in now, businesses were able to determine what margin they had with sales by starting with all of the costs that were relevant, and then adding on a reasonable amount for the profit margin, and call it a day. However, the prevalence of screens in our day, either on the phone or a computer screen, means that everyone is a bargain shopper and can look around to find the best deal.

What this means is that companies are not only competing against the other similar companies in their area but also with those that are all around the world. Since customers can get online, they can compare and then pick out products to be sent to them for better prices, the competition for many smaller companies is steep. As a result, there are only going to be a few options available for a company when it comes to squeaking by with any profit margin at all. Most companies need to either find a way to add perceived or real value to the product, or they can reduce how much waste is in the process to make and distribute that process, and then save money as well.

Many times a business is going to find that it is better to figure out their margins by looking at what the customers are most likely to pay for the goods and services, and then work their way back from there. Ideally, you would like to be able to reduce that first price by at least five percent to make you more competitive, while still providing good customer service. It may not be a huge amount, but in a world where the customer is always looking for a discount, it can be a difference.

No matter what your business does or produces, you will find that there are several principles of Lean that you are able to implement. This can help you to improve how much value you can provide to your customers, and in the process, you can still show them that you appreciate the business that they send your way and that you respect them as individuals. This may seem like a lot of things to bring together, but the Lean methodology makes it happen.

Often, you will be able to manage this simply by listening to your customers and figuring out their specific wants and needs. Value is often going to be generated when you are able to add in something tangible, something that can either modify or improve the most common aspects of the service or the good being provided. The goal is that this improvement must be something that the customer will actually pay for, so when they get that benefit for free, they see it as a viable reason for your service to cost more in the beginning.

You will find that it is also important that the added value is as easy for the customer to claim as possible. Otherwise, they are going to feel like you have deceived them along the way. By making the added value something easy to see, easy to show off, and something of value can make a big difference.

The next thing we need to focus on is cost reduction. Every business wants to reduce costs as much as possible. This allows them to stay competitive in the market, helps them to provide a better price point for their products, and can help them make more money.

To help your company reduce the cost, you need to focus on reducing the amount of waste that you have. There are three types of wastes - Muri, which is waste that is going to come when there is too much variation in your most-used processes. Muda, the name given to the seven types of waste, and Mura, which is any waste that happens due to fluctuations in demand.

Muda is often the one that is the easiest to control and eliminate out of all of them, and the seven wastes that are included in it include:

Transportation waste: This is going to form when information, materials, and parts for a task aren't available because the processes for allocating these resources aren't working the way that they should.

Waiting waste can be created when there is some part of the production chain that has time periods where they aren't working on a task. This could happen because they don't have the right parts or they are waiting for another group to finish first.

Overproduction waste can occur when the demand is exceeding the supply, and the business doesn't have a good plan in place to help deal with this. The Lean system is designed to make sure that this ends up at zero to help the supply and demand for a product to be in balance.

Defective waste is another part to watch out for. This type of waste is going to appear when a part of your operating process starts to generate some issues that must be sorted out later on, often when the product is in the hands of the customer.

Inventory waste is often going to appear if the production chain ends up being idle in between runs. This can happen because that part of the chain doesn't have all of the physical materials that are needed to run all the time.

Movement waste can occur when information, materials, and parts must be moved around in order to complete that part of the process.

Additional processing waste can be generated if the work completed doesn't end up adding any kind of value for the company.

Sometimes there is an eight form of waste that needs to be considered. This is any waste that occurs because of the underutilization of the team. This can occur anytime that a member of the team is placed into a position that doesn't let them use their full potential. It could also refer to any waste that occurs when members of your team are working on tasks that they have not been trained to do.

Chapter 23. Creating A Lean System

Lean leadership

With so much emphasis placed on improving efficiency, the Lean process naturally puts a lot of emphasis on team leaders who should be working hard to directly inspire their teams to adopt the Lean mindset. In the end, many Lean systems live and die by the leadership involved, which means it is important that those who are put in charge of leading the Lean transition are able to not only explain what's going on but are truly committed to the work that is being done as well. Some of the things that Lean leaders should strive to emphasize include:

Customer retention: When it comes to customer retention, Lean leaders need to take the time to consider not only what their customers want at the moment, but what they are likely to want in the future as well. Additionally, it is important to understand what a customer will accept, what they will enjoy, and what they will stop at nothing to obtain. The Lean leader should also work to truly understand the many ways the specific wants and needs of their target audience throughout the customer base.

Team improvement: In order to help their team members be their best, Lean leaders should always be available to help the team throughout the problem-solving process. At the same time, they are going to need to show restraint and refrain from going so far as to take control and just do things on their own. Their role in the process should be to focus on locating the required resources that allow the team to solve their own problems. Open-ended questions are a big part of this process as they will make it possible for the team to seek out a much wider variety of solutions.

Incremental improvement: One of the major duties of the Lean leader is to constantly evaluate different aspects of the team in order to ensure that it is operating at peak efficiency. The leader will also need to keep up to date on customer requirements, as this is something that is going to be constantly changing as well. Doing so is one of the only truly reliable ways of staying ahead of the curve by making it possible to streamline the overall direction of the company towards the processes that will achieve the best results.

In order to ensure that this is the case, the Lean leader will want to make time in their schedule to look at the results and then compare them to the costs as a means of discovering the best ways to use all the resources available to them at the given time. This will include things like evaluating the organization as a whole in hopes of making it more efficient and reliable. It will also involve evaluating the value stream to ensure that it satisfies the customer on both the macro and micro levels.

Focus on sustained improvement: It is also the task of the Lean leader to ensure that improvements that are undertaken are seen through to the end as well. This will often include teaching the team members the correct Lean behaviors to use in a given situation and also approaching instances of failure as opportunities for improvement and innovation.

Three actuals

Lean leaders typically use a different leadership style than many of their peers, largely because being a Lean leader requires an understanding that the best way to analyze a situation is to physically be in the space where the situation occurred. Once there, the Lean leader needs to consider what is known as the three actuals, the broadest of which is known as Genchi and is the issue that led the leader to come to the place in question. Genbutsu is the idea that it is important to view what is being created or provided in action before making any moves. Finally, Genjitsu says it is always best to gather as much information as possible before making a decision one way or the other.

Creating a Lean system

In order to create a Lean system that lasts, the first thing you will need to do is consider the absolute simplest means of getting your product or service out to the public and put that system into effect. From there, you will need to continuously monitor the processes you have put in place to support your business in order to ensure that improvement breakthroughs happen from time to time. The last step is to then implement any improvements as you come across. While there are plenty of theories and tools that can help you do go on from there, the fact of the matter is that creating a Lean system really is that simple.

There's more to business than profits: When using the Lean system, the end goal is to determine the many ways that it might be possible to improve the efficiency of your business. While an increase in profits is often a natural result of this process, this should not be the primary motivating factor behind undertaking a Lean transformation. Instead, it is important to focus on streamlining as much as possible, regardless of what the upfront cost is going to be since you can confidentially expect every dollar you spend to come back to you in savings.

There are limits to this, of course, and at a certain point, the gains won't be worth the costs. To determine where this line is, you can use a simple value curve to determine how the changes will likely affect your bottom line. A value curve is often used to compare various products or services based on many relevant factors as well as the data on hand at the moment. In this instance, creating one to show the difference between a pre- and post-Lean state should make such decisions far easier to make.

Treat tools as what they are: When many new companies switch to a Lean style of doing things, they find it easy to slip into the trap of taking tools to the extreme, to the point that they follow them with near-religious fervor. It is important to keep in mind that the Lean principles are ultimately just guidelines and any Lean tools you use are just that, tools which are there to help your company work more effectively. This means that if they need to be tweaked to better serve your team and your customers, then there is nothing stopping you from doing just that. Your team should understand from the very beginning the limits and purpose of the Lean tools they are being provided and, most importantly, understand that they are not laws.

Prepare to follow through: Even if you bring in a trained professional to help your team over the initial Lean learning curve, it will still ultimately fall to you, as the team leader, to ensure that the learned practices don't fall by the wayside as time goes on. It takes time to take new ways of doing things and turn them into habits, and it will be your job to keep everyone on until everything clicks and they start operating via the new system without thinking about it. Likewise, it is important that you make it clear just why the Lean process is good for the team as a whole and for the individual team member as if they are personally invested in it, then it is far more likely that they will stick with it, even if the going gets tough.

Chapter 24. The 5 Principles of Lean Manufacturing

Many businesses are beginning to switch to lean thinking and lean manufacturing to develop the kinds of products that have a good chance of penetrating the global market. Aside from consistently meeting customer demands, it also enables them to earn more profits and enhance product quality with less cost.

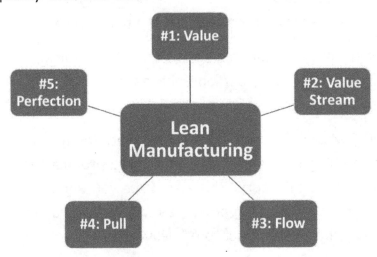

Lean thinking gave way to the five lean manufacturing principles that have greatly improved the workflow of many successful companies today. These are often considered as key factors in improving overall efficiency in the workplace.

Defining Value

The first step of lean manufacturing begins with learning what exactly the customer values in a particular product or service. This will help a business determine how much a customer is willing to pay for what, which then allows them to set a reasonable target price. After which, the cost of manufacturing the product will then be defined.

To properly establish value in a lean system, it is vital to learn about the market's recognized and latent needs.

While some customers may already know what they want exactly, others may not be aware that there might be a product or service out there that they actually want or need. Or perhaps, they know they need a particular something, but cannot express what it's supposed to be.

That's where market research comes in. This is typically done through interviews, demographic assessment, web analytics, user testing, surveys, etc.

By defining what your customers really want, you get to create something of great value — not just a product that seems innovative in theory. This also helps you understand your customers' purchasing power, as well as the way in which they want this product to be delivered to them.

Determining and Planning the Value Stream

The value stream consists of all the activities that allow you to conceptualize and create the most useful yet most profitable product that matches the customer values that have been defined in the first step.

This is the product's journey from the raw materials stage all the way to the customer usage stage. The stream even includes the customer's eventual disposal of the product, which paves the way for considerable upgrades in the next release.

Naturally, activities that do not provide value at the end of the value stream (customer) are regarded as wastes. These wastes can be subdivided into two types: necessary waste (e.g. quality control) and pure waste (e.g. supplier delays).

The latter should be completely eliminated, while the former should be continuously perfected so they don't get in the way of the value stream. Otherwise, they'd only delay the rest of the process.

Creating Flow

A river will always make its way to the ocean eventually, provided that nothing stops the water in its tracks. However, a significant amount of debris in one part of the river system may cause the water to be trapped and unable to follow its natural path.

This is exactly what waste does in a value stream. It interrupts the natural flow of the production process, causing delays that might start out small. Eventually, however, it might end up becoming a massive setback that prevents everything from moving further forward.

That said, a company must take their time to fully understand their flow systems to eliminate wastes effectively and completely. The concept of flow in lean manufacturing is all about creating a series of steps that are in sync with each other — one that hardly ever gets interrupted.

Setting Pull

One of the most significant wastes involved in manufacturing is inventory. To solve this, a pull-based system must be established. This system aims to minimize inventories and works in progress as much as possible. Relevant materials should always be available to maintain the company's flow.

Instead of creating products way ahead of schedule based only on market forecasts, a pull-based system encourages you to begin working on something only when a customer expresses the need for it. Thus, you'll only begin production at the moment of need, and only in the quantities requested.

This allows you to develop the most efficient way to assemble a product, as you need to deliver your promise within a reasonable timeframe.

Pursuing Perfection

The first four principles of lean manufacturing are all about identifying and reducing wastes as much as possible. This last principle is the crucial point that holds all lean thinking concepts together. Perfection based on company standards helps deliver products in the best state possible to the end user.

Although a perfect product can never technically exist, pursuing perfection is what inspires companies to continue serving their customers to the best of their abilities.

This is what ultimately sets them apart from the competition. After all, if small mistakes can be removed from the value stream every single day, there will come a time when errors will be close to non-existent.

The shift towards lean thinking may not exactly be an easy task, especially if you've just realized that you have major roadblocks in all the steps of your value stream. But when you've identified what exactly your problem areas are, you've already taken the first step in creating a more efficient business. Applying the principles of lean thinking and lean manufacturing gives you a more competitive edge, simply because you've addressed all of your wastes.

Chapter 25. The Types of Waste

Manufacturing wastes come in various forms. We already know in theory that the lean manufacturing framework is all about keeping your value stream and final products aligned by minimizing wastes. But what are wastes, exactly? How do they play out in the real world?

Defects

A defect refers to any mistake that needs additional effort, money, resources, or time to rectify. In non-lean productions, defects typically halt the flow of the value stream because of a component that needs to be completely remade.

The truth is, all wastes can never be fully eliminated. However, if you can work on eliminating defects, the rest of the lean wastes will follow suit. This can usually be accomplished by standardizing all aspects of the production process and applying stricter quality controls at every point of the value stream.

Overproduction

This is often the result of not following the pull-based or JIT-jidoka systems. As we have learned, lean systems try to minimize wastes by producing and assembling parts only when they are needed. Overproduction can get the value stream stuck when the flow ends up in a bottleneck. This is generally caused by:

- Just-in-case production as opposed to just-in-time production
- Producing based on uninformed forecasts
- Changes in product design and engineering
- Long production and assembly times
- Unassessed customer needs
- Ineffective automation processes

To solve issues with overproduction, it's important to focus on what the customer really cares about and then develop the most straightforward value stream. This ensures that none of the company's efforts will ever be put to waste.

Waiting

This happens when there's been a hold-up somewhere in the value stream. For instance, everything may have to be stopped because of machine breakdowns, lack of complete supplies, lack of approval from higher-ups, or overwhelmed staff. All of these may happen due to:

- Insufficient or unreliable staff (and managers)
- Staff absences
- Uneven workloads
- Unexpected downtimes
- Poor communication and processing

Just like overproduction, this waste is typically due to process bottlenecks. One way of solving this is by having enough staff so that the workload is evenly distributed at these points.

Although you may think that having a smaller staff can help you save money from salaries, it may actually incur even more expenses. This is because waiting and delays cost more money than simply paying a few more people to do the job well.

Non-utilized Talent

This wasn't part of the TPS' original list of lean wastes, but this has become quite a common occurrence in many modern businesses. This happens when a company fails to utilize its staff in the best way possible. This is often seen through:

- Poor communication among departments
- Poor management
- Insufficient staff training
- Lack of cooperation
- Inefficient workflow at the admin level
- Mismatch between an employee's skills and their given tasks

Improper utilization of staff's skills and talents may not seem like a big deal, but its bad effects over the long-term are usually made apparent when the whole company fails to reach its goals within their scheduled timeframes. It's also one of the main reasons why there is a resounding lack of employee engagement within a company. On the other hand, businesses usually thrive once they begin to give employees the recognition that they deserve.

Transportation

This doesn't only refer to actual transportation by a vehicle from one place to the next. Transportation is a general term that covers any process that involves getting something from Point A to Point B — even if the task is purely digital in nature. For instance, sending memos via e-mail can already be considered as "transport". Oftentimes, transportation wastes are results of:

- Wasteful steps in the value stream
- Workflow that is out of sync
- Poorly-designed processes and systems
- Bad office layouts and/or poor planning of office locations

The longer it takes for a product to get where it's supposed to, the higher the transportation costs will be. Not only does this waste time, but it also makes the product more prone to deterioration and damage. Transportation wastes can be eliminated by simplifying workflows, improving layouts, or simply shortening the physical distances between steps.

Inventory

More often than not, inventories are necessities for a business — especially for one that is highly in demand. Production lines will need raw materials and manufactured parts that are value-adding to the final product.

The retrieval processes for these materials need to be well-documented in order to spot any errors more conveniently. Additionally, having enough stock will allow you to be more adaptable when it comes to following through with the customer's needs.

The thing is, inventory can sometimes be the source of problems in lean systems. This is usually illustrated using the ship metaphor.

However, what you don't know is that there are problems lurking beneath the surface — as represented by the rocks.

Just because you're able to move, as usual, it doesn't mean that problems aren't there. In fact, it may only take a slight shift in water level before your ship finally hits one of those rocks. Examples of issues that are hidden by inventory are:

- Poor documentation and management
- Incompetent monitoring systems
- Unclear communication
- Lack of foresight
- Defective deliveries
- Unreliable suppliers
- Inconsistent manufacturing speeds
- Untrained or mismatched staff

Still going by the metaphor, this means that you need to dive deep into your inventories to figure out whether rocks are just waiting for their turn to bust through your ship. Once these issues have been detected, you must do whatever it takes to eliminate those rocks so you can steer your ship in any direction — without worrying about the water level.

Motion

Wastes relating to motion are quite similar to transportation wastes. This involves non-value adding steps that are covered by machines or employees. In contrast with transportation wastes, motion wastes are found in any unnecessary movement within the value stream. Generally, motion is affected by:

- Bad workstation or shop layouts
- Badly designed processes
- Bottleneck in workstations caused by shared tools
- Poor staff training

Eliminating motion wastes can be as simple as making the movement between workstations more convenient. More often than not, the reason why people aren't driven to do what they have to do is that the layout and circumstances make doing the task utterly inconvenient and difficult.

Excess Processing

While lean systems are all about providing quality, sometimes even quality controls can be over the top. Customers will only need a few key things, and constantly checking for something that goes beyond that only adds to waste. That's because you're investing time and resources in certain things when the customers have zero interest in what you're trying to offer.

Chapter 26. What Are the 5S's and How They Work

The next topic that we need to look at is known as the 5s's. When it comes to determining what processes your company has that are considered wasteful, it is important to ensure that the work environment is in optimum shape for the best results. The 5S organizational methodology is one commonly used system based around a number of Japanese words that, when they are taken together, are the first rate when it comes to improving efficiency and effectiveness by clearly identifying and storing items in the right space each time.

Now, the goal that comes with this kind of system is to allow for more standardization in your company across more than one process. When you are able to do this, you will notice that there is a significant amount of savings that show up in the long term. The reason that this method can be so effective is that when you have the human eye work to track across a messy workspace, it can take a bit of time, even if that time period is short, for the person to locate what they want and then process everything that is in the room. While this amount of time may seem small at a glance, if it happens constantly, and the whole team is doing it, then it results in a ton of time that is lost, and finding ways to reduce this and keep your employees at the job can help save you time and money in the process.

So, how do we work with the 5S organizational method? There are five parts that come with this and they include:

Sorting

The first part of this method is going to be sorting. Sorting is all about doing what you can in order to make sure that the workspace is as clean as possible, and that nothing that isn't required to complete the work is kept out. When sorting, you need to make sure that the space is organized in such a manner where you can remove anything and everything that could potentially create an obstacle when it comes to your team completing the task that they need to do. You will want to ensure that the items that are critical to the process have their own unique space, one that is labeled and easy for everyone on the team to find.

You don't want to make your workspace a mess. If things get easily lost, if there are items there that aren't necessary to the production phase, and if you run into issues with items always being somewhere else, even in other parts of the building, then this can slow things down. Taking some time to organize things and putting them in the locations that are the most convenient to find later on can make a big difference in how well you will be able to find them, and how well the team can get the work done.

After you organize the area, it becomes so much easier to keep the space free of any new distraction. Your leader should encourage the team members to prune their personal workspace on a regular basis to ensure that no new obstacles, and extra stuff, end up getting in the way.

Set in Order

When you are trying to organize the items in your workplace, it is important to ensure that all of the items are organized in the manner in which they are going to be used the most. While doing so, it is so important that you and your team take care to make sure that all of the items and tools that you need for the most common steps are nearby and easy to get. Your goal here is to reduce the amount of movement waste for getting items as much as possible.

You will find that over time, keeping the items that you need in the same space each time is going to help you get faster and faster at completing the project each time. Muscle memory can take over, and the team members are able to reach for and grab things without even needing to think about or look at the item that they need.

You need to have an open mind when you are working on this step because you may find that promoting the ease of workflow can be more than just organizing the area. It could even require some serious reworking of the facilities and how they are laid out at this point. In addition, you must make sure that all the items are arranged in the correct manner to make it easier for you to create steps for every part of the process. You want it to not only be easy for the people who are already on the team, but also for those who are new to the team so they can catch on and not slow down the process.

Shine

The next thing that we are going to take a look at is known as Shine. Keeping the workspace as clean as you can, and making sure that there isn't a lot of a mess around so that you maintain the most effective workspace possible. You want to talk to your team and emphasize how important it is to have some kind of daily cleaning to ensure that the overall efficiency of the team is boosted and to ensure that everything stays where it needs to be.

This is also a good time for you to set up a schedule for regular maintenance, if any is very needed, which is going to serve to ensure that the whole office stays as safe as possible for everyone. The end goal here is that any member of the team should be able to walk into the workspace and understand, within five minutes or less, where the key items in the process are located.

Standardized

The standardized step in this methodology is going to be all about ensuring that the processes in the organization itself stay in line in such a way that you can take these same ideas and apply them throughout all the areas, the departments, and everywhere else throughout the whole business. The reason that you want to do this is to make sure that order is maintained, even when things get hectic. It makes it so that everyone is going to be held to the same standards of quality and reliability.

Sustain

Finally, we are going to look at the idea of sustain. Sustaining the process is going to be vital because it could take a week or more to set up this process. If you spend that much time learning about the process and getting it set up, you don't want to have it fall apart in just a few months. This makes all that hard work a waste of time, and it can be discouraging overall.

It is important to make sure that this new organizational method becomes a vital part of the business starting from day one and moving into the future. If things are truly sustainable in this kind of regard, then the team is going to successfully move through the process, without the management or the leader expressly having to ask them to do it.

Of course, while sustainability is something that you should strive for with this method, it isn't something that you can expect overnight. It requires lots of training and adoption of the ideas of Lean and more, to become a part of the culture for your business. This does take time as everyone gets on board with the ideas and as they start to learn more about the process. But once it happens, you will really start to see all of the benefits that come with this method.

It's a Great Starter Tool

If you have some big plans for your business and these include transitioning yourself to more advanced concepts of Lean over time, then working with the 5S method is going to be a great way to help move employees in the right direction to make this happen. This method can be really effective with any employees who seem to be stuck in their ways. Once these individuals get on board, they will find that it is hard to deny all of the benefits of the Lean system and these organizational versions, and they will jump on even more. When they see these benefits, they are more likely to jump on board with some of the additional changes that you want to add in the future.

One thing to remember when you are rolling out a new system like this one, you may find that the team members are only going to care about two main things. These include the way that this kind of new system is going to affect them specifically and whether the Lean process is actually going to provide some results.

These concerns are also what make the 5S system a great place to start. It comes with some answers that are easily understandable for anyone who has a question and who wants to see if Lean and the other methods we have discussed in this guidebook will actually provide some results.

Is the 5S System Actually a good choice for my business?

While the 5S system is going to be a good choice for many businesses, no matter what kind of industry they are in, it isn't a solution that fits everyone. This is why it is so important for you as a business owner to have a good idea of both the strengths and weaknesses when you get started. One of the biggest strengths with this system is that when it gets implemented properly, it is going to help your team define their processes easier while helping them to claim some ownership on the processes that come.

Remember that with Lean the goal is to not have one manager or one leader calling all of the shots. The point is to bring in all of the team members and hear their opinions and get everyone on board. When the team gets their voice heard and can have a say in what happens, it is going to add some more accountability in the process. And when everything goes according to plan in this manner, it is going to lead to performance that is improved even more, which then leads to better conditions of work for everyone on the team.

In addition, implementing this process has the potential to make long-term employee contributions thanks to an internalized sense of improvement. In an ideal world, this is something that will continue on until the main ideas of continuous improvement start to become the order of the day. When the company and the team are able to use the 5S system in the proper way, it can provide them with some bigger insights into the worlds of work standardization, equipment reliability, and value analysis.

However, while there may be a lot of things to love about the 5S system, there are also some drawbacks that businesses need to be prepared for. One of the biggest weaknesses that occur with this is that if the system and its purpose are not communicated to the team in the proper manner, then members of the team can sometimes make some mistakes. This is because they may see the system as more of an end goal, rather than as a means to an end.

The 5S system needs to be the flagbearer of any kind of success that is going to come in the future, rather than the sum total of the journey the company made with the processes of Lean. Specifically, businesses whose movement is constrained quite a bit by some external factors (which they are not able to control), may find that it is hard to use the 5S system, and companies who run into lots of storage problems right now may need to solve these issues before they try to transition into the method.

In addition, just because this method is a good fit for many different kinds of companies doesn't mean that it is automatically going to fit in with your business and your team. This can be seen when we are talking about some of the smaller teams, or for any team that has all of their members take on many roles at the same time. Just because the 5S system is seen as a very popular way to implement the Lean principles doesn't mean that it is going to fit for everyone.

Choosing to ignore this information and moving ahead anyway and enforcing organization just because you think you need to, or just because another business has done it, won't do much of anything when you take a look at the results that it generates. In fact, if you try to implement this system into a process where it doesn't belong, you are just going to generate more waste in the long run.

This is going to be even more true for any kind of business that works with a large variety of interactions with humans, various styles of management, and other management tools. However, when the different aspects work together in the proper manner, they may be able to generate some extra value to their customer, which of course is seen as a very vital part of a business that is able to see success in the market.

While the 5S system can be a great way to help your business, if you blindly press forward with it, you are going to find that it is easy to lose sight of the proper outcome for your customer because you are trying to pursue the perfect outcome or a perfect implementation of the 5S principles. If this method isn't going to help you to serve the customer properly, and it wastes more time than it is worth, then don't worry about implementing it into your business.

Finally, when you are trying to implement this system, you must take the time to stress to all the members of your team that 5S is something that needs to be a part of their natural routine and the best practices that are standard for the business. It should never be seen as any kind of additional task that they need to do outside of their daily work.

The goal of the 5S system is to enhance how effective the workflow for your business is at every step of the process. If you try to separate out this system into a new layer that is in addition to the work, rather than going along with the work, then you are doing the complete opposite of what the process stands for.

Chapter 27. Applying The Lean Method

With so much emphasis on improving efficiency, the Lean process naturally places a lot of emphasis on team leaders who have to work hard to immediately inspire their teams to adopt the Lean mentality. In the end, many Lean systems live and die because of the leadership involved, which means that it is important that those in charge of leading the Lean transition can not only explain what is going on, but are really committed to it. work that is being done too. Some things Lean leaders should try to emphasize include:

Customer loyalty: when it comes to customer loyalty, Lean leaders must take the time to consider not only what their customers want right now, but also what they probably want in the future. Moreover, it is important to understand what a customer accepts, what they will like and what they will stop at nothing to have. The Lean leader must also work to understand the many ways in which the specific wishes and needs of their target audience are present throughout the customer base.

Team improvement: To help their team members be their best, Lean leaders must always be available to help the team during the problem-solving process. At the same time, they must be cautious and refrain from taking control and just doing it themselves. Their role in the process must be to focus on finding the resources that the team can use to solve their own problems. Open questions are a big part of this process because they make it possible for the team to find a much wider variety of solutions.

Incremental improvement: one of the most important tasks of the Lean leader is to constantly evaluate different aspects of the team to ensure that it performs optimally. The leader must also keep abreast of customer requirements, as this is something that will constantly change. This is one of the only truly reliable ways to stay ahead by allowing the overall direction of the company to be streamlined to the processes that will achieve the best results.

To ensure that this is the case, the Lean leader will want to make time in his schedule to view the results and then compare them with the costs to find the best ways to use all available resources at the given time. . This includes things like evaluating the organization as a whole in the hope of making it more efficient and reliable. It also includes evaluating the value flow to ensure that it satisfies the customer at both macro and micro levels.

Focus on sustainable improvement: it is also the task of the Lean leader to ensure that improvements that are made are implemented until the end. This often includes teaching team members the correct Lean behavior to use in a given situation and also approaching failure cases as opportunities for improvement and innovation.

Three Actuals

Lean leaders usually use a different leadership style than many of their peers, mainly because Lean leaders require an understanding that the best way to analyze a situation is to be physically in the room where the situation has occurred. Once there, the Lean leader must think about what is known as the three actuals, the widest of which is known as Genchi, and the issue that led the leader to the place in question. Genbutsu believes it is important to see what is created or put into action before you make a move. Finally, Genjitsu says it is always best to collect as much information as possible before you make a decision in any way.

Create A Lean System

To create a long-lasting Lean system, the first thing you need to do is to consider the simplest way to bring your product or service to the public's attention and operate that system. From there, you must continuously monitor the processes that you have set up to support your business to ensure that breakthroughs in improvement occur from time to time. The final step is to implement improvements that you come across. Although there are many theories and tools that can help you move on, the fact that creating a Lean system is really that simple.

Business is more than just profit: when using the Lean system, the ultimate goal is to determine in which ways it is possible to improve the efficiency of your company. Although an increase in profit is often a natural result of this process, this should not be the main motivating factor for a Lean transformation. Instead, it is important to focus as much as possible on streamlining, regardless of what the costs are beforehand, since you can confidentially expect that every dollar you spend will come back.

There are, of course, limits to this and at a certain point in time the revenues are not worth the costs. To determine where this line is, you can use a simple value curve to determine how the changes are likely to affect your bottom line. A value curve is often used to compare different products or services based on many relevant factors and the data currently available. In this case, making one to show the difference between a pre- and post-Lean state should make such decisions much easier.

Treat tools the way they are: when many new companies switch to a Lean style to do things, they find it easy to fall into the trap of taking tools to the limit, to the point that they follow them with almost religious zeal. It is important to remember that the Lean principles are ultimately guidelines only and all the Lean tools that you use are precisely the tools that will make your business work more effectively. This means that if they need to be adjusted to better serve your team and your customers, there is nothing to stop you from doing exactly that. From the start, your team must understand the limits and purpose of the Lean tools they receive and, above all, understand that they are not laws.

Prepare to continue: even if you hire a trained professional to help your team with the initial Lean learning curve, it will ultimately be up to you, as a team leader, to ensure that the learned practices do not fall out of the boat while time passes. It takes time to find new ways of doing things and making habits out of it, and it's your job to keep everyone on until everything clicks and they start working through the new system without thinking about it. Similarly, it is important to clarify why the Lean process is good for the team as a whole and for the individual team member as if they were invested in it personally, then it is much more likely that they will stick to it, even if it becomes difficult.

Setting Lean Goals

In order to ultimately make the right changes to your company, you must first ensure that you set the right goals. To ensure that your goals put you on the right track, you must ensure that they are SMART, which means that they are specific, measurable, achievable, realistic and current.

Specific: Charities are specific, which means that you want to be sure that the goal you choose is extremely clear, especially when you first start, because goals that are less well defined are much easier to avoid in favor of activities that provide more positive stimulation in a shorter period. Keeping specific goals in mind makes it much easier for you to continue with the tasks that you are currently performing.

If you are not entirely sure whether the goal you have chosen is specific enough to actually improve your chance to change for the better, you might find out by looking through who, why, where, when and how of the goal . In particular, do you want to consider who will be involved with you when it comes to achieving the goal? What exactly will be achieved? Where will it take place, why is it important that you ensure that it is completed as quickly as possible and how exactly you can expect you to do it. If you can answer all five major questions, you know that you have a goal that is specific enough to generate the kind of results you are looking for.

Measurable: SMART goals are goals that can be divided into small, easy-to-handle chunks that can be tackled piece by piece. A measurable goal should make it easy to determine when exactly you are on course, so that you can correct yourself as quickly as possible. Measuring your progress will make it easier for you to continue the good work.

Reachable: Perhaps more important than anything else, if a goal you set is unreachable, especially the first goal you set with this system, then you unknowingly waste valuable time and energy while creating negative patterns that end with failure. What's more, you will eventually strengthen fixed mindsets, making this a bad choice no matter how you look at it. This means that when it comes to setting goals, you want to have a clear understanding of the current situation and everything that is going on in the company, making it less likely for that purpose.

Realistic: a good goal is a realistic goal, besides being achievable, which means that you can expect success without something that is highly unlikely to push reality to your advantage. An ideal goal is one that requires a lot of work to achieve, while still not being too difficult to become unrealistic. Moreover, you will want to avoid goals that you can achieve without really going to much trouble, because too easy goals can be demotivating, because then it becomes easy to postpone them until they eventually fall into oblivion.

Timely: Studies show that the human mind is more active in problem-solving behavior when there is a time limit for successfully completing the task in question. What this means for the goals you set is that if you have a fixed end date in mind for when you want to reach your goal, you will work harder in the period prior to that date. This means that you want to choose completion dates that are strict enough to really motivate you to do what you have in mind while at the same time not being so strict that there is no realistic way to complete the task on time. The goal here is to put a little extra effort into your step and not force you to keep a tiring schedule, so make sure you can always follow the schedule that you have set for the best results.

Implementation Of Policy

Also known as Hoshin Kanri, policy implementation is a way to ensure that SMART goals that are set at management level are ultimately measurably filtered to the rest of the team. By making good use of policy implementation, you essentially ensure that everything you intend to implement does not accidentally cause more problems than has ultimately resolved. It will also help to ensure that as little waste as possible is generated as a result of issues such as inconsistent messages from management or poor communication. The goal in this case should not be to force different team members to act in a specific way. It is about generating the kind of vision for the company that everyone can appreciate and understand how it relates to both the team and the customers.

Implementation of the plan: After all relevant SMART goals have been completed, the next thing you want to do is to group them based on which team members are ultimately charged with solving them. Keep in mind that the fewer goals there are, the more likely it is that they will be executed within a reasonable time. If your goals cannot be generalized in such a way, it is important to start with the goals that definitely make the biggest difference and then work out the list from there.

Regardless of which goals you ultimately choose, it is important that you make sure that there are no goals to which no one has assigned specific instructions to track overall progress and at the same time provide status reports when needed. This person must also be someone who can be counted on to make clear to other team members how important the goal is for the company as a whole and how it will make things easier in the long run.

Consider your tactics: those responsible for achieving the goal must in turn be the ones who decide how the goal can best be achieved by the team as a whole. However, this process must still include interaction between all levels of the team, only to ensure that the tactics and the goal are well aligned. Tactics are likely to change if the goal is on its way to success, which means that it needs to be studied from time to time to ensure that it remains fit for the goal in question.

Progress: Once the tactics have been agreed by all parties, it is time to actually put them into practice. This will be the phase where the team can really take over, although quality goals still require a buy-in from relevant parties. During this period, it is important to ensure that all communications from management are up to date, to ensure that actions and wider goals continue to align.

Check from time to time: it is important to remember that once the action is implemented, the team leader must change the action if necessary. This means that they will also follow things while hopefully going according to plan. Remember that Lean systems are always being improved, which means that your goals and their implementation cannot be different.

Simplify Lean As Much As Possible

All products and services generated by your company have a combination of three different value streams that can ultimately be used productively if you take the time to fully understand them. These include the concept to launch stream, creating customer stream and the order to customer stream. To ensure that you get the greatest overall value from all the processes that your company completes, it is important to look at a value flow chart, as it is an excellent way to ensure that you maximize efficiency at every turn.

The average value flow card contains everything that ultimately comes together to generate value for the customer, including activities, people, materials and information. To properly visualize a value stream, you want to follow the Plan / Do / Study / Act process, also known as the Lean cycle. To begin with, you want to plan the task ahead by focusing on one goal at a time. From there you want to make a list of everything that needs to be done to ensure that the task is successfully completed. This is then followed by the step of following, where the results are studied and where necessary monitored.

Make Your Own Value Flow Card

A well-constructed value flow chart is an essential part of the process, as it allows you to see the big picture by mapping the full flow of resources from their different starting points all the way when they come together and ultimately in the hands of the customer. As such, it makes it much more of a manageable task to determine the points in the process that hamper the overall efficiency of your company's process and thus take the first steps to take over Lean processes.

Although one person can certainly go through the following steps, the value flow cards that prove to be the most effective are often the cards made by the entire team, so those with the most knowledge of each step can give them two cents. Your initial value flow card should be seen as a very rough sketch and must be constructed as such, which means that you must plan it in pencil and expect a lot of rewriting as you proceed.

Consider the process: the first step in this process is to consider what exactly you want to map. For companies that first start with the Lean system, you first want to consider the different processes that ultimately prove to be of the utmost importance to the team as a whole and then complete the list from there. If you still can't decide where to start, you want to turn to your customers, consider what they have to say, and start with the areas where you regularly receive the most complaints.

What is known as a pareto analysis is currently an effective tool because it can make it easier for you to find the right starting place if you are not sure where your efforts can best be used. It is a statistical analysis technique that can be especially useful if you are looking for a few different tasks that will certainly produce serious results if you can only decide which one to use first. The goal in this case is to focus on the 20 percent of your business that, if cherished, could eventually generate 80 percent of your total results. Your initial value stream card can be focused on just one service or product or on multiples that share a significant part of the process.

Choose your shorthand: the symbols that you use to indicate different phases of the process that you are mapping do not have really hard and fixed guidelines, because they will be unique for every project and every company. Regardless of what you and your team ultimately choose, it is important to make a list of all the symbols that you use and what they mean, so that anyone coming in after the fact can be easily entangled. From there, it's important to stick to the designated symbols and not to invent anything on the spot. If the company is working on more than one value stream card at the same time, it is important that the symbols match between the two. Otherwise things can quickly turn into illegibility.

Set limits: If these are used wide enough, almost any value flow card for your company can be connected to other value flow cards or go into more detail. At some point, however, this will be counterproductive and you have to set limits on what the value flow card will explain if you ever hope to continue successfully. Similarly, if you let this part of the process get out of hand, the map may lose focus and therefore become less useful.

Start with clearly defined steps: After you have a clear start and end for the mapping process, the next thing to do is make a list of all the logical steps to be taken from start to finish. This should not be an in-depth look at every link in the chain, but instead should be an overview of the most important phases that need to be considered as the process approaches.

Consider the information flow: An important step in the value flow allocation process that distinguishes it from other similar allocation processes is that each value flow card also takes into account the way information flows through the entire process from start to finish. It also shows the way in which information is passed on between team members. You must also ensure that the ways in which the customer interacts with your company and how often such interactions occur are taken into account. You must also ensure that the communication chain includes suppliers or other third parties with whom the company deals.

Further details: when it comes to splitting the process to the most detailed level, you may also want to include a flow chart with your value flow chart. A flow chart is a great way to chart the deepest details of how a certain process is completed. This is also an excellent way to determine which types of muda you are dealing with, so you can consider whether they can be removed from the process.

If you are interested in the ways in which your team physically moves through your space, a string diagram can also be effective. To generate these types of charts, map the workspace of your company by drawing what each team member should do and where they should go to fully complete the process. You want to draw different team members or different teams in different colors to prevent things from becoming too confusing. From there, mapping the flow of information with regard to this data can lead to surprising conclusions about errors that would otherwise go unnoticed for years.

Collecting data: when it comes to mapping your original map of a value stream, you may find that certain aspects of the process require additional data before something can be determined with a certain degree of certainty. The data that you may need to find include:

- Cycle time
- Total stock at hand
- Availability of the service
- Transition time
- Uptime
- Number of teams required to complete the process
- Total available working time

When it comes to collecting this data, it is important to always remember to go directly to the source and find the details that you are looking for instead of making assumptions. Furthermore, it is important to get the most recent figures instead of looking at older, better available figures or hypothetical benchmarks. This can mean something as practical as physically monitoring every part of the process so that you can make relevant notes.

View the inventory: even if you are relatively certain of the inventory requirements for the process in question, it is vital that you check this again before you commit to the value stream card. Minor miscalculations at this point can dramatically skew your overall results and essentially destroy all your hard work if you are not careful. This means that you absolutely have to take two measures to see the best results. After all, inventory is susceptible to construction for various reasons and there is a good chance that you will only know if you look closer and take a look at what is really at hand. You can also use this step as an excuse to take stock of exactly what the team is working with and to determine to what extent it will stretch effectively.

Use the data: once you have finished visualizing the steps you have found in your main process, you can now use it to determine where any issues are located. You will want to pay particular attention to processes that re-perform previously completed work, anything that requires a longer period of resetting before work can begin again, or long holes where parts of the team cannot do anything except wait for someone else, in the Finally, keep an eye on those who take more resources than your research indicates that you should, or even those who for no reason seem to last longer than they should.

Generate the ideal version of the value stream: after you have determined where the bottlenecks occur, you want to create an updated value stream map that indicates how you want the process to continue after you have sorted everything properly. This gives you an A to C scenario, where figuring out the pain points represents B. Ideally, it also gives an idea of how you can remove the waste from the process to create an idea that you can really strive for in both the short and the long term.

After you have determined the ideal state for the process, you can work out a future value flow chart that will serve as a plan to take the team from where you are currently to where you need to be. This type of plan is often subdivided into sections that last a few months depending on what needs to be done. In addition, most future value flow cards will contain multiple iterations, as they will have to be changed several times as the project is almost completed.

When you go through different variations of the value flow card, it is important to pay close attention to the lead time available for different processes. The lead time is the amount of time required to complete a certain task in the process and, if not used as efficiently as possible, it can easily lead to a wealth of bottlenecks. Remember that when it comes to creating the best possible flow chart, no part of the process is further investigated.

Chapter 28. Lean Thinking

Lean businesses always identify ways to maximize the value for their customers, which is the core objective of lean thinking. Most people are under the notion that lean thinking can only be implemented in sales and marketing departments since those departments work directly with customers.

This is not true since lean thinking is now being used to deliver value products to stakeholders of all departments.

Most people view lean as a tool that can be used to eliminate waste from processes and internal mechanisms thereby maximizing the value for the customer. But lean is a business process and kaizen is its cultural center. This is an important aspect to consider when a business wants to identify the value of long-term processes.

Most businesses still believe that lean thinking is a way for the demand side since they are not looking at the value stream. These businesses can make better profits since the demand for their products exceeds their supply.

However, most businesses are in a market where supply exceeds demand. Take mobile phones for instance. Numerous companies have been set up in different parts of the world that develop new phone models every day.

However, most people choose to purchase Apple products, because the business has catered to the demands of the product and has always tried to identify ways to maximize the value of the customer. Therefore, businesses must remember that lean is not only about removing waste from the process, but also about identifying ways to enhance the value stream to maximize the value of the product.

There is no company in today's economy that rejects more prospects or refuses orders. The business must always look for ways to drive revenue. Therefore, a business must improve continually to enhance and improve the processes in the value stream. So, how does a business use lean thinking to identify value?

- Understand the demands of stakeholders and customers
- Identify elements in the process that are waste contributors and those that affect the quality of the product

If a business is implementing lean thinking, it must eliminate processes that contribute to waste and those that do not add any value to the product or service. A business will view every activity that it performs and views the steps to see if each of them adds value to the final product or service.

An activity is defined as a waste contributor if it adds cost and takes time to complete but does not improve the final product that is delivered to the stakeholder or customer. Every business focuses on how to shorten the timeline and how the value flow between the business and customer can be improved.

The value is identified by becoming a faster, cheaper and better business. In simpler words, a business must always change its processes to produce goods and services that a customer is willing to pay for.

Another way to identify value is by defining the internal customers or stakeholders. These internal stakeholders are members of each department that use outputs of one department as input to achieve their business goals and objectives. Regardless of whether a business is working with internal or external customers, it must focus on how the customers are satisfied rather how well they are satisfied. The fundamental of lean thinking then changes to the following – "if a process is improved, the value of the process is also improved."

Most businesses are product-focused. These businesses cannot view the market or access the market to become the best. They also make the mistake of looking at the value of the product or service and how it will help the customer. Businesses must remember that the idea of value is abstract and there is no real definition. The business must always identify ways to create, identify and deliver value to its customers.

Ways to Add Value

Faster and Better

The business must identify ways to deliver products of high quality to customers either before the promised time or on time. Every individual is impatient and a person who has finally taken a look at a product will want it yesterday. If the business can deliver faster, more customers will flock towards the business since there is a direct perceived correlation between the value of offering and the speed at which it is offered.

Better Quality

The key is to remember that every customer wants products that are of better quality. Therefore, every business must develop products that are of greater quality when compared to the products of its competitors. A business must remember that the customer defines quality. A business must always find out what its customers want and develop products with high quality for them.

Always Add More Value

Always add value to the product. Most businesses in an industry deliver the same or similar products. For any business to stand out, it must offer something that other businesses do not offer. Apple is an excellent example of this point.

Increase convenience

You have to identify ways to eliminate processes that make it difficult for customers to place their orders with ease. There are issues when the customer needs to go through elaborate processes to place an order. If that is the case, customers will choose businesses where it is easy for them to place their orders. Lean thinking plays a key role here since the business will need to identify waste contributors and remove them thereby adding value to the process.

Improve Customer Service

It is important to remember that human beings are emotional and this is a factor that every business must include in its customer service. The business must identify a way to tap into the emotions of its customers by being warm, friendly, cheerful and helpful. A business must ensure that it always helps its customers regardless of how big or small the request is.

Changing Lifestyle

Businesses must identify how lifestyles are changing and how these changes impact customers. They must collect data and make sound decisions to improve the value of their products and services. It is important to understand that every customer has a different taste and a business must find a way to tap into those tastes and deliver products of excellent quality.

A business can also have the ability to move into new markets and provide customers with better products and services.

Offer Discounts

Planned discounting will add value and wealth to a business. If a business has a surplus of products, it must identify ways to sell those products in higher volumes. Most supermarkets, like Costco, give customers the chance to buy large volumes of a product at a lower rate. The business can also pass on the savings to the customer and also make profits by selling more significant volumes of some products.

When a business wants to identify ways to enhance the value of its products and services, it will look at ways to increase the speed at which it delivers products and also find ways to improve the quality of the products.

This is when they begin to innovate and identify new processes that can maximize the value of a product for the customer. Businesses must always function with the customers in their minds since they define the business.

If a customer believes that a business is honest and the products delivered are of great quality, word will spread across the market and more customers will switch to that business. Therefore, a business must always identify ways to enhance value for its customers.

Chapter 29. The 7 Principles of Lean Thinking

Lean thinking primarily started as a required practice in Toyota's manufacturing floor. The term "lean thinking" was first coined by James Womack and Daniel Jones in their book, Lean Thinking: Banish Waste and Create Wealth in Your Corporation.

All of their insights were a result of their comprehensive study of the Toyota Production System (TPS). They noticed that Toyota focused on creating system frameworks that makes manufacturing a lot more value-adding and efficient. Most lean strategies that you'll come across can be traced back to the wide success of the TPS. It remains the primary reference where most lean manufacturing methods are based.

Any business that is trying to get into the lean mindset will need to integrate the following principles into their processes:

Eliminating Wastes

Wastes found within the knowledge workflow are usually linked to the management and to the people doing the work, and not exactly on the production floor. Examples of wastes involved in the knowledge work are:

Context Switching: This occurs when people need to switch from one tool or platform to the other just to complete a single task. This may involve opening a ton of programs or apps all at once.

It usually requires a certain order to accomplish so it's prone to confusion. In a way, it overlaps with multitasking since your attention is scattered across various tasks.

Poor Appropriation of Tools: Sometimes, slow completion time can mainly be blamed on inappropriate tools. Oftentimes, when employees are forced to use a tool that certainly isn't the best for the job, the production flow doesn't move as quickly as it should.

Inefficiency of Information Systems: This is related to the previous point. If the workflow relies heavily on information systems, yet company reports say that these systems aren't helping like they're supposed to, you can't expect that things will be accomplished as planned.

It's even worse when user feedback isn't integrated into the design — either before the system was launched or after a system overhaul had been made.

Ineffective Communication Among Teams: The phrase "communication is key" isn't emphasized in many contexts for nothing. The lack of open communication and transparency is often the cause of many delays during the production process.

Lack of Viable Market: Any factor in your product that your customer wouldn't be willing to pay for is ultimately considered a waste in the whole workflow. What's the use of something if nobody wants it?

Creating Knowledge

For companies to become a truly lean business, knowledge and learning must be integrated into the organization. When employees are constantly given the chance to learn the industry's best practices from experts, not only can they add more value to the work they do, but they also learn how to be valuable in other ways. This is typically done by:

Having retrospectives

Cross-training employees

Holding regular discussions about employees' work processes

When a company values knowledge creation, they will be able to perform their tasks with more value at a much faster rate. This is a way for them to constantly update their skills and competencies.

Integrating Quality

A company that envisions long-term growth needs to utilize systems that are as error-free as possible. Lean companies usually do this by automating tasks that are repetitive, mentally uninteresting, and prone to human error.

As a result, employees can pour their time and focus on skills that actually engage them mentally. This allows them to devote themselves fully to the pursuit of both personal and company growth.

Delivering on Time

Lean thinking is primarily driven by the idea that focus is the root of all high-quality outputs. When your work environment isn't conducive enough to maintain an uncluttered mind, this slows your work down. Top-quality work is hard to produce when an employee is constantly distracted.

Lean systems always have steady workflows. This means that everything is delivered and accomplished on a consistent, predictable basis. A bad workflow, on the other hand, is always unpredictable because of unsustainable and unreliable work habits.

Lean teams are always refining their workflows to optimize value at every level. They do this by greatly limiting their WIPs (works in progress) and providing a good work environment so nothing gets stuck in the workload traffic. Multitasking is prohibited because it only prevents people from finishing tasks on time.

Deferring Commitment

Careful planning is necessary to accomplish long-term goals. In lean thinking, however, it is discouraged to plan for a product's release way out in advance. This prevents having stocks that may only end up being useless.

Instead, it recommends that you decide to pursue something at the last responsible moment — during the time when you've thoroughly considered all the factors that would help you come up with the best decision possible.

This goes back to the main goal of all lean systems: eliminating wastes.

Deferring commitment helps you decide more smartly by going over the data and reports that accurately reflect the current market situation. This prevents you from pursuing seemingly innovative projects that don't really translate into an urgent or even viable market need in reality.

Respecting People

The root of a lean system's success all boils down to one basic thing: respect.

First, the concept of lean was born out of a desire to respect the customer's needs and preferences. Second, lean systems are able to thrive because their employees are well-respected by their superiors. They are provided with environments that encourage them to perform at their best.

On an individual level, respect generally entails maintaining kindness and courtesy to everyone that you're working with — whether it's your superiors, your colleagues, your employees, or your customers. Respect is also often shown through:

Providing safe environments for idea sharing

Encouraging employees to develop themselves in whatever way they wish

Trusting employees' decision-making processes

Respect goes a long way in lean systems because trust is required to maintain good workflow. After all, building good relationships is the key to creating a stable system that produces high-value outputs.

Optimizing the Whole Organization

All decisions in a lean company must be made relative to the whole organization. For instance, decisions to optimize processes must not only involve one team — it must involve everybody else.

Naturally, an improvement in one component can already be enough to see significant differences in the workflow. However, to become truly lean means to address all possible sources of waste.

Building a lean enterprise all starts with creating a lean business. The next step would be to find others who also share the same lean ideas as you do. Maintaining collaborations among companies can already be difficult enough since each member will have their own goals and agendas. However, if all of you can work towards operating under the same lean system, then overall work and production is going to be a breeze.

Chapter 30. Kaizen

Kaizen translates to continuous improvement which is an important goal to consider when creating a Lean system that works for your business. The goal of this strategy is to get the entire team to focus on the idea that small improvements should be happening all the time. Everyone on your team will have different talents and specialties, the goal of Kaizen is to have all of that talent focused on improving wherever and whenever possible.

Kaizen is unique among Lean strategies as it is as much a general philosophy as it is a direct plan for future action. The goal of Kaizen should be to create a culture that supports improvement while also creating groups focused more directly on improving key processes to reach well-defined goals.

If you are already using or thinking about using a standardized work process, then it is likely you will want to take advantage of Kaizen as well because they complement each other nicely. Standard practices lead to current best practices that Kaizen can then improve upon.

Kaizen can be useful for essentially every process that your team uses with any regularity, but first, it is important to determine the goals of the updated process. After that, it is important to follow up and ensure the improvements work as expected. Consider using PDCA or DMADV for the same results.

Teaching team members to use Kaizen as a plan of action, simultaneously teaches them to apply it as a philosophy as well. The type of thinking that is formed habitually by constantly looking for paths to improvement also allows team members to approach their daily processes from new and innovative ways as opposed to simply sticking with what works. This mindset should be nurtured whenever possible as it only produces more fruitful results the longer it is active.

While constantly improving existing practices is a great place to start, it is important that the Kaizen your team is practicing does not only occur after the fact. When new processes are created, it is in everyone's best interest that they are held to the same stringent examination process as well. Hindsight is good, foresight is better.

Steps to better Kaizen

- Start by standardizing your process, not just the process that you are looking to actively engage in Kaizen, but all your processes to ensure future improvements are as beneficial as possible.
- Compare processes to determine what steps being used in some areas can be used in others. It is important to look at real KPIs and not anecdotal information during this step as it can be easy to get off on the wrong track without realizing it.
- Once you know where change should occur, work with what is available to determine easier ways of completing the process. Consider the beginning of the

process and then its end, then simply visualize alternative ways from 'a' to reach 'b'. It is important to only move forward with useful innovations as innovating simply for the sake of innovating will simply create waste.

- Repeat, turn the innovations into new standardized procedures and begin the entire process anew. The only bad idea, when it comes to Kaizen, is resting on your laurels.

Create a Kaizen mindset

While it can be great to get your team together now and then for Kaizen centered events where everyone takes a look at a specific process and determines the best way to get to the solution. It can be more difficult to train your team to always be in a Kaizen mindset. The best way to begin to train them to this improved way of thinking is to start by making the elimination of waste a top priority. Keep this idea in the team mindset, every day and during every meeting. Once team members start noticing waste without thinking about it they will be well on their way finding ways to work around it instead.

From there, set aside time specially to allow team members to look at the processes they use most regularly and really think about them. The human mind loves pattern and repetition which is why it is so easy to follow well-worn steps regardless of their total efficacy. Providing your team with the opportunity to really think about their processes, instead of simply working through them, will push them into seeing the flaws that they may otherwise have been blind to for years.

Taking this exercise a step further can be useful as well. To do so, provide team members the time to talk to others about their processes which will, in turn, give each process a fresh set of eyes. This is also a great way to find logical blind spots in complicated processes, just be sure that everyone takes notes during the entire process to make sure valuable insight is not lost in the shuffle. It is important to emphasize that there are no wrong answers during this stage, a free and open dialogue can provide innovative solutions to problems you didn't even know you were facing.

Chapter 31. Six Sigma

Many times you may have heard of Lean Six Sigma, or even Six Sigma on its own, and you may be confused about what the differences are. It is possible to implement the Six Sigma methodology on its own, and it is also possible to implement the Lean process on its own too. You can also implement them together in order to get even better results for your process and your business. Let's take a look at the Six Sigma methodology and how it can work together with the Lean process we have been discussing in this guidebook.

Six Sigma is known as the shorthand name of a system that measures the quality with an overall goal of getting as close to perfection in the process as possible. If a company is using Six Sigma properly, then they are going o generate as few as 3.4 defects per million attempts at the given process. Z-shift is going to be the name that is given to any deviations that are available between a process that was completed in a poor manner, and a process that was completed to perfection.

The standard Z-shift is one with a number of 4.5, but the ultimate value that businesses are aiming for is a 6. Processes that haven't been viewed with the lens of Six Sigma are going to earn about 1.5. A Six Sigma level of 1 means that the customers are able to get what they expect from the customer about 30% of the time. If the Six Sigma level is at 2, it means that about 70% of the time, the customers are able to get what they expect. If you can get to a Six Sigma level of 3, this means that about 93% of the time, the customers are satisfied with what they are getting from you.

If we move up the scale and get to a Six Sigma level of 4, this means that your customers are satisfied with the level of attention and the quality of the product they are getting more than 99 percent of the time. this means that reaching a Six Sigma level of 5 or 6 indicates that the satisfaction percentages with your customers will be even closer to 100 percent, or almost perfections.

In addition, you will find that the process of Six Sigma can be broken up into numerous certification levels. Each one is going to have a different amount of knowledge with it to help the individual know more about this process, how to implement it, and how to reach the near perfection levels that are required with it.

The executive level of Six Sigma is going to consist mainly of management team members who are going to be in charge of going through your company and actively setting up the Six Sigma method. A Champion of Six Sigma is someone who is able to lead the projects you set up, and who will be the voice of these projects specifically.

There are also white belts in this system, and they are the rank and file workers. These are the individuals who have an understanding of Six Sigma, but it is going to be more limited than the higher two levels. The yellow belts are going to be active members on the Six Sigma project teams, and they have the responsibility of figuring out some areas where improvements can be used.

Next, are the green belts. These individuals work with the black belts on some of the projects considered high level, while also working to run some of their own yellow belt projects. Then there are the black belts who will run their own high-level projects while still doing some mentoring and some support for the other tiers we talked about. The Master black belts are going to be those who the company brought in specifically to implement this system in the business, and who can help to mentor and teach anyone, no matter what level they are at.

Implementing

Giving your team some compelling reasons to work with Six Sigma can be so important to how successful the whole process is. To make sure that the Six Sigma process is implemented in the right way, you need to find a way to motivate the team. Explaining the Six Sigma process to them and discussing how important it is to implement this new methodology can be a great place to start.

One tactic that works with this is to use a burning platform. This is a kind of motivational tactic where you are going to explain the situation that the company is in right now, and why that situation is so dire. Then you can explain that implementing Six Sigma is the only way to get long-term survival to last for the company. Of course, before you make these assertions, you should have some statistics that can help you to make this point.

Ensure that the Right Tools Are Available

Once your team has gone through the initial rounds of training that they need, it is important that you set up a kind of program for mentorship along with some additional refresher materials ready for any team member who may need them. You will find that at this stage, one of the worst things that can happen is for someone to be confused about one of the important parts of Six Sigma, and then they are rebuffed because they don't have the right resources to help them out.

The more information that you are able to provide to your team, and the more opportunities you provide for them to learn and understand Six Sigma in the beginning, the easier the implementation of this process will be. You will be able to see that everyone is on the same page, that everyone understands the importance of this process, and everyone has the right training and knowledge to make this process happen.

The Key Principles

Now that we know a little bit more about Six Sigma, it is time to take a look at some of the key principles. This process is going to work the best based on an acceptance of five laws. The first is going to be the law of the market. This means that before anything is implemented, the customer should be considered. The second is the law of flexibility. This is where the best processes are those that can be used for the greatest number of disparate functions.

Then there is the third law, which is going to be the law of focus. This one states that a company that follows Six Sigma should put all of their focus on the problem that they are experiencing, rather than on the business itself. Then there is the fourth law or the law of velocity. This one states that the more steps that are in a process, the more likely that some of those steps aren't needed, and that the process is less efficient. For the last law, we look to the law of complexity. This one states that the simpler the processes are, the more superior they are for the business.

So, how do I choose the best process? When it comes to deciding which of the processes that you should use with Six Sigma, the best place for you to start is with any process that you know to be defective, and that needs some work to reduce the number of deficiencies that occur. From there, it is simply going to be a matter of looking for situations where Takt time is out of whack before you figure out which steps where the number of available resources can be reduced as well.

The Methodologies to Work With

When you are ready to work with the Six Sigma process, there are going to be two main methodologies that you can choose to work with. Both are going to be efficient and can work, it just depends on which kind of industry you are in and what works the best for you. The two main methods are going to be DMAIC and DMADV.

First, we need to take a look at the DMAIC. This is an acronym that is going to help you and your team remember the five phases that come with it. This is useful when it comes to creating a new process and fixing any processes that need some extra work to be more efficient and deal with less risk. The way that DMAIC works includes:

Define what the process needs to do. To figure this out, you need to get some input from the customer and then work from there.

Measure: This is where your team needs to measure the parameters that the process will adhere to. Once this is done, you can ensure that the process is being created in a proper manner by gathering all of the information that is relevant.

Analyze: Here you will need to analyze all of the information that you have gathered. You may be able to see that there are some trends coming out of that information or find out that you need to do some more research and analyze it before continuing.

Improve: This is where the team can take that information and the analysis that you did, and make some improvements to the process.

Control the process. You need to work to control your business process as much as possible. You can do this by finding ways to reliably decrease how many times a delinquent variation starts to make an appearance in your process.

In addition to working with the DMAIC process, you can work with the DMADV process as well. This is very similar to the method that we just talked about before, and the five phases are going to correspond with the DMAIC process as well. The five phases that come with the DMADV method will include the following:

Define the solutions that you want the process to provide. You can look at your own mission statement, how the product is supposed to work, and input from the customer to help figure this one out.

Measure out the specifics of the process so that you are able to determine what parameters need to be in place.

Analyze the data that you and your team have been able to collect up to this particular point.

Design the new process with the help of the analysis that you have.

Verify any time that it is needed.

Both of these methods can be very effective at helping you to see results when you try to implement Six Sigma into your business. Often they work in very similar manners. You will need to consider the situations around your process, what deficiencies you need to fix, and more to help you determine which process is the best one for you.

Is Six Sigma the right choice for me?

While this process is something that can work for many different businesses across a wide variety of different industries, and Six Sigma has something to offer for teams of all sizes and shapes, it doesn't mean that this process is going to be the best fit for everyone. This can be really apparent as implementing it successfully means that a number of specifics need to come into play. This will start with the conviction of those who are looking to implement the system in the first place, as well as the overall culture that is found in the business and how open it is to the new change.

This is why many companies decide to ease into the process and will start with the 5S method. This is seen as a lower impact method that can adjust the team to what you want to happen before you move into some more advanced techniques, like what you find with Six Sigma. Once the team has accepted what you are trying to do, it becomes so much easier to implement all of Six Sigma and all of Lean into the business and its culture.

When you are taking a look at the Six Sigma method and trying to determine if this kind of transition is actually something that you can do, you must make sure that no one in the business, especially upper management, sees this as a fad or a trend that the business is just trying out. In fact, Six Sigma, and the whole Lean philosophy needs to be seen as an evolution of the ideals that the company already put in place.

In most cases, the more involved you can get the leadership of the team right from the beginning, the more onboard the team will be, and the more participation you will be able to get out of everyone. This is why it is so important to get all of the employees on board, whether they are in top management or hold another important position within the company.

In addition, it is so important for the culture of your company to be seen as one that is in full support of this kind of positive change, and to remember that if your upper management, or anyone on the management team, isn't able to come up with a consensus on the new program, that it is better to hold off a bit to reach that consensus. Jumping in when not everyone is on board, especially if some of those are the upper management, means that the idea and the process will be dead from the start.

Of course, this doesn't mean that every single person on the team must be committed to the idea of Six Sigma or the Lean methodology right from the start. But it does mean that the changes that occur need to be seen as institutional. This ensures that the front that you send to the public shows that everyone is united under the ideas of the method.

Implementing Six Sigma into your business can take some time, but when you add it together with the ideas of Lean, then you are going to see a big shift in the company culture and so much more. But when both of these ideologies are used together, you will find that it results in more satisfaction with your customers, less waste, more efficiencies in the process, and more profits in the long term of your business.

Chapter 32. Deciding If Six Sigma Is Right For Your Company

While the Six Sigma system has something to offer teams and companies of all sizes and complexities, that doesn't mean that it is automatically a good fit for your particular business. In fact, implementing Six Sigma successfully depends on a myriad of different specifics including the conviction of those implementing the system, and the company's overarching culture. As such, understanding the concepts related to successfully implementing 5S will make the transition to Six Sigma much easier to accomplish.

Is The Leadership Involved?

When suggesting a transition to Six Sigma, it is important that it not be framed as another "fad" management style and instead be seen as an enhancement of what is already in place. As a rule, management is going to be opposed to the change which means it will be important to get buy-in from the person at the top and work down from there.

This doesn't mean that every person in the organization must be committed to Six Sigma, but it does mean that the change must be seen as institutional which means the public front must always appear united. The human brain is a creature of habit, especially when it is confronted with new systems that seem complicated which Six Sigma often does, if it is at all apparent that the new system is optional, most people will opt out every time. Don't give them an avoidance opportunity, do what you can to ensure that opposition is voiced in private.

Is The Correct Infrastructure In Place?

Six Sigma is founded on the principle of leaders mentoring those underneath them and in order to make Six Sigma work, this needs to be a full-time job for some people, at least until new, positive habits form. While it may not seem cost-effective to dedicate one or more people to the task of actively mentoring others on Six Sigma specifics, it is a sacrifice you must be willing to make if you want Six Sigma to be more than a flash in the pan with your team.

Unfortunately, this will never be the case if the person who is responsible for mentoring others is also bogged down with additional work as that additional work is almost always going to ultimately end up in front of additional mentoring duties. Prior to implementing Six Sigma, it is important to ensure that you have the infrastructure to support it long term, otherwise, you are ultimately just wasting everyone's time.

What Will Cause The Rank And File To Fall In Line?

Once you have the support of management and have ensured that you have the infrastructure to support the undertaking for as long as it takes, the next thing you need to determine is if you have a way to motivate the remaining employees to stick with Six Sigma to the point that they internalize it so that it becomes second nature. Regardless of how their progress is tracked, it is vital that each member of the team feels an immediate and compelling reason to commit to the new program, at least at first.

Companies are like any other body that is in motion, the larger the company, the more inertia it displays when it comes to making large changes, and for many companies, Six Sigma is a very large change. This is why a tangible incentive must be attached at every level of the company to ensure that everyone remains united in their drive to obtain the incentive. The side effect from this will, of course, be they are also internalizing the ideas behind Six Sigma without actively trying to do so.

How Common Is The Practice In Your Field?

While Six Sigma has proven value in a wide variety of fields, that doesn't mean that all of those fields are ready to adopt the process with open arms. While being a forward thinker is never a bad thing, if your industry has yet to adopt Six Sigma as a common practice, it is important to be ready for additional pushback from the institution when attempting to move forward with the change.

Be prepared for resistance and stand your ground, using examples of successful companies who have already adopted the Six Sigma system will also help to silence naysayers. The research behind Six Sigma speaks for itself, be ready with specific examples of how it can help your company specifically and the facts will ultimately speak for themselves.

What Are The Objectives Of The Training?

Depending on the size of your company, training the team at the same overall level of Six Sigma may make sense. Eventually, however, the size of the team will necessitate the use of numerous training levels. If this is the case, it is important to consider the qualifications for each level as well as how training will be staggered for maximum efficacy. Don't forget to determine how the length of the training will affect other duties as well as the areas that will be focused on the most.

Taking the time to identify the specifics unique to your desired training scenario before you start will make all the difference in the overall implementation of Six Sigma and should not be ignored. There are no one-size-fits-all options in this scenario, planning out the specifics of your team's training could very well make the difference between success and failure in the long term. What's more, it can help point out potential issues that may arise which may otherwise have not been visible until the training was already in progress.

Which Projects Are Going To Be Used As The Flagships For The New System?

Once Six Sigma training is completed, you will want to already have a few projects waiting in the wings that can be ultimately connected to the new system and pointed to as signs of success further down the road when the question as to whether or not it is a good idea to continue with Six

Sigma arises. Your goal should be to increase the level of involvement surrounding one or more Black Belt or Green Belt projects and do whatever is required to ensure they are successful.

During this period, it is important to ensure that the initial round of Black Belt and Green Belt employees don't find themselves on so many projects that they begin to miss measurable objectives. Your goal above all others during this time should be to maximize success as much as possible. Take the extra time to ensure that the first round of projects has the appropriate amount of buy-in from management or other key stakeholders, again, there is nothing more demotivating than seeing projects fail after a new system has been implemented. Ensure that the management team is committed to making sure that doesn't happen.

It is important that the projects chosen are not just "feel good" projects and are instead those that are truly beneficial to the company as a whole. If enough early Six Sigma projects are well-publicized but produce little of measurable value than the entire system is at risk of collapsing from the inside as it will be seen as a fad with little in terms of substance.

Don't let this happen by instead choosing projects that have a clear value regardless of whether the person making the decision is trained in Six Sigma or not. Public opinion is crucial at this stage to allow everything to settle down to provide Six Sigma the time it needs to become a habit.

In order to ensure that Six Sigma is properly implemented, it is important that you properly motivate your team by explaining how crucial the adoption of a new methodology really is. The most common choice in these situations is to create what is known as a burning platform scenario.

A burning platform is a motivational tactic whereby you explain that the situation the company now finds itself in is so dire (like standing on a burning platform) that only by implementing Six Sigma is there any chance of long term survival for the company. Having stats that back up your assertions is helpful, though, if times aren't really so tough, a bit of exaggeration never hurt. Adapting to Six Sigma can be difficult, especially for older employees and a little external motivation can make the change more palatable.

Ensure The Tools For Self-Improvement Are Readily Available

Once the initial round of training regarding Six Sigma has been completed, it is important that you have a strong mentorship program in play while also making additional refresher materials readily available to those who need them. The worst thing that can happen at this point is for a team member who is confused about one of the finer points of Six Sigma to try and find additional answers only to be rebuffed due to lack of resources.

Not only will they walk away still confused, but they will have been rebuffed for trying and not rewarded for taking an interest in the subject matter. A team member who cannot easily find answers to their questions is a team member who will not follow Six Sigma processes when it really counts.

Give Priority To The Right Activities

In every situation, there are a number of potential outcomes when it comes to resolutions. While talking about Six Sigma is nice, it is important that team members see those in leadership roles commit to prioritizing the correct types of choices in every situation. It is important that determining criteria that are quality critical, listening to the customer and ensuring Six Sigma leads to measurable goals are all seen as vital activities for team members regardless of their level of Six Sigma certification.

Ensure The Six Sigma Initiative Is Owned By Everyone

When tutoring your team regarding Six Sigma it is important to make personal connections between it and individual team members so they feel more closely linked to the program's success. Whether it is by achieving buy-in from the team as a whole or making everyone in charge of enforcing Six Sigma principals, take the time to ensure that everyone feels connected to seeing Six Sigma succeed and the individual retention rate is sure to rise.

Ensure You Have A Way To Measure Results

Creating a realistic metric that can determine levels of success before Six Sigma was implemented, as well as after it is adopted, can provide you with the motivating data that you and your company need to keep it up over the long term. Alternatively, if it turns out that the system is actually ineffective in your case, the metric will be able to determine that as well. Either way, having a metric by which to measure aptitude is certain to come in handy.

Additionally, it will be a reliable motivating factor (assuming the results are positive, of course) and provide yet another way to reinforce the benefits of sticking with Six Sigma until its processes become habits.

Reward Excellence

When all else fails, rewarding those who take to the Six Sigma system with the most ease will always motivate the rest of the team to work as hard as possible if only to earn whatever reward you have promised. The goal with this type of motivation should be to choose something that is valuable enough to be worth working towards without being so extravagant that eventually removing the external motivation would cause all forward momentum to cease.

One common reason that Six Sigma implementation fails, is that many of those in management positions have never heard of the system and as such have a number of off the cuff questions or preconceived notions about it. Forewarned is forearmed, however, so many of the common critiques of Six Sigma, and their rebuttals, are listed below.

Six Sigma is just a fad like any other flavor of the month management style

In all actuality, Six Sigma can trace its origins back to the early 1900s where it was pioneered by the likes of Walter Shewhart, Henry Ford, and Edward Deming. What's more, it separates itself from the pack of related programs dedicated to continual improvement by being more focused on the use of data to make appropriate decisions that focus on the customer and ultimately always provide a solid return on any given investment.

We don't have the resources or time to dedicate to teaching and learning Six Sigma

Time is undeniably the most important resource that any company has as it is the only resource that is truly finite. Instead of considering the amount of time and resources that investing in Six Sigma will require, a better metric would be to determine what not adhering to a more effective system such as Six Sigma will cost in the long run.

It is important to remember the story of the pair of lumberjacks who worked day after day in the forest. One man worked himself to the point of exhaustion every day while the other man spent the time preparing properly and at the end of the day both men had always chopped the same amount of wood. If your team has the opportunity to work smarter instead of harder, why wouldn't you provide them with the tools they need to make that the new norm.

What's more, the cost of training the team in the specifics of Six Sigma can be mitigated over time by spreading out training courses as needed. While you won't start seeing the benefits from the higher levels all at once, training the whole team to Yellow Belt certification will still produce noticeable results. In addition, any funds put towards this type of training can also be seen as investing in the future of the business and should be considered accordingly.

We're Too Small For Six Sigma To Be Effective

Six Sigma offers up a new way of looking at the day to day business interactions that will increase productivity, and ultimately profits, regardless of the size of the team in question. Will a 10-person team need as many training sessions and resources committed to the project as a 50-person team? Of course not, but the individual results will be the same.

In fact, for smaller businesses, taking the time to determine areas of waste and specific bottlenecks, can actually lead to greater periods of growth as the issues that have been addressed may not have otherwise been noted and, when left unaddressed, could have led to serious issues further down the line. Taking the time to streamline processes and improve customer relations is always the right choice.

Six Sigma Doesn't Apply To Us

While Six Sigma originated in the manufacturing sector, studies show that industries based around providing services are actually more likely to generate unnecessary waste, not less. This is caused by the fact that so much of what is provided is essentially intangible which makes standardizing processes much more difficult. However, all of the processes that are already in place to track the services being provided

can ultimately be leveraged to implement Six Sigma
successfully.

Six Sigma Involves Too Many Statistics To Be Used Practically

Despite its reputation for being all about the numbers, a
majority of the tools and principles that are used in
implementing Six Sigma require more common sense than
mathematical formulas. For example, mitigating waste is
one of the most important facets of Six Sigma, a facet, that
only requires an understanding of the process in question
and how to do it in the most effective way possible.
Operating under Six Sigma is more about fostering a
mentality that allows employees to get to the root cause of
an issue, regardless of how long it takes. The formulas and
mathematical equations simply justify it after the fact.

Lean Is A Better Fit For Us Right Now

Lean and Six Sigma aren't opposing processes, and indeed
they work incredibly well together, so much so, that Six
Sigma is often referred to as Lean Six Sigma. When used in
conjunction with one another, Lean will improve the
throughput and speed of your processes while simplifying
and allowing the team to do the best with what is available.
Six Sigma then takes those improved processes and makes
them as high of quality as possible by reducing deviation
and related defects. Combing the two will only lead to better
results overall. Starting with 5S is recommended, after that

there is no harm in combing Lean and Six Sigma for the best results.

We've Tried It Before And It Didn't Work

The Six Sigma system has a proven track record with some of the biggest corporations in the world including Starbucks and Coca Cola. This means that the reason for the failure is likely related more to the way the program was managed in the past as opposed to a lack of efficacy when it comes to Six Sigma in general.

Chapter 33. Methodology of Lean and Six Sigma

As defined in the very beginning, lean is "elimination of all forms of non-value-added work from the customer's perspective in business transactions and processes."

Lean Methodology

When we look at any business or process, different operations are the building blocks of them which combine to form that business or process. Some operations add value, and some do not. So, it is important to understand the concept of value from the customer's perspective so that lean can be applied successfully. The operations can be categorized according to the value they produce from the customer's perspective as follows.

Business Non-Value Add Activities

The operations or activities which do not result in any value addition or produce any beneficial outcome but are still necessary for running the company or organization are termed as business non-value add activities.

The most common example of it is the operations that must be carried out to achieve the regulatory requirements imposed by the government. These are generally the tasks that do not add any value from the customer's point of view but they still can't be eliminated.

Essential Activities

These are the operations, tasks, and activities which produce valuable outcome from the customer's perspective and the customer is willing to pay for it.

Wastes

The activities or operations which do not produce any beneficial outcome or result in value addition from the customer's perspective are termed as waste in the lean philosophy.

In a typical business process, more than eighty percent of the activities can be classified as wastes or non-value add activities. This is indeed a tremendous amount of activity that produces nothing. The proportion also signifies that one can achieve an extraordinary edge over average businesses just by limiting or eliminating the non-value add activities. When you are able to control the amount of waste activities, you will be able to increase the proportion of activities for which the customer is actually willing to pay for. And this will make all the difference between your extraordinary efficient and profitable company against the average runt of the litter company.

This calls for an increased scrutinization of the processes so that waste can be identified. After many years of efforts in finding various types of wastes, experts have boiled down their analysis of waste and found them to be of the following seven types.

- Motion
- Transportation
- Waiting
- Overproduction
- Inventory
- Over-processing
- Rework

Motion

It is the movement of the employee who is performing a certain operation. If an operation involves a lot of movement on behalf of the employee, it produces no such feature for which the customer is interested in paying, hence it is classified as a waste. Examples of such waste are going to different offices, going to the printer, searching for any missing information.

Transportation

This might come as unexpected to you, but any conveyance of a product is considered waste. Assembly lines, shipping or mailing move a product from one place to another, but they do not add any value to it. Transportation really does not transform or change a product; all it does is move that product from one place to another. Amazon is the company that has tremendously gained by curtailing this waste by building warehouses all across the United States of America. This greatly reduced the need for transportation to deliver the product to the customer which resulted in an extraordinary profit for the company.

Waiting

This is perhaps the most common form of waste in almost all fields all over the globe. Delay in the process or improper flow of the procedure results in waiting. The most common examples of waiting that the customer has to endure are waiting for clarification, delivery of the order and waiting to finalize the deal.

Overproduction

Overproduction is the waste which is a result of producing the goods or services in quantities which are higher than the demand for them. Overproduction generally happens when the planned production rate is based on a forecast of the sales rather than the present market demand.

Inventory

Any type of service or supply, raw materials, etc., which is kept in quantities higher than the minimum required to produce the product and get the job done can be termed as inventory. Inventory is something which also ties up the resources of the company as well as takes up space and demand special facilities in some cases. Too much inventory also results in unnecessary motion as well as transportation, in other words, it is a non-value-added activity which produces other types of wastes as well.

Over-processing

In many instances of producing a product, extra work is done which the customer is not interested in paying for. This type of work involves expenses but does not give any profit or revenues in return. If the product is made extra shiny but the customer is not affected about whether the product is shiny or not, then shining that product may be categorized as a waste because of over-processing. Of course, if the customer does care about whether the product is shiny or not, then shining the product should be classified as an essential activity rather than over-processing, in the end, it all boils down to the customer's perspective.

Rework

Any modifications or improvements in the product which are done in the product after its final step of manufacturing is termed as rework and is classified as a waste in the lean philosophy. Because lean stresses on doing the right thing the first time, if a product is not defective then it will not need any rework, hence rework is an additional step that can be avoided without affecting the quality or standard of the product.

Lean Tools

Many techniques and simple creative thinking are done to develop tools that help make the process and business lean. Lean tools, basically, are just a practical application of common sense in business management to make it more impactful, efficient and profitable.

Some tools of lean are enlisted below.

- The 5S
- Mistake-proofing

- Kanban
- SMED
- Andon
- Bottleneck analysis
- Continuous flow
- Muda (waste)
- Root cause analysis
- SMART goals
- Jidoka
- KPI
- Production leveling
- Gamba
- Hoshin Kanri
- Value Stream Mapping

Detailed description and analysis of the tools used in the lean methodology might require a separate book of its own, however, a brief discussion on some of the most important and extensively used tools of lean is done in the proceeding paragraphs.

The 5S

The 5S is basically a workplace organization tool. The 5S which constitute the following steps.

- Sort
- Set in order
- Shine
- Standardize

- Sustain

These are the guiding principles that, if followed, result in an efficient work environment.

Mistake-proofing

Mistake proofing is known as po-ka yo-ke in Japanese. It is a design approach that makes it impossible for a mistake to occur or once a mistake or error occurs, it becomes obvious right away. An example of po-ka yo-ke is the plug and socket having different shapes of each hole of the socket and leg of the switch so that they can be connected in a specific order.

Kanban

It is the lean approach developed by the pioneers of lean, Taiichi Ohno. The name, Kanban, is taken because of the cards used in this methodology. It is an inventory management approach focusing on the Just in Time (JIT) principle which Mr. Ohno introduced in the Toyota factory where he worked.

SMED (Single Minute Exchange of Dies)

It is a technique applied to significantly lower the time required to complete the change of equipment. SMED, short for single minute change of dies, focuses on converting as many steps of Chang over of equipment to "external" as possible. So that the process may continue while the changeover of the equipment is done. This approach streamlines the workflow and reduces downtime.

Andon

It's a management term that refers to the system to notify management, maintenance and other processes of quality and process problems. The workstation has an alert to indicate if a problem arises, it can be activated by a worker or by an automatic system. It informs the system that it may include some issues which should be resolved. The whole system is stopped so the issue can be corrected. It brings immediate attention to the problem so that it can be resolved.

Bottleneck analysis

A bottleneck refers to a process that causes the system to stop or delay the outcome of the system, a process that takes the longest cycle time. Bottleneck analysis should be done when the expansion of capacity is being planned. Only increasing the capacity of the other processes will not increase the overall output as they will still be limited by bottleneck processes. Bottleneck analysis identifies which steps of the process limit the overall throughput and improve it. It improves performance by finding the weakest part of the manufacturing process and strengthen it.

Continuous Flow

Continuous flow is the movement of the product or service through the production process to finish without hindrance. In an efficient continuous flow, the cycle time is equal to the lead time. Continuous flow can reduce the wastage of time when done properly and can significantly reduce costs. It lowers the inventory level. It improves the on-time delivery as there is no waste or unwanted goods piled up and only the right goods are moved forward through the system. It delivers high-quality products as mistakes in continuous flow only affect one part of the process.

Muda (waste)

Muda is anything in the process that does not add value from the customer's perspective and the customers are not willing to pay for it. The primary goal of lean manufacturing is to eliminate waste.

Root call analysis

It is a methodology to solve problems that begin by solving the problems related to the core of the system rather than fixing the problems on the surface which only give temporary solutions.

SMART Goals

SMART goals are the goals that are: specific, measurable, attainable, relevant and time-specific. It helps to achieve the goals.

Jidoka (Autonomation)

Autonomation is described as intelligent automation or automation with a human touch. This type of automation advises some supervisory functions instead of production functions. This means that if an abnormal situation occurs then the machine is stopped and workers stop the production line. And for this, the Jidoka follows the steps of the first detection of the abnormality, stop the process, fix or correct the immediate condition and find the root cause of the problem and install a countermeasure. Autonomation prevents overproduction, over inventory and elimination of the waste and focuses on solving problems and make sure they don't occur again.

KPI (key performance indicator)

The key performance indicator indicates how well the company is performing and effectively working towards the achievement of its goals. Organizations use key performance indicators at different levels to evaluate their success possibilities. High-level KPI refers to the performance of the overall organization and low-level KPI refers to the processes of the departments.

Production leveling

Production leveling, also known as production smoothing or, in Japanese, as "heijunka", is a technique used to reduce waste. The goal is to produce goods at a constant rate so that further processing can be done at a constant and predictable rate. It reduces the lead time and inventory by keeping the batches smaller.

Gemba

The term Gemba refers to the personal observation of the work- where the work is happening. Gemba is derived from a Japanese word Gembutsu, which means "real thing" or, sometimes, "real place". Observation in-person, the core principle of the tool, observe where the work is done, interacting with the people and the process for the change.

Hoshin Kanri (policy deployment)

It is a process that identifies the business's critical needs and demands and develops the capabilities of the employees, achieved by the alignment of the company's resources at all levels. Policy deployment increases the efficiency of the business. It focuses on achieving the company's goals by meeting the demands of the customers, employees, shareholders, suppliers and the environment. Policy deployment is an ideal report structure.

Value Stream Mapping

Value stream mapping is an amazing tool that helps to identify major non-value add activities (wastes), which must be removed from the process to make it lean.

What do we mean by a value stream map? A value stream map is a graphical representation of all the activities which constitute any process under consideration. The activities represented in the value stream map can be essential activities, wastes or non-value add business activities. It contains a lot of information regarding the process under consideration and is extremely helpful in understanding the flow of the procedure.

What do we get by drawing a value stream map? When a value stream map is constructed, understanding of the mechanism of the flow of activities and their significance becomes clear to the management and anyone studying the value stream map. It also helps to identify the nonessential steps in the process which must be eliminated from the process to make it lean.

Tips for developing a value stream map:

Value stream map is a simple tool for making the business lean. If applied efficiently, it can result in great value generation with minimal investment of time, mental capabilities and physical efforts. Some of the tips that might come in handy when you are developing a value stream map for your organization are discussed with you in the entailing paragraphs.

Use Sticky notes

Sticky notes are fun to work with, but that is not their main appeal or attractive feature. You can comfortably make changes in them and you can color-code them as well. For instance, you can designate green colored sticky notes only to be used for essential activities, red sticky notes for wastes, and grey colored sticky notes for non-value add business activities. This way, it becomes easy to identify the different types of activities when the value stream map is studied.

Make sure that your workstation is spacious

When developing a value stream map, things can become very messy very fast. If you are working on a value stream map in a congested space, it will become very difficult to avoid cluttering up different things. The more spacious the workstation is, the easier it will be to manage it. It would be much preferable if you work on a big whiteboard or a giant desk when you are developing a value stream map.

Don't develop the value stream map all alone

It is best to develop the value stream map with a team of professionals who are personally involved in the process. It eliminates or reduces the possibility of overlooking a step or classifying an essential activity as waste or vice versa. It also allows you to have an eagle's view of all the steps involved in the process and find the loopholes in the process.

Six Sigma Methodology

"Six Sigma is a statistical-based methodology used to reduce variations and remove defects in various processes and business transactions."

We have already discussed the pertinent concepts of six sigma such as standard deviation, mean, upper specification limit and lower specification limit so we will not repeat those here. However, a concise discussion of variations must be done to continue the topic in an orderly fashion, so it is discussed hereunder.

Concepts and Tools of Six Sigma

Apart from calculating the mean, standard deviation, determining the upper specification limit and lower specification limit and finding the defects per million opportunities (DPMO), many handy tools are developed and utilized to reduce variations and minimize defects. These tools and techniques are termed as six sigma tools and some of them are listed hereunder.

- Fishbone Diagram
- Why-Why-Why Diagram
- Pareto Diagram
- Correlation Chart
- Punchlist
- Failure Mode Analysis
- Zero Defect

Detailed description and analysis of the tools used in the six sigma methodology might require a separate book of its own, however, a brief discussion on some of the most important and extensively used tools of six sigma is done in the proceeding paragraphs.

Chapter 34. The Motorola Case

The Six Sigma methodology gained traction in the 1980s after it was endorsed by Motorola. In that time period, Motorola had been trying to measure the defects their company was turning out on a granular level. This was quite the shift from previous methods, which had been measuring things on a much larger scale. Their hope, in putting their mistakes under the microscope, so to speak, was to reduce the amount of waste being created, while turning out a better product for their customers to use.

In implementing Six Sigma, the return on their investment was a massive increase in the level of quality in several of their products. Motorola even received the first Malcolm Baldrige National Quality Award, which is in its third decade of being awarded for performance excellence in United States companies. Shortly thereafter, Motorola shared their Six Sigma method with the world, causing several other companies across the country to start earning these awards in performance excellence as well. By 2003, the total estimated savings caused by the use of Six Sigma was topping out over $100 billion.

Chapter 35. How to Harness Lean to Foster Innovation and Develop New Ideas

There is a lot of talk about innovation and how companies have started to innovate their processes to work efficiently. But, what is the impact of using lean to foster innovation in business? The potential is huge, and it is essential that every business harness that potential if some criteria are met.

The word innovation can either excite or terrify us. Many people are skeptical about the innovation of processes in their company. But, there are others who are embracing this innovation with open arms.

The former group is stuck in their old ways while the latter are willing to unlock their creative potential to improve the business. However, there is one thing that is certain – the leaner a business, the easier it is to innovate the business.

The debate on how lean thinking can foster innovation is one that has gained popularity. But, what is innovation? Innovation can be defined as the process of changing or transforming a process or an idea into something new, which will make the lives of the employees in the business more accessible.

Regardless of what process the business is transforming – manufacturing technology, products, services, software and business models – any innovation should always lead to the maximization and creation of value for the stakeholder or customer. This means that the business should meet not only the needs and demands of the customer but also anticipate them. Apple is one company that has understood its customer group very well.

I am sure you know where this is leading. Lean is one process that is customer-driven, and every principle and tool is based on the idea of freeing up the business's resources by removing waste and also maximizing the customers' value.

This helps to include newer projects and also allocate some resources to those processes. Many people believe that a lean business can innovate processes since it encourages the employees to identify innovative ways to improve its processes.

The business community has realized that lean thinking is one model that should be used to foster innovation in business. Many organizations have used lean thinking as a foundation to innovate their ideas and processes.

Take Pixar, for instance, which is a company that has implemented feedback loops and team-based collaboration. This has helped employees overcome their creative block thereby triggering innovation.

It is also important to remember that it is not only businesses that can benefit from lean thinking. Social, economic and environmental problems have become driving forces behind innovation. People and businesses should be respectful and mindful of the resources of our planet before they begin to innovate.

This innovation should contribute to solving the challenges of our time. Toyota Automotive has taught the world that lean thinking improves the society. This is further proof that lean thinking and innovation are a perfect match.

It has been proved that lean thinking is more superior to traditional manufacturing. But, one has to remember that lean thinking is more about improving the management system and leadership behavior. Lean drives innovation and is an approach that is based on learning. However, certain conditions have to be in place for lean management to succeed.

Organizational Structure for Lean Innovation

An organization must have the right structure to foster innovation through lean thinking. Companies must always be inclusive in the sense that every stakeholder must participate in the decisions that the company makes.

For example, employees, engineers, suppliers, scientists and customers must agree upon every decision that is made by the company to maximize value for the customers. Every function that takes place in a business must be included in innovation, and this is what lean thinking teaches us.

The phenomenon of "open innovation" arises when every team in an organization is included in the process of innovation. This concept suggests that every innovative idea must be welcome even if it is coming from outside the organization. Businesses can take ideas that were coined by college students, scientists, young entrepreneurs and sometimes amateurs as well.

A striking example of this phenomenon is Wikipedia. Any person who has additional information about a particular concept can make changes to pages in Wikipedia. Some traditional organizations are catching up and accepting products that were invented outside the organization.

A company that is open to innovation must have a flat organizational structure since vertical structures have been known to fail. Business leaders must always identify the processes or layers in the structure that add value to their customers. There are a few strategies that a business can use to foster innovation through lean thinking in their organization.

How to Start the Process of Innovation and Experimentation

Understand why

Most businesses have started to innovate their processes. The ideas can be taken from outside the business. This does not mean that a business should always choose ideas from outside the organization. If the business is unable to sketch or draft an idea that can maximize value for the customers, it does not understand the process fully. Additionally, it cannot implement new ideas successfully if it does not understand how those ideas benefit the company and the customer.

Business Factors

The management must always look at the business factors in their business and their competitors' businesses. If the factors used to conduct processes are the same, no innovation has been made to the process. This reduces the competitive advantage that the business may have over its competitors.

Business Model Diagram

If there are any competitive barriers, they must be removed to start improving and innovating processes. The management must outline the key activities, partners, cost structure, revenue stream and value propositions and observe them keenly to understand if any changes can be made.

Value Matrix

If there are any products or services that the customers do not appreciate or want, these can be removed from the value stream to enhance the process. This allows businesses to invest in fewer resources and add more value to the products and services. Businesses will have the ability to elevate the elements of the business that are bringing in more value and also create different purchases that are in line with the demands of the customers.

Strategy Profile

Businesses must revisit their business strategies and their competitors to identify areas where they can innovate and newer areas of business that can be tapped into. This will help the business identify new areas of work and also develop products and services within that area of work.

Business Model Diagram

Businesses must always identify ways to solve problems and also identify new ways to develop and enhance customer relationships. There was one landscaping company that passed the following message to different households by flinging Frisbees into their yards – "We work on your neighbor's lawn. Let us work on yours too!"

If the customer had never thought of hiring a landscaping company before, they might think about it twice since it will make their life easier.

Experimentation

Every business is allowed to fail. If there is a new concept that has been developed, the business should put it into action to see how the customers view it. There is a possibility that the idea may fail, but it is all right to fail. This helps the business identify what can be done better the next time an idea is implemented.

Renewal

Ideas that have been implemented should never be ignored. The business must revisit the ideas and see what can be improved to enhance customer experience. Always make upgrades to existing ideas since innovation is an ongoing process.

Chapter 36. How to Foster Learning and Experimentation through Lean

A learning organization is not different from lean management. Learning is a process that is embedded in lean management. An organization where teams learn from everyday processes and also experiment with innovations and changes made to a process is called a lean and learning organization.

Every employee in an organization must learn every day about the processes and enhance their knowledge of the processes. This will enable the employees to cater to any problems that may occur during the process. Every employee must focus on the following questions:

- What have I learned today?
- Have I implemented any new changes to an existing process?
- Have I experimented with new processes?
- What is the data trying to tell me today?

Learning organizations are not the current trend, and there are very few businesses that have begun to learn about the processes and have tried to innovate those processes. What every business must remember is that learning provides the business with an environment where employees are given the freedom to think and also embrace the idea that solutions to work-related problems are found in their mind.

The employee must always tap into his or her knowledge base and use that knowledge to develop concepts and ideas that will improve the process.

In a lean business, learning is not restricted to training only. Training does help the employees develop some skills and also grasp and understanding of how the company functions. But, through learning, the employees will develop better skills and more knowledge that can enhance the profitability of the company.

Learning Model

The following learning model can be implemented in businesses to enhance learning.

Level 1

Every employee must learn the process, procedures, understand why a process is being done the way it is and also some essential facts about the process. This is a level of learning that applies to processes where only minor changes can be made.

Level 2

Learn new skills that can be transferred to situations at work. If the employee is in a new situation or has been shifted to a new process, he or she must have the ability to respond to changes in the process. The business can also choose to bring in outside expertise for this level of learning. There can be training that will help employees enhance their skills.

Level 3

Employees must always learn to adapt. This is a level of learning that applies to situations that are dynamic and where every solution must be developed. Experimentation and learning from failure are two ways of learning in this level.

Level 4

This is where an employee learns to learn. This is about how an employee can be creative and innovate processes. He or she can learn to design processes for the future. Knowledge is reframed at this level, and every assumption made by an employee is challenged.

Learning organizations set employees free. They are not required to be passive players in the business but can learn to express their views and ideas and also challenge those ideas and their skills to improve the work environment. Employees can create an environment where they can create and achieve the results that they truly desire.

Learning Culture

It is difficult to establish a learning culture in organizations that are not lean since they are comfortable in old practices and rarely find the necessity to change their processes. That being said, it is hard to establish a learning culture in any business.

External or Future Orientation

Organizations that have external or future orientation can understand their environment. Some teams comprise of senior members of the organization who take some time out of their busy day to develop a plan for the future. Additionally, the business can also choose to employ advisors who can help them plan their business.

Free Flow and Exchange of Information

There should be some systems in place that ensure that there are experts available whenever needed. Employees must have the chance to expand their horizons and also network with employees or professionals from other companies. This will give them an opportunity to enhance their knowledge of different processes, which will help them become experts in the process.

Commitment to Personal Development and Learning

With the support from the top management, employees must have the chance to learn. Employees who make an effort to learn regularly must be rewarded. This act will ensure that other employees also step forward and learn more. The employees must also be given the time to learn and also be encouraged to think lean which will help to remove waste from processes.

Trust and Openness

Every individual must be encouraged to develop or create ideas that will improve processes. They must also be allowed to voice their opinion, even if it is different from what other employees think since that gives rise to diversity. Views should be challenged.

Valuing Employees

Any idea that is developed by an employee should be tried and tested. An employee must be valued, and his or her thought process must be stimulated. If the idea is experimented and fails, the employee must learn from that failure and develop an idea that overcomes any errors.

In simpler words, a learning organization does not only implement ideas developed by senior management. It also allows employees to express their views.

Lean thinking is about creating a learning organization

It is important to remember that lean businesses are not only about the processes, it is also about learning. Every process is a great tool to transform an organization into a learning organization. This should be the goal that every organization must achieve in the current market and economy.

The disruption, complexity and change are going to continue, and the rate at which these phenomena are occurring will only increase with time. The only competitive advantage that any business has in this economy is the ability to adapt, and the only way a business can adapt is by learning continually.

If a business wants to compete in the information-saturated economy, it is necessary for it to remain competitive, dynamic and to look for ways to improve its processes. It is essential to remember that change is the only constant in every organization and every business must rid itself of the traditional hierarchy that often averse to change.

A learning organization embraces change and creates reference points that help to rebuild the structure. Learning organizations are healthier since they:

- Increase the ability to accept and manage change
- Garner and encourage independent thought
- Improve quality
- Give employees hope that things can always get better
- Develop a committed organization and workforce
- Stretch and expand perceived limits

To create a learning organization the management or leadership must be effective. This means that leadership cannot follow the traditional hierarchy but must consist of a mixed group of people from different levels in the system.

The business must also accept that every employee can solve some problems that may occur in the organization. The business must give employees the benefit of doubt and encourage them to voice their opinion, which will help the business forge ahead and create a bright future.

An organization must never consider itself separate from the world. It is only when it connects to the world that it can build a learning culture and environment.

One of the biggest challenges that every business must overcome is the way it identifies people within the organization. Only when every employee is considered equal is there a possibility to develop a learning organization.

Conclusions

Thanks for downloading this book. It's my firm belief that it will provide you with all the answers to your questions.

Lean thinking is a way of business and not just a business project. There are only some businesses that have begun to use lean thinking to enhance and improve processes and also maximize customer value. The group of businesses that do not implement lean thinking is afraid of change. However, change is the only constant in the market and life.

Lean thinking requires a change not only in the processes but also in the management and leadership since the business has to be open to new thoughts and ideas.

Through lean management and thinking, a business can encourage its employees to identify ways to improve processes and also innovate or develop new processes that maximize value. This creates a sense of equality in the organization since every employee has the right to voice his or her opinion.

Section 3: Lean Six Sigma

Some things are that obvious – and that is a good starting point. It cannot also carry fluff and unnecessary baggage with it. That is what lean connotes, isn't it? So, we have bagged those initial marks; let us now find out what Six Sigma then is.

Simply put, Six Sigma is a method of working where you focus on minimizing wastage in whatever it is that you are doing. We have in mind the service sector; the manufacturing sector; and even the trading sector. Six Sigma helps you monitor, through observed data, how well you are doing. What you do in Six Sigma is analyze the data within your project and establish the degree of poor performance – and that is what you work on reducing.

Surely, you understand what we are essentially saying. For example, if you happen to be manufacturing a brand of alcoholic drinks, there is no way you will anticipate sending out to the market some cartons with empty bottles well corked. This is because your plan is not to short-change your customers and chase them away, but to supply them with cartons of full bottles of the drink. You do not also want to send out some batches with lower alcohol levels than stated on the label. Six Sigma is basically that – no complicated stuff.

If you are running a salon, you want your clients to leave your parlor with their heads looking like the picture you both agreed on – or maybe close. And if your role is to supply materials to a manufacturing entity, you cannot surely afford to be that notorious supplier costing your customers hours upon hours of downtime because of your unreliable deliveries. You need to have set timelines within which to make deliveries after receiving the orders.

In short, Lean Six Sigma calls for systems whose performance can be measured. And after gauging your performance against what is expected, you deduce where losses are occurring in terms of wasted inputs and so on; and then you correct that.

So what are the guidelines in Six Sigma?

First of all, you need to know what you would like to achieve: your intended specifications

Then you need to measure the results of your performance at every stage of the process. For purposes of credible assessment, you need to then get the average of various results that you get over a set period of time, and that is the figure you then take as your mean for purposes of calculations.

Those two – your intended results and your actual mean results – must be as close as possible for you to speak of efficiency and impressive performance. The wider the variation between those two levels, the worse you are performing. In short, you do not want to deviate from what you planned with a big margin. You want to be as close as possible to what you initially planned. And you know what they call such kind of discrepancies? Well, they are called deviations. And that is because you are deviating from the planned results. You are deviating from the best way of doing things; the reason your performance is not optimum.

Your Expectations for Lean Six Sigma

At the end of the day, what you seek to achieve when you introduce this methodology of doing things into your organization is:

Alignment of projects with the organization's strategic objectives

This you do by having clearly defined roles for everyone involved and having set protocols for measurements

Objective assessment of processes

You want to know how ready the processes are to deliver the required output at the quality anticipated – and that is as close as possible to excellence

Modification or even overhaul of existing inefficient processes

The extent to which this is done, of course, is determined by the results of the processes assessment.

But how do we use Six Sigma to evaluate performance?

That is easy – always is, when you are using specific data and clear procedure. To help you gauge if you are doing well using the Six Sigma method, you are given an accepted deviation against which to compare your success. As such, if your mean performance is within the accepted standard deviation from your set goal, you can give yourself a pat on the back. Your performance, whether in production; in trade; or even in service provision can be termed good.

But why, really, can you not be even closer to your goal than that; not deviating at all? What would happen if you smelt or even touched success; or the best performance possible? Would you not be the best rated in your industry? Would you not be reaping the most profits that you could? Would you also not have a well-oiled system where things work whether you are around supervising or not?

Essentially, you would be utilizing every bit of input to its optimum and incurring no losses or waste. The implication of such efficiency is that every input and every effort contributes directly and unmistakably to revenue creation. No input is in excess and none is redundant. In the same vein, inputs are not insufficient in a manner to cause downtime or bottlenecks. Lean Six Sigma is about smooth running processes utilizing only inputs that are relevant and necessary to produce the desired results as per plan.

That is the working of Lean Six Sigma when implemented by knowledgeable people: getting rid of the sticky stuff that lines the performance passage slowing it down. Think of the doctor's recommendation as far as your heart is concerned – clear the bad cholesterol that lines up your arteries, and if there is plaque do the same; and the blood will serve your body like you are just beginning your youth. That is what the call is in all spheres of life. You need to clear anything that slows down your performance.

Now, you will agree that you need to know exactly what this sticky stuff is in order to know what kind of brush to use to get rid of it. It is even important, before then, to ascertain if it is cleanable in the first place, because if it is not, a major decision will need to be made regarding the viability of the whole project.

Here are the eight categories of waste that you need to set your eyes on:

- Downtime
- Overproduction
- Waiting
- Non utilized talent
- Transportation
- Inventory
- Motion
- Extra processing

Shorten it as DOWNTIME, and you will not forget it.

Wow! That technical sounding term – Lean Six Sigma – boils down to bringing down DOWNTIME as far as humanly possible...? It surely does; even when what is humanly possible involves using machinery and technical knowhow. It is essentially about making best use of resources at your disposal, and reducing redundancy all round.

For those who know nothing about reducing DOWNTIME, waste within an organization becomes like a disease or a cultural weakness. Individuals do not tie their wasteful actions to the organization's end results. And that is what

Lean Six Sigma seeks to clean up. Every move and every piece of resource has an impact on the organization's end results, and this is what every employee is made to appreciate when working within Lean Six Sigma projects. And since the processes are data based and all evaluations are clear at every stage, it is easy for individuals concerned to appreciate when they are doing well for the company and when they are doing the organization disservice through inefficiencies.

Whereas the Lean Six Sigma way of working may seem to keep everyone on their toes, once they get the hang of it, it becomes a morale booster as great performers stand out through measurable results.

Chapter 37. What is the Lean Six Sigma Method?

Six sigma lean is a discipline which conveys client esteem. Not from the company's perspective, but from the client's perspective. It conveys client's value through productive activity, and quality. This implies that, lean six sigma conveys steady quality.

What is Lean Six Sigma?

Lean six sigma can be an idea of management, known for adequately improving job forms, in view of the mixture of the various tools of Sigma Six and Lean. Sigma Lean six is a procedure improvement technique intended to remove issues, eradicate inefficiency, waste, and improve working conditions to give a great response to client's needs.

It joins the techniques, instruments & standards for Six Sigma Lean all unto one prominent and incredible strategy for improving your company's activities.

Lean six sigma's group-oriented approach has shown results in amplifying productivity and increasing profits for organizations around the globe.

Lean manufacturing comprises 25 significant ideas, for example, proofing of error, SMED source of the quality, Kanban, 5s Balancing of Line, Cellular Manufacturing, Standard Operations, and Value Stream Mapping. A couple of associations put in a few years executing these wonderful guidelines into their organization. Six sigma includes a 5 phase approach DMAIC (Define, Measure, Analyze, Improve, Control), utilizing a few instruments all through the stages.

Incorporate the two strategies and these devices, and it is anything but difficult to understand the disappointment in activities. But on the off chance that the affiliation has the bent to manage the execution and help center the endeavors, the program transforms into a shotgun approach and is bound to come up short. Most affiliations couldn't withstand the perplexity and postponed costs without significant recompense.

The two six sigma and manufacturing of lean standards have been tested to work. Numerous organizations have expanded business, decreased costs, expanded throughput, and brought down process durations utilizing the two methods. It is reasonable to use all the tools that are available and accessible to get the most advancement possible.

It is basic for organizations to let the problem decide the tools that are required, as opposed to decide the tool and force it's utilization. Not many of the works shows plainly the assembling lean thought. In the occasion, if a machine has a short set up time and it is the bottleneck, by then a SMED undertaking is basic. It may be a straightforward SMED (Single moment trade of bite the dust) or a piece of a kaizen rush.

There are clearly various exercises which will be founded on a six sigma. For example, a clump strategy plant using 12 unmistakable fixings with various methodology at different temperatures, rates, and viscosities, would require a six sigma task to choose the best blend of machines and speed to get incredible results. A segment of the six sigma instruments used would be speculation trying, investigation of fluctuation, factual examination, and plan of trials.

There are different sorts of activities where both six sigma instruments and lean collecting would best loosen up the test. For instance, expect a bunch getting ready issue incorporated the different temperatures and speed. The best methodology may be a sure blend of machines, yet the best one has a 5 man bunch with a 2 hour course of action time.

It is the perfect open door for the lean gadgets to diminish the cost per man hour utilizing SMED, just as OEE (Overall Equipment Effectiveness).

An average use of lean gear or devices in a six sigma undertaking is during the Improve arrange. The issue is being Define, Measured, and Analyzed by six sigma venture, anyway a lean gadget is essential to explain it. Another six sigma instrument/hardware will help Control it. In case the association simply used one of lean assembling or six sigma devices, the issue may not get unraveled.

The greatness of six sigma is the proficient method to manage conditions. The advantage of lean assembling mechanical assemblies is the speed of use. Right when the two gadgets are merged and used when important to settle business openings, the best result and most noticeable compensation will be gained.

What are DMAIC Cycles?

DMAIC are the information propelled procedure that are used to process improvement cycles. The abbreviation represents 5 indoor associated steps or stages that are; face has a particular purpose with a general objective.

In the Define face; an undertaking charger is made, to define the business issues, problem team, objectives, high project timeline, and target.

The motivation behind the Measure face; is to decide the gauge execution of the procedure. This means that, we have to quantify how the procedure performs today.

In the Analyze face; the group may break down information and the procedure stream to distinguish the main cause of waste, defects, and variation

The Improve face; is tied in with creating and devaluating, to dispose of or lessen the recognized root cause.

The major goals of the control face; is to get gains. This is achieved by creating or updating standard operating procedures, and ongoing managing of process performance based on a control plan.

The motivation behind the Control face; is to support the increases. This is accomplished by making or refreshing standard working methods, and ongoing managing of procedure execution dependent on a control plan.

DMAIC has gain credibility and reliability over the years, as an improvement technique that is simple to apply, reasonable for group, and efficient at conveying execution upgrades.

Who Are The Main Players?

While applying Lean Six Sigma, people all over the level of organization and business functions needs to play certain role towards a prosperous execution of this strategy.

The important ones are; Black or Green Belt, Champion, Project Team, and Process Owner.

Sponsor

The role of the executive sponsor is vital and important for the success of this initiative. The set of people are known members in a management or board members, and actively follow the implementation of sigma lean six. For the organization, they provide the resources and budget required for the program, and individuals for the projects.

Champions

These are probably the single most important role within the lean six sigma. They take the vision, and the directions from executives, and establish organizational objectives that need to be looked into by using lean six sigma. In addition, they also identify and prioritize project ideas which they assign to the black or green belt. As department head or manager of an area, champions are the ones responsible for the success of projects in their division. Once a project has been started, they provide motivation and consultation, and assist the black or green belt, and their team in removing any issue that might stop the project from being successful.

Green Or Black Belt

These are professionals that acts as project leader of lean six sigma projects. They also serve as teachers and mentors of the team members. The most important role and responsibility of a black or green belt is to deliver solution to business issues to the process owner.

Well, Black Belts sell mostly 100% dedicated resources to lean six sigma, and responsible for large scale projects.

Green Belts are traditionally only dedicated to part time within companies, and manage small to medium projects.

Process Owner

Another key player is the process owner. The process owner is a professional. This professional is the one meant for the procedure of business which are the goals of the lean sigma six initiative. One of the most important roles that the process owner has is to help for an execution prior for the problem solved that is brought about by the black or green belt, and typically control to improve procedure after the project has been closed. He also assist with the identification of future project opportunities, because he is the one that usually know the process intimately, and feels the pain of any issues we have in our processes.

The Team Members

The team members help the black and green belt to execute a project. They assist with things like, experiment, data or information collection, experimentation, and other duty related to executing the project. The reason why this people are incredibly important and need to be well selected, is because they provide the expertise needed to analyze a process appropriately.

When To Apply The Lean Six Sigma

When confronting a business issue, the accompanying criteria ought to be met to effectively be a part of this initiative.

These issues are connected from a dealed procedure: A business procedure is the tedious sequence of tasks or activities that produce a particular product or services for a specific client.

The procedure runs often: This implies that the procedure happens all the time, and annually. The more often the procedure runs, the more advantage can be produced over a specific timeframe.

There isn't a known answer for the issue: If you know the issue, you needn't bother with lean six sigma. Just take care of business.

The underlying cause of the issue isn't known: Lean six sigma is a critical solving technique, concentrating on recognizing the underlying cause forgiven issue. It just bodes well to apply the apparatuses and ideas, if those jobs does not need to be finished.

There is information accessible: Data availability and accessibility is basic to the achievement of lean six sigma and the speed. It is additionally the most basic condition to be met when applying lean six sigma. Without information, we can't gauge, and without having the option to gauge, we can't measure and devaluate the procedure execution, before and after development have been made.

This topic is the information driven procedure, used for adequately improve business forms.

Lean Six Sigma Methodology

These strategies pay attention to disposals. Waste incorporates utilizing too many staff individuals to finish a work. This makes a business spend an excessive amount of cash on work and even tries harder which can hinder, or slow production. Waste likewise incorporates making pointless buys on resources, assets or tools that you truly needn't bother with. One can figure out how to distinguish the waste and diminish it, just when you experience lean six sigma certification training. This can help a business reduce expenses, and also improve efficiency with workers. Congestion happen and hence hinder a business procedure fundamentally. At the point when representatives go attend lean Six Sigma certification training, they are instructed to recognize congestions inside a whole association right down to explicit procedures. Being capable of recognizing congestions offers your organization the chance to dispose them and amplify efficiency. Lean Six Sigma courses give brilliant training thinking basically and concocting imaginative answers for fix issues.

Another crucial part of lean six sigma is client loyalty and satisfaction. Clients are the place the cash originates from and in the event that you can't fulfill them, at that point you may not be good to go for a really long time. Organizations that have seen they have had an enormous loss of clients frequently send their staff individuals to Six Sigma Lean Certificate training in order to make something happen. Sigma Six Training will help workers get an in-depth comprehension and recognize the necessities of a client and how to meet their demand. This will surely help as a business accomplished and manufacture better client connections and expand your client base.

Lean Six Sigma techniques are designed for upgrading business forms in different ways. Your business can profit by removing waste, congestions, hindering efficiency, and improving client loyalty and satisfaction. These courses will profit the representative, and furthermore your business. You will realize that better productivity is an outcome alongside higher incomes at last.

Chapter 38. Introducing Lean Production

Lean is an end of the types of non-value added work from the client's point of view in business transactions and procedures. Lean centers on effectiveness; it limits delays, mistakes, and waste.

History Of Lean

Lean has its root traced back to the 90's of the nineteenth century. Frederick Taylor was an American mechanical engineer. He is called the management of scientific and was a primary administration consultant. Taylor started make out and see persons work techniques to find the most ideal approach to carry out each work. The outcome was institutionalized work, and time study. At that point, Ford Henry came into field. An American Industrialist and an Originator of the Ford Motors Industries he was. He presented auto-mobile, American industry, and revolutionized transportation. He formed the primary extensive assembling procedure. His island park plan generation by setting fabrication equipment in procedure sequence. The outcome was, a lot higher generation, and quicker production time.

In the 60's of a century ago, a man named Taiichi Ohno, created what is normally referred to today as the Management. He was a Japanese business person, and a supervisor for Toyota. Taiichi is the pioneer of the Toyota production framework. Which became lean Manufacturing in the US. Ohno perceived the role of inventory, and created functional strategies to execute the idea of "Just the nick of time". He likewise distinguishes the seven different ways, which should be disposed of as the focal point of lean, to increase profitability, and business forms.

As per Lean terms, reliably, esteem is described by the customer. There are three unique approaches to arrange esteem;

Squander: This is by and large alluded to as a non-esteem include exercises.

Basic Activities: These exercises are known as worth includes exercises for which the customer needs to pay for. There are a few activities that fall somewhere in the center. These activities are generally known as Non-Value Activities. The jobs can be finished, regardless of whether they are not customarily characterized as value add. A good example of a business non-value add activity, will be test required to meet administrative or lawful prerequisites. These activities are not characterized as increasing the value of a procedure from the client's perspective. In any case, they can't be avoided. In a regular business process, whether transactional or manufacturing, an enormous measure of the activities is non-value add. Most procedures are 3 percent to 5 percent value add, and possibly 10 percent to 15 percent non-value add. Be that as it may, most of procedure are the non-value add.

To comprehend the concept of Lean, of importance it is imperative of note is to understand the concept of what waste is. As a focal point of lean, is about the decrease of waste.

Lean gives the definition of seven kinds of waste. These are; Transportation, Motion, Inventory, Rework, Waiting, Over-processing, and Overproduction.

Transportation: Any movement of an item is viewed as waste. Mails and Shipping are move services and items, however don't add value. Transportation doesn't change an item or services. It just conveys it.

Motion: This refers to the real conveyance of an individual. This may be an unnecessary movement inside the work station, or movement in a task that takes much time and effort to finish.

Inventory: This is any sort of materials or provisions that are kept, over the base, to take care of job. Inventory occupies room. An excess of inventory in term of work in progress is a significant contributor to long live time.

Rework: Rework is any fix or repair, change to an item after it has been made, or any correction that was not done right the first run through. One of the essential part of lean is value, and something only have value if it was done well the first run through.

Waiting: This waste shows waiting for data or information. An absence of data or information, or the delay in the process is an instance of waste, and something we need to remove completely. The objective is to be able to respond to the client's needs, with no delay to goods or services.

Over processing: This waste is about activities that add cost, however no value. We do activities that the client couldn't care less about, or doesn't request. At the end of the day, over-processing just means, accomplishing things that are repetitive.

Overproduction: This implies delivering excessively, or too early. It is producing to forecast, rather than to request. Overproduction exhaust our assets with things the clients don't require, and has not requested. If we listen to the client's prerequisite carefully, we can respond with goods that satisfies those needs.

Stream Value Mapping

This can be seen as the most fundamental & amazing principle and tool of Lean. Value stream mapping helps to visualize and map the business procedures. A stream value covers entire plans and procedures, which can be needed to create an item, or service. Moreover, a value stream map ought to incorporate procedure data, to evaluate and exhibit the procedure execution in a graphical form. By making a value stream map, a typical comprehension of the present condition of the procedure is figured out. Most important, it distinguishes waste, opportunities for development. Data is what different a value stream map from a standard procedure map. The objective is to get as much data, in terms of process execution measurements as possible.

Value stream metrics are; cycle times, process times, rework rate or defect rate, and circle times. Now, that the process cycle is visualized, and customary execution measurement are visible, we have an ideal basis to recognize waste, in and between procedure steps, as this is the main reason of creating the value stream maps. It makes it easy and simple to point at weak points along the process. When talking about weak points, it means the seven types of waste.

Within this extent of the waste analysis, the procedure improvement group ought to research the value stream map, and in the process, trashs are recognized. To show kind of trash, issue area at a value stream maps. Graphic signs can be utilized and added to the map appropriately. This genuine mark areas is for development to concentrate on, when creating ways and answers to lessen the non-value time spent in a procedure.

Before you begin to make your value stream map, there are some tips to remember.

Use sticky notes

Instead of using a software tool to document your process, it's easier to make changes, and most important, it contributes to employing engagement and involvements.

Use enough space

Don't restrict your mapping activity to a single shit of paper. Find a large piece of paper, or a white board, to document your map.

Create value stream maps with a team

Really, only one person has all of the process knowledge, to make sure that the right amount of knowledge is given, you should answer the question of who was involved in the process. When building the team, in other to develop a business procedure to the eradication of waste may include some tools and principles.

Chapter 39. Introducing Six Sigma

Six Sigma is a known as a measurable based methodology used to diminish variety, and discard blemishes in business strategies and exchanges.

History of Six Sigma

Six Sigma has its initiation in the 20's of a century back. Walter Shewhart was an analyst, physicist, and specialist. He displayed the differentiation of unique sections basic reason variety, and the control diagram.

In the twentieth century, Six Sigma was exhibited by Bill Smith, at Motorola. Smith, who was an American architect, known as the pioneer of six sigma. As an administration thought, six sigma seem to improve the nature of system, by perceiving, and disposing of the reason for disfigurements, or errors, and restricting varieties in business techniques.

In 1995, six sigma ended up being prominent, after Welch made it a point of convergence of his business method at general electric. Welch was executive, and CEO of General Electric. He expressed, six sigma is the most huge activity General Electric has ever utilized, as six sigma is tied in with reducing variety, and clearing out imperfections. These terms ought to be clarified.

What is Variation?

Variety is the extent of complexity, between the measurable mean, and all information indicates that are used make sense of the mean. All things considered, it is how much methodology execution changes around the normal. In six sigma, variety is assessed by figuring the standard deviation.

What is an imperfection?

A deformity is a quantifiable thing or administrations characteristics that doesn't meet a customer essential. It is any methodology execution outside of described specs.

Imperfections, in six sigma are assessed by figuring the DPMO

DPMO is determined by separating the aggregate sum of imperfection, by the absolute units.

DPMO (Defects per million chances) is dictated by isolating imperfections by unit, by circumstance per unit, duplicated by 100.

Why six Sigma is called Six Sigma

Similarly, as imperfections unto million chances, the level of sigma is an extent of methodology capacity. Methodology limit reveals to you how extraordinary, or poor the technique is performing. The level of sigma is evaluated by deviations of standards from the system mean (or normal) to an objective, or a stipulation limit. Each sign parts associate to a related deformity for each million open doors esteem.

Chapter 40. Why You Should Use the Lean Six Sigma Method

Lean Six Sigma can be linked to the most diverse formations, not just to the engineering ones. Can only engineers take Lean Six Sigma training? Whenever someone asks me this question, I rebut with another question: "Do only engineering students learn statistics during college?" The answer is simple. Of course not, after all, even in a psychology course the student may have contact with statistics. So you mean that anyone can become a Green Belt or Black Belt? Before answering this question let's take a brief reflection.

Engineers are, by definition, people of logical reasoning who use mathematical calculations to turn numbers into efficient processes and functional products. Another ability of your profile is to transfer the ideas from the clipboard to the real world, but for that to happen you also need to have a good understanding of social and economic issues. What I mean is that in the market, there is a very thin line between different areas of knowledge. In practice, every profession has a little of each area, without exceptions.

Let me give you some examples that prove this. A biologist must have knowledge of the social sciences to deal with his patients. A journalist needs to be knowledgeable about the accuracy of interpreting numbers that will give credibility to a story. An engineer needs to know the numbers to understand the social impact of new technology.

And what does this have to do with the Lean Six Sigma methodology? It goes without saying that if you think that only an engineer or an expert in the field of numbers can learn a managerial methodology that involves statistical calculations, you are making a serious mistake. This mistake may cost a better job position in the future, as companies are increasingly looking for multi-disciplinary professionals who are able to solve problems and generate results.

The studies of the last decade have consolidated the definition of the term Lean Six Sigma as a managerial philosophy that allows companies to leverage their profits by improving operations, improving quality, and eliminating defects, failures and process errors. Because it is so broad, this is a methodology that is not restricted to only one area, not least because it is applied not only in the operational sector of companies but also in the administrative areas. Today we have several examples of good results that Lean Six Sigma has brought to the HR, legal, commercial, and even marketing areas of a company. So if in each of these administrative areas, I'm talking about employees with different backgrounds, that is, this methodology is suitable for managers, advertisers, psychologists, economists, engineers, and many other types of professionals. So, anyone can do Lean Six Sigma training? The answer to this question is YES. Anyone can learn and apply the methodology.

The only prerequisite to take on a Lean Six Sigma training is to be willing to face the challenge. It is necessary to know that in the course there is an extensive statistical section that is part of the Six Sigma professional training, but if you are interested in learning to apply the methodology and to face this challenge, you have everything you need to become a professional more valued by the marketplace. Look for stimuli! The ideology of planning is trained in psychology and worked at the core of Human Resources. So it's easy to see: not only engineers or people who work with numbers can learn and apply Lean Six Sigma.

How Can Lean Six Sigma Help Me?

To ensure the success of Lean Six Sigma and therefore ensure its great contribution to achieving results, it is necessary to train people with the appropriate profile and we have already proven here that this does not mean the need for specific training. Duly trained employees will become sponsors of the program and specialists in methodology and quantitative and managerial tools, which will have a great impact in their areas of action and in their chances of reaching new goals and paths. By committing to learning, the consequences will be visible in your activities. Lean Six Sigma can be a possible system for many, just by wanting and having willpower.

Lean Six Sigma in Government Operations

As problems do not distinguish businesses, they occur in the most diverse economic segments and sizes of establishments and in almost every company there is a need for improvements. In the food industry, for example, there may be bottlenecks in the production chain, which can increase the cost of the commodity and generate a number of negative consequences for the organization. In the financial services sector, the difficulty of doing the credit analysis of clients can be an obstacle even to the survival of the business, because this segment is very competitive.

Six Sigma in the Industrial Area

In the industrial area, a manufacturer of auto parts must have a high degree of accuracy to meet the needs of automotive factories. Otherwise, defective items will represent a major loss to the business. In a credit card company, a challenge may be to increase sales to ensure the financial health of the company. Therefore, practically any type of company lives in search of perfecting some process to leverage its own results. What many of them do not know is how to do it.

The differential of Lean Six Sigma methodology in the search for improvements is that it has a very structured method, capable of scientifically proving whether the changes implanted in an organization have in fact resulted in improvement of productivity and quality. Therefore, by having a method, Lean Six Sigma can be applied to different realities with satisfactory results.

When they do not have this methodology, companies tend to want to solve their own production system failures. However, many of them take very inefficient and costly paths to the business, such as putting pressure on employees to get better results. Another unsuccessful way of raising performance is to find scapegoats internally but

318

without any scientific criterion of performance analysis. In such cases, the company walks in circles without finding solutions to its own problems.

By using an improvement road map and using statistical tools to prove or reject hypotheses, the Lean Six Sigma methodology seeks to combine efficiency and effectiveness in the search for better business processes. From the point of view of the projects, it is much more advantageous to invest in this type of work, to solve and to prevent problems, than to bear the consequences of perceived failures by the clients.

Six Sigma in Services

A service provider whose quality is evaluated during the execution of the activity can suffer damages due to defects in the processes. In the case of a bank, if the customer is dissatisfied with something, he can try to solve it at first by self-service, either over the internet or by telephone. If he cannot, he may consider going to an agency to talk to the manager. If this still does not resolve the situation, the customer can complain on consumer protection websites or file a complaint. If all this happens, the banking institution will create a great liability for the institutional image, not counting the possible sanctions of the supervisory entities. Therefore, it is much more advantageous to proactively decrease the rate of complaints than to learn to live with negative results.

Six Sigma in Health Organizations

Other companies that perform closely with their customers are those of telephone companies and those of the health sector. In these cases, the consumer already forms an almost automatic value judgment regarding the enterprise. Therefore, such organizations should be careful not to sacrifice their own business because of a lack of "listening" to complaints and the observation of opportunities for improvement.

In the case of the health sector, the needs of companies are increasing due to a series of factors, such as increase and aging of the population, growth in costs to maintain adequate structure and technology for care, risk of damages to patients, etc. Because this sector deals with the highest good for a person, which is life itself, the degree of excellence in business performance must be enormous.

Over the last few years, various applications of the Lean Six Sigma methodology in the health sector have shown that it is possible to improve three aspects of this area: the care of the population as a whole, the patient's experience in care, and the reduction of costs with the decrease of waste. As you may realize, the Lean Six Sigma approach not only considers economic factors but also customer satisfaction. In the case of the health area, it is not enough for the patient to get treatment for a certain illness, but he must also feel welcomed and cared for.

Six Sigma in the Public Sector

It is necessary to mention that even in the public sector it is possible to have applications of Lean Six Sigma. Entities and government agencies have a great history of dissatisfaction on the part of users of the services. Cases of friction between these parties are common.

In order to overcome this dissatisfaction in the public sector, managers must lead improvement policies in their respective areas of activity, to bureaucratize processes and speed up service delivery. It is clear that proactive initiatives presuppose a certain degree of political will on the part of those responsible for the operation of the public machine, yet they demonstrate that it is possible for Lean Six Sigma to operate in this sector. In Scotland, for example, the model of improvement is a state policy in the country, so it transcends the political plans of some rulers.

Chapter 41. Benefits of Six Sigma

Associations face increasing expense, and rivalry consistently. In particular, the demonstrated advantages are assorted.

Faster forms

With lean six sigma, associations accomplish quick procedures, by expelling all kind of non-esteem included work, as demonstrated by the seven sorts of waste.

Higher quality

Lean six sigma expects to accomplish higher caliber in term of procedure, soundness, and capacity, through the decrease of variety, and the end of imperfections.

Increased consumer loyalty

The essential wanted advantage of all procedure improvement exercises inside length of six sigma lean is a decrease for cost, by accomplishing stream line forms that are totally quicker, and all the more productively. Less assets are required, bringing about diminished cost. Moreover, less variety and imperfections prompts less

Cost of low quality incorporates cost that emerge because of the hole between the ideal and genuine item, and administration quality. Lean six sigma expands pay, by empowering an association or an organization to accomplish more with less assets.

Improved worker spirit and aptitude

Lean six sigma expands a worker's commitment, and adequacy. Lean six sigma don't just decrease cost, and expands income. It decidedly influences individuals by connecting with them in improving the manner in which they work. By including representatives in lean six sigma ventures, they increase a more noteworthy gratefulness for the effect of the work they do on primary concern business result. Too, as a thankfulness, or how crafted by different workers in offices additionally add to progress. When representatives get settled with lean six sigma scales, learnt through preparing or tasks. They can develop effectively, and keep on improving their business forms, in view of a genuine set up procedure.

The prime mandate of business: better, less expensive, and quicker. However, when squeezed for a clarification of what that truly implies, most administrators can just express the craving to get the most work, at all time, with the least individuals. When examined further on what's going on with their business forms, reactions are fluctuated however unsurprising. We need more individuals. The PC frameworks are lousy. The client's requests are unreasonable.

Most officials neglect to see the genuine issue. The genuine issue is the poor arrangement of the business procedure to the client needs and the abundance steps in the process that carries no an incentive to the client experience.

Other than consumer loyalty, putting resources into administration process improvement can rapidly add genuine dollars to the primary concern. It is settled that roughly 80% of an organization's contributed capital is the expense of individuals performing administration related obligations. So contributed capital is extremely the "Cost of individuals." Combined with observational information that has demonstrated that administration expenses are swelled by 30% to 80% waste, it bodes well to concentrate vitality on improving assistance side procedures.

How Lean Six Sigma Improves The Bottom Line

Services, typically encompass an organization's service framework, such as, Operations, Finance, Sales, Marketing, Human Resources, etc. A major characteristic of most service procedures is it that they depend on people to accomplish their objective.

Service process improvement is challenging for the following reasons:

They are moderate and costly on the grounds that there is in every case a lot of Work-in-Process (WIP). This is principally because of an inability to control WIP speed (for example work is pushed into the procedure regardless of work leaving the procedure).

- Less than 20% of administration procedure time includes worth or upgrades a client's understanding.
- The less obvious nature of administration procedures makes the procedure harder to track and issues harder to distinguish, measure, and fix.

- They have a convention of uniqueness, opportunity, and innovativeness.
- They are portrayed by an absence of significant information for basic leadership.
- People, your significant resource, are likewise the significant reason for process variety.
- Customers can't be dealt with like stock.

Sigma six lean for Services can be seen as augmentation of Sigma Six, not a substitution. Sigma six lean for Services & Sigma Six work pair.Six Sigma brings restrained, client driven, information driven devices and procedures to measures process mistakes, recognize changes, dispose of them, and bring the procedure under Statistical Process Control (SPC). Lean Six Sigma for Services centers around speed and productivity.

Lean Six Sigma for Services is ideal for improving help forms for the accompanying reasons:

- It isolates "esteem included" from "non-esteem included" work with Six Sigma devices to dispose of the major points of included non-esteemed exercises & (therefore) their expense.
- It gives a way to measuring and dispensing with the expense of multifaceted nature.
- Like its Six Sigma partner, it centers around consumer loyalty and quality by perceiving openings and wiping out client characterized surrenders.
- It perceives that variety thwarts the capacity to dependably convey top notch administrations.

- It requires information driven choices and joins a complete arrangement of value devices under an incredible system for successful critical thinking.
- It gives an exceptionally prescriptive social foundation for practical outcomes.

I have discovered that it is smarter to bring a procedure into measurable procedure control initial (Six Sigma), at that point take a shot at improving its ability (Lean). As it were, expel variety at that point raise execution level. At the point when a business procedure has been "Inclined" it has the accompanying qualities:

- The procedure is under factual control (for example assignable cause variety have been wiped out)
- The procedure works at a cycle productivity, more noteworthy than 20%. (Cycle effectiveness is known as the worth include time inside a procedure)
- It utilizes a draw framework where new work is discharged into the procedure just when old work has left.
- It utilizes visual controls to oversee and screen the procedure.

Lean Six Sigma for Services augments investor esteem by accomplishing the quickest pace of progress in consumer loyalty, cost, quality, speed, and contributed capital. It is a procedure, set of standards, and devices that attention on quickening the speed of all procedures over the endeavor by taking out waste and non-esteem included advances.

Organizations who have put vigorously in business process improvement have perceived a few crucial facts:

- Getting quick can really improve quality
- Enhanced quality can really improve speed
- Reducing unpredictability improves speed and quality

As you embark for improving business processes, stay focused on the above fundamentals using Lean Six Sigma for Services and you will see an improved bottom line.

Chapter 42. The Lean Six Sigma Method

It is not always easy to determine what to improve even when the organization decides to do so. There are so many things to check and many issues to point. It is always hard to know how to start and where to start. The Six Sigma approach is considered to be the best in the world as it answers all these questions. Keeping in mind the core principles of Lean Six Sigma, one can directly head towards improvement.

The Lean Six Sigma covers each and every step of processing in a systemic manner – here are its core principles:

Giving Priority To Customers

It is the first principle is related to customers in Six Sigma as they hold much importance in its functioning. The business advice of the past is considered true today that a customer is always right. Customers play a key role in the success of any organization. They are necessary for any business to mature. Therefore, no matter what business you do, you should give the first priority to your customers always. Keep in mind that without fulfilling the demands of the customer, your business might stop to grow further.

Each choice you make ought to carry your organization closer to conveying the greatest esteem. It's a good pre-practice to be sure about maintaining the degree of quality you have guaranteed your clients before making any minor or intense changes. Your new process implementation should focus on your goals without affecting or only improving the quality of your product or service.

Improving the value of the customer is the key thing. Lean Six Sigma offers companies and individuals the core principles to drive the business forward, a holistic view for the whole business, not just one component of it. It defines your proper goals and tells you where you must stand. Like trying to optimize the production process of some items that no one likes, it carries almost no value in doing that, rather than advancing the production process of products that people enjoy and want the most.

The PDCA cycle or Deming Cycle could be used here. It checks out the six sigma idea of continuously improving the quality model. An unmistakable idea of what comprises quality in your business shapes how you are willing to improve items and processes. You have to comprehend what your worth is and how it can be further improved.

The model PDCA Cycle has four logical and continuous learning steps that include Plan, Do, Check, and Act. Sometimes, it is also referred to as the PDSA Cycle in which 'Check' is changed with 'Study'.

If you are evaluating the production and supply process, remove the steps which don't contribute much profit; using this practice you can comprehend what is inefficient and what is not. Of chance, if you do not evaluate then you just cannot viably figure out what is inefficient. Hence, you can not make changes to improve.

Process improvements lead to ending what is not important and not ending the process and customer value gives a clear picture of it.

Six Sigma focuses on understanding the needs of the customers by using all means. Changes should be made for improvement, but the quality should be sustained.

Understanding The Heart Of The Process

Where your process is standing right now? Its evaluation is the only means to make the right decision and move forward. Designing of the value stream is what makes Lean Six Sigma special. It gives the complete idea of every step involved in your process and draws attention to the waste.

A couple of bits of plastic and glass on a mechanical production system, at last, become a LED TV? There is a value stream map for every progression that is involved in this process from buying all the necessary components, gathering them, running a quality inspection to dispersing the completed item. This stream map allows the organization to figure out which steps include more worth. Rest which does not work can be expelled from the procedure immediately.

Automated process mining is one of the core principles of Lean Six Sigma where whatever you do is process-driven. You can't simply leave things over a hunch, possibility, or any capacity because a process should be all smooth and practical.

All things considered, one of the initial steps is to make sense of and comprehend the issues.

The bottleneck seems to be the common and most clear inability to accomplish a smooth process stream. It is a zone of the process that is performed below the standard. It brings all levels down depending on it to its own level or the opposite of it where a zone of the process has the capability to perform far more than other levels.

When process mining is used during any process, programmed software is used according to the user's need; it can call attention to most bottlenecks as a feature of its analysis. Automated Business Process Discovery (ABPD) tools, in general, have the ability to recognize bottlenecks and bring them to light.

You can generally use the strategy of 5 whys to figure out the root cause. Usually, when the problem occurs, it is due to the malfunctioning of the system or when any process is lacking. The 5 whys are for only small operations. Here is one example that might help you – it is the example of your car stopped on a road.

- Why did the car stop? (First why) – The engine has seized.
- Why did the engine seize? (Second why) - There was insufficient lubrication inside the engine, it locked the crankshaft.
- Why was there insufficient lubrication? (Third why) – The oil pump on the engine is not circulating enough oil inside.

Using five whys technique lead to the root cause of the issue which can be solved using Six Sigma strategies.

Eliminating Waste Without Compromising Quality

When you have assembled your present value stream, you can distinguish issues with your work and tackle them. Remove activities that have no value at all. Lean Six Sigma philosophy is tied in with finding where issues emerge, fixing them, and averting future events. There is no need to showcase the sectors that are working flawlessly as it will diverge the attention from the main problem. Though it will make your employees happy to see the progress, but it is better to remain focused.

In an event where your value stream guide does not explain precisely where the issue lies, you can use a few different approaches, like logical result graphs, cause and effect graphs also called the fishbone diagram and any other statical method. They can assist you to look at another angle to find the root cause. Affinity diagram could also come in handy; you can brainstorm issues with it by taking help from the involved group to make things fast and more effective.

Anything that does not contribute towards production is a waste. Remove it out in order to prioritize the company's value.

Focusing on eliminating waste is called "Muda" within a manufacturing system. It is a Japanese word meaning uselessness or wastefulness. It is the basic concept of Toyota Production System (TPS); it gives insight on each level of production from raw materials to resources needed to mold materials into a complete product and improves overall revenue.

Under the TPS, seven basic Muda are identified as:

- Overpopulation (waste)
- Inventory (waste)
- Transportation (waste)
- Defected stock (waste)
- Over-processing (waste)
- Waiting (waste)
- Motion (waste)

Understanding the 7 Muda is easy but figuring out how to get rid of them as much as possible is a difficult job. Here are a few tips that are presented to eliminate waste for each Muda.

1. Overpopulation - Synchronize processes. Man and machine should work accordingly.
2. Inventory - Measure the waste and keep raw material and finished goods inventories clean.
3. Transportation - Utilize the most straightforward routes to reach a destination.
4. Defected stock - Be accountable, develop a system for quality assurance.
5. Over-processing - Get customers' standards and expectations on time.

6. Waiting - Be conscious, increase the reliability of processes.
7. Motion - Reduce travel time between stations. Decrease unnecessary machine movements.

When a specific classification of waste is identified, it's conceivable to execute techniques that will handle specifically that waste. The same goes for another Muda. Once it's identified which sector in the organization produces which sort of waste, you can take countermeasures to get the quantity of waste to near zero.

For example, you can counter waste overproduction through synchronizing processes (Man and machine). When things are accordingly, production will go smoothly with almost no waste. Or it can be encountered with Lean manufacturing techniques. On the other hand, One Piece Flow Assembly systems can be used to counter waste excess processing itself.

Having A Smooth Workflow

Nothing is going to change unless you take the first step. Make up your mind on how you want to fix or improve things, go for it. It's like the law of inertia. If a ball is rolling, it will continue to roll unless friction or some other force stops it. A body in motion tends to stay in motion and a body at rest tends to stay at rest. The same goes for any organization or company or even an individual. Nothing is going to change unless you induce a change.

Labor will continue to work or not work; they will continue the similar undertakings until someone from the management chooses something else for them. Convey new guidelines and practices to follow if you want the change. Be certain that every representative or worker gets proper training and look out for criticism. Otherwise, the problem will not be solved.

Lucid chart can be used to create a simple process map to convey to your workers what's new about their work process. Knowing about the change and its results can work like a force that will keep them motivated in doing the work.

The work must go smoothly. The obstacles should be managed beforehand to gain the best results.

Make The Change Acceptable Throughout

Lean Six Sigma requires a ton of progress and change. You have to welcome a change and ask your workers and labor to accept it too. If you'll put yourself in your labor shoes' you might fear or panic by hearing the news of change. As so much of work is now computerized, it could result in losing their job. Make things clearer from your end on how these computerized operations will help workers in making things much easier. Show them how convenient you have made their work.

As a major aspect of this move, your organization should consistently search for better approaches to streamline the process and counter waste. Watch out the data, examine it, and regulate your procedures where important.

Although directors and experts can settle on astounding choices looking down the workflow from where they stand, labor or workers involved are not behind. In each step, they might have a better understanding and significant knowledge as well because they are the ones doing the job.

The fact of the matter is, workers who are involved in the processes every day might have a useful opinion that would, in fact, result in product improvement. They know about machines and resources very well because they deal with them daily. Their contribution can improve the process and guarantee the company's growth. This is the approach adopted by Toyota.

It tells to go and see the work where it is actually happening as nothing can provide process details better than that.

Inside Six Sigma, various individuals from different teams liable for the improvement task are given titles:

- Process owner
- Process champion
- Black belt
- Green belts

All these titles have various duties, some of which can be about engaging with other staff and convey messages to representatives. Getting different groups in the organization to perceive the issue and to make arrangements to solve is an important aspect of Six Sigma job.

Including staff in the improvement process is the best way to approach a problem and to solve it. Running an association is not like coding a personal computer. People are included, you have to make things easier for labor to ensure the process runs smoothly. Six Sigma focuses on the team that is not burdened but relaxed while producing the top quality results.

Having A Systematic And Scientific Approach

On a basic level, the motivation behind why Six Sigma is so popular approach is that it defines a framework through which your company can improve its processes. It's the era of information; Six Sigma has a logical quality that takes advantage of the information drive world. It only seems fair to take the benefit of the collected data and use it for making enhancements and improve further processes through it

This same feeling goes right back to masterminds like Frederick Winslow Taylor and W. Edwards Deming who in real launched a logical way to deal with business tasks.

Ideas like the TPS are originated from Japanese culture with Deming being one of the minds behind it. He went to Japan after the 2nd world war and is credited with the process improvement of Japans' post-war interests.

One aspect of Six Sigma is using a scientific approach to achieve results is present in the form of the DMAIC process. It tells how to define the problem and measure the success rate even before the initiation of the process.

Chapter 43. Improving Customer Satisfaction

Six Sigma Strategies improve a business process or product. Its goal is to identify the root cause of the problem and find solutions to it so that the process or product is close to perfection. Sig Sigma eliminates any service problem or product defect to satisfy the customer. Using viable metrics, it focuses on monitoring progress to improve customer service.

A business can use a Six Sigma model that meets its needs in improving its present processes or create new procedures to serve its customers. It can measure its progress through the Six Sigma DMAIC (Define, Measure, Analyze, Improve, and Control) process. It can also use the Six Sigma DMADV (Define, Measure, Analyze, Design, and Verify) process to improve and execute the new process. The business must ensure that it finishes either of the processes to complete the Six Sigma.

One problem of using the Six Sigma model to improve customer service processes is to search for ways to measure improvement. Customer experience is not quantitative but qualitative therefore it is difficult to search for the right metrics to monitor progress accurately. As such, it is important that the company choose its metrics for its Six Sigma model.

Factors to Consider in Choosing Customer Service Metrics

First, the business must consider variability. It must be able to adjust its metrics to consider the differences of its customer service with the other businesses.

Second, the business must ensure that every personnel providing customer service is on the same page when it comes to measuring progress. It must create a positive environment within the department to effect the changes.

Third, the business must employ quantitative metrics, if possible. It can monitor the time spent by customers waiting for a customer service staff or the number of complaints received.

Fourth, the business must use sales figures by repeat customers in measuring customer loyalty. It can also use different metrics to measure abstract goals and customer satisfaction.

Fifth, the choice of metrics will depend on the customer service area that the business wants to focus on. As such, it is important that it is able to narrow down the processes to at most two at a time so that it will not overwhelm the customer service staff, as well as those who will supervise the Six Sigma process.

The identification of improvement areas in customer service is just one process of Six Sigma. A business must be able to monitor the metrics precisely and carefully so that Six Sigma will be effective.

Problems in Measuring and Improving Customer Service

Customer service is important in most companies. A business allots a large part of its operating margin in service processes. As such, most efforts of Six Sigma are in these processes to improve, modify, measure, and model them. The usual problems in these processes are in the choice of quantitative and qualitative measures that are right to the service process, in particular, and to the business, in general.

For example, a fast food business may see a need to measure quantitatively the time it takes to complete a process. On the other hand, a gourmet restaurant may regard fast completion as a negative indicator. It aims to offer a relaxing dining experience instead of rushing its customers to finish eating.

Another problem is how to balance the various qualitative aspects with the rates of response that the customers expect. Most clients do not want to answer long surveys. They may decline or abandon them.

An issue in measuring the service processes for Six Sigma purposes is the characterization of defect, which can be quantitative or qualitative. Data measurement can be continuous or discrete, depending on the context. There must be a conversation from qualitative customer satisfaction measurement to its equivalent quantitative measure.

Usually, a business can rank overall satisfaction from one to seven. If the rank is below six, it can consider it as a defect if customer service is critical in the operations. On the other hand, it can be acceptable if customer service does not play an important role in the business process.

Lastly, defect can be context-sensitive. A newspaper delivery business must be able to bring the morning newspapers to its customers within the cutoff time. On the other hand, delivery of mail to the mailbox must be within the day for it to be timely. Customers of the Postal Service do not require delivery of their mails within a specific period during the day.

How to Make Sensible Measurements of the Service Processes

One way to measure service processes is to use the right measurement level. It is important to have the correct abstraction level in order to have a meaningful measurement.

Service processes also use the 80/20 rule, which means that 20% of the processes contribute to 80% of the time it needs to implement the service processes. The rule also means that 20% of customers account for the 80% of customer dissatisfaction. If it focuses only on some important elements, the business may be able to generate an excellent result. Detail usually does not create significant incremental value.

Another way to measure service processes is to take into account important variations in execution of tasks. For example, an underwriter in an automobile insurance underwriting can consider a regular car for a driver with no record of accidents as a regular case. On the other hand, it can consider a customized vehicle or motor home as a special case.

Assessments of the cases for Six Sigma purposes can differ significantly. Not all measurements are applicable for all cases. Therefore, it is necessary for the business to make the necessary adjustments in terms of deciding what and how to measure service processes.

It is also possible for a business to emphasize on quantitative instead of qualitative measures strategically. Some business can emphasize on qualitative measures when their customer service representatives have face-to-face encounters with their customers. On the other hand, they can put more value on quantitative measures if the service processes focus on quick service.

Lastly, a business can put emphasis on managing support and communication. There are large-scale service processes such as insurance claims processing that require various groups of people. As such, it is possible for these groups to resist any improvement in the processes through Six Sigma methodologies. These people may be doing the same process for a long time so they may feel confused about their role in the process improvement.

To remedy this problem, the company can offer information sessions to these groups in order to explain to them the bigger picture. This way, these people will not feel threatened. It is also important that the management provide significant support in the implementation of the process improvements.

The Customer Oriented Approach

Large companies like Motorola, Citibank, and General Electric adopted the Six Sigma methodology successfully because they adhered to the customer-oriented approach instead of the product-oriented approach.

Customer satisfaction, according to Hansemark and Albinsson, is the general attitude of the customer to the service provider. It is also an emotional reaction between what the client expects vis-à-vis what he receives. Customer loyalty, as defined by Anderson and Jacobsen, is the outcome produced by a business when it creates a benefit to maintain or increase the customer purchases.

The purpose of the Six Sigma methodology is to improve the business processes through quality improvement and elimination of mistakes. The customer-oriented approach has for major steps: quantifying customer satisfaction; gap identification between customer needs and the company's performance level; analysis why the gaps exist; and developing a plan to eliminate the gaps.

The customer-oriented approach gets rid of mistakes; improves product quality; and initiates product changes. To eliminate mistakes, it empowers the Six Sigma project team to offer solutions in important matters. It aims to encourage employees to do things right the first time.

For the service sector, it is important for the project team to understand customer satisfaction in order to eliminate mistakes. For example, improving doctors' scheduling of appointments in hospitals can produce significant results because it strives to understand customer satisfaction. Having to wait for hours is a significant issue for patients, after all. Thus, the Six Sigma strategy can devise ways to improve the scheduling appointments to minimize patients' waiting time.

For assembly line projects, an error can add to the cost of production and can affect product quality. It can influence customer satisfaction directly thereby affecting customer loyalty significantly. For example, if it employs the product-oriented instead of the customer-oriented approach, the Six Sigma model can make delivery time faster by changing the process of packing.

However, a change in the packing process can have an impact on product durability that can affect customer satisfaction. It is important for the Six Sigma project team to understand the customer preference in order to devise ways to improve product delivery without sacrificing product durability.

Chapter 44. The 5 DMAIC Phases

DMAIC is a strategy to implement Six Sigma into a business. DMAIC stands for:

- Define
- Measure
- Analyze
- Improve
- Control

It is a five-phase strategy that leads to solutions to the problems of unknown causes.

Define means to know the problem that is in need of fixing? Define means to get answers to some of the questions like defining:

- Who are the customers?
- What are their needs according to the product or service?
- What is the initiation point of the process of the problem?
- What is the finishing point of the problem?
- When will the problem be considered solved?
- In what direction and flow will the process flow?

Understanding the voice of the customer is important. Once understanding the need of the customer the team can then move to the next step of the DMAIC for further processing.

Measure means to know how the process is currently flowing. Measure means to collect data from:

- Multiple sources to know the defect and metric types.
- Comparison of customer surveys to know what is lacking?

Analyze means to make use of data collected from measure to determine the possible defects and how to solve them. Look into matters like:

- Identify gaps between the current process and the object to reach
- Know the different types of sources from where the data was collected
- Make room for opportunities for overall improvement

This is the most crucial part of the process as analyzing the root cause of the problem is very important. Failing to come up with root cause makes the process even more complicated and teams find it impossible to provide a solution to the customer's problem.

Jumping to conclusions without proper leaves a big question mark the whole time for the customer and the team solving the problem. No matter how many methods are implemented the solution doesn't seem to arrive.

Improve means to modify the secondary process by providing a creative solution to solving and preventing problems

- Make creative solutions to solve the problem
- Make and set up implementation plans

To improve is to refine the overall structure of the solution process here is the part where teams get to know the core reason for the problem and make it easy to counter it.

Control means to keep the improvements merged with the new process. Keeping the new processed maintained is demanded from the team and it does so by monitoring the plan to track the plan's success. Once the process is considered a true success the current process is updated to the best solution available.

The systems and structures are modified to the latest solution and are referred first to the future problems. The 5Ss are used to keep the process at its most efficient level.

Tools used in DMAIC

DMAIC stands for Define, Measure, Analyze, Improve and Control. The DMAIC comes under the methodology of implementing Six Sigma. Knowing what tools can be used in the five phases of DMAIC makes it easy to implement the methodology.

Define

Define phase can be used in a step by step process:

- Describe the problem by building a Problem Statement
- Describe the objective or goal by making a Goal Statement
- Describe the process using Process Map
- Describe types of customers and what they need

- Make it clear to others involved in the Project process

The following tools can be used in Define phase to outline the steps:

- A3
- Swim lane Map
- Tree Diagram
- Project Charter
- Relationship Map
- Value-stream Map
- Voice of the Customer Translation Matrix
- SIPOC (Supplier, Inputs, Process, Outputs, Customers)

Measure

Measure phase can be used in a step by step process:

- Know the current state of the process
- Build a plan on collecting data
- Make sure data is from a reliable source
- Collect the data from point zero
- Modify the project charter

The following tools can be used in the Measure phase to outline the steps:

- Check sheets
- Project charter
- Data collection plan
- Operational Definitions

Analyze

Analyze phase can be used in a step by step process:

- Carefully observe the process
- Display the data collected in graphical form
- Look for the root cause of the problem
- Verify the reason(s) the problem occurs
- Modify the project charter

The following tools can be used in the Analyze phase to outline the steps:

- 5 Whys
- Box Plots
- Run Charts
- Histograms
- Pareto Charts
- Project Charter
- Fishbone Diagram
- Value Stream Map
- Root Cause Hypothesis

Improve

Improve phase can be used in a step by step process:

- Brainstorm the possible solutions to fix the problem
- Select the solution which is practically implementable
- Develop Maps of Process depending upon the various solutions
- Choose the best solution(s)
- Apply the Solution(s)

- Measure to make sure there is an improvement

The following tools can be used in the Improve phase to outline the steps:

- To-Be Map
- PDCA/PDSA
- Plot Checklist
- Benchmarking
- Brainstorming
- Swim Lane Map
- Value Stream Map
- Impact Effort Matrix
- Implementation Plan
- Weighted Criteria Matrix
- Classic Lean Improvements

Control

Control phase can be used in a step by step process:

- Make sure the process is properly monitored and managed
- Make the document of improved process
- Make modifications to other sectors
- Celebrate and share your success
- Make continuous improvements to the process using Lean production principles

The following tools can be used in the Control phase to outline the steps:

- Control Plan

- Gallery Walks
- Control Charts
- Documentation
- Monitoring and Response plan
- Innovation Transfer Opportunities

Chapter 45. Lean Six Sigma Implementation Method

Sigma's six principles use statistical and numerical methods to reduce the number of defects in the output. They emphasize the simplicity of the process, the quality of the parts and the logistics, and the responsibility of the employees to achieve the promised results.

Key Points to Implement a Project

There are some key points which are necessary for the implantation of project. Mandatory are as follow:

- Project
- Training
- Team
- Plan
- Execute
- Evaluate

Choose Project

The best way to implement the Six Sigma program is to start with a pilot project. You can identify a company process that is usually causing production problems or having other problems.

The process of identifying the pilot project involves the workforce involved and their input needs to be considered. Six Sigma only works when everyone is involved.

Training

The person who guides the implementation of the Six Sigma project should know six principles and principles of Sigma. In Six Sigma's terms, he should be a "black belt" expert.

In small businesses, a black belt is usually sufficient for a pilot project. A qualified new employee in the business can hire or train in the ranks. Training can be an overlap for Black Belt certification and pilot project implementation.

Team management

Once the company has chosen a Black Belt Team Leader, it has to assign team members who will assist in the process.

The company has to consult the workers involved in the pilot project. The team needs good staff, but also to run the Six Sigma Pilot Project after implementation.

Make plan

The team plans to implement it. The aim is to have an organizational structure that simplifies the production target preparation process to minimize defects.

Projects Manager (Black Belt holder) identifies areas of the problem, and workers at work assist with the solution. The project describes the steps the team has proposed to reduce team waste, increase worker efficiencies and eliminate barriers.

Execute

Six Sigma requires initial effort and then it is a continuous process. The pilot project will have to take preliminary steps and keep the organization in place for permanent application.

The team makes the necessary changes according to the plan and then wears a black belt to run it. The Green Belts support the new project and take on specific aspects.

Evaluate

Upon completion of the pilot project, an evaluation describes what worked and where the problems were encountered. The workers involved are a key source for diagnostic standards and parameters.

Assessment is the basis for permanent application in other areas of the Company's work. In a small business, the second round might include all the rest of the production activity.

Beneficial Tips

Without understanding what is being done and why, there will be very limited scope to improve Lean and Six Sigma. So, let's take a look at the top 10 tips for successful implementation of Lean and Six Sigma.

- Change in behavior
- Make Lean Six Sigma Compulsory
- Strong Platform

- Top-Down Approach
- High Profile Identification
- Right Measurement Systems
- Awareness of cultural Difference
- Having Communication Channels
- Perfect to start Lean Six Sigma (σ)
- Communities or Forums

Change of behavior

Industry experts believe that change of behavior is essential for effective implementation of change. This tendency in people is to work around it rather than to solve a problem, and this is where Lean and Six Sigma's willingness to permanently eliminate problems arising in the business process.

Even when people pledge to change their behavior, the tools will be added seamlessly. Training your manpower in Lean & Six Sigma is one thing, but without a change in attitude, the whole process will be educational only with no practical implications.

Make it Compulsory

Incorporating Lean & Six Sigma as part of the organization's goals and core strategy is one of the key components to its successful implementation.

And without it, the entire initiative will have a short-term life where people reject the process even before it is properly established in the organization.

Moreover, when an organization has a basic mechanism for the center of everything, combining lean and six sigma increases its chances of success.

Strong Platform

Strong platforms make a good impression on any customer. Which naturally inclines you towards it. A robust platform acts as a backbone for any organization.

Top-Down approach

Organizations around the world can apply Lean and Six Sigma to a bottom line. But industry experts believe that trying to involve senior and middle managers before ways to improve the process is worthwhile.

Their involvement in implementing Lean and Six Sigma towards improving key business processes will strengthen other affiliate practices that will also help increase adoption by others. Without the involvement of senior and middle managers, it is a difficult task to successfully adopt Lean and Six Sigma throughout the organization.

High Profile Identification

You need to choose projects that are endorsed by senior and middle management that passionately care about bringing people faster results.

This increases overall confidence in the lean and Six Sigma approach and will lead to widespread acceptance in the organization.

Right Measurement Systems

Practitioners can use data to make informed decisions and decide on baseline performance with the proper measurement system in place. And when people understand the potential of lean and six-sigma, plans will quickly improve.

Awareness of Cultural Differences

Each organization has its own distinct culture, and experts believe that the culture is different between different geographical areas and different types of organizations such as local, corporate, small or medium, public, private and government.

It is better to avoid the assumptions about how you need to adopt lean and sigma and avoid the use of jargon unless this organization wants it. Doing so will facilitate the smooth implementation and integration of the lean and six sigma procedures between the two entities.

Having Communication Channels

Keeping open communication channels in an organization is an important aspect of timely completion of lean and six sigma projects.

On many occasions, addressing a small group or talking face-to-face to discuss important things is more effective than mass email communication.

Perfect to Start Lean Six Sigma

It is better to start with just a handful of people who will take over the leadership and responsibility of Lean and Six Sigma implementation and tell them that this will work for them, rather than just wasting their time and energy on skeptics or unbelievers. The word will spread positively through the networks of internal champions.

Communities or Forums

Knowledge management plays a key role in sustaining the growth or improvement of key business processes through lean and six sigma practices.

Lean and Six Sigma practitioners play an important role in knowledge management techniques to ensure learning from each other's experience, improving their capabilities with respect to the Lean and Six Sigma principles and tools regularly used in an organization.

Steps for Successful Implementation

There are 8 major steps in order to implement a successful project management. By following them, you can easily win a project management & can be applicable for a successful project implementation.

The steps are given below:

- Burning Platform
- Keep resources in the place
- Teaching

- Prioritize Activities
- Ownership
- Right Measurements
- Govern Programs
- Recognition

Burning Platform

To implement or think about lean or six sigma modes, we must have a burning platform. A burning platform can take many forms.

For example, some common or rare are like:

We are experiencing huge quality losses and this accounts for more than 45% of our cost

Our competitors are gaining 12% of our market share every quarter

By this, organizations are rarely motivated to implement continuous improvements to TPS (Lean) or Six Sigma or TQM or any improvement.

With the completion of this task, ever since Six Sigma became a visionary in the organization, everything else began to fall into place. So in order to increase organizational vision and value across our workforce, customers, partners and suppliers, we need to leverage our key leadership towards a common vision.

This ensures that the organization's environment is viable for change and capable of driving change, leveraging innovation and technology as key tools.

Finally, we need to take steps to achieve our vision. This ensures that we have visibility and strong support from the leadership. Leadership sponsors make sure we meet our organization's vision, thereby achieving excellence.

Keep resources in place

It is important to know what to look for in potential resources. Resources don't just help us succeed. We need to deploy them as a team, and this team must act as a change agent.

As an organization, we need to emphasize taking the initiative to empower the team, so we need domain expertise and knowledge. We also need to take care of our resources in terms of wages, and also have the resources to fit and realize the common vision.

Teaching Methodology

Lean Six Sigma Organizations need to train their team members as powerful change agents in order to survive. Yellow Belt, Green Belt and Black Belt training can help increase organizational awareness with skilled teachers. Employees identified for training should share the organization's vision.

Prioritize activities / Tasks

We need to know what to ignore and where to take the risk, and the question here is whether we can meet the key expectations of our organization's goals in terms of risk mitigation and expectation management.

Organizations should make it a top priority:

- Listen to the customer
- Identify quality standards by quality
- Ensure that the Lean Six Sigma efforts are aligned with business goals

Ownership

This includes setting up a committee to determine who is responsible for the entire team.

Ownership feels empowered and proud, and team members who are more committed, responsive and committed.

Right / Accurate measurements

Practitioners can assess baseline performance and use data in objective decision-making and variable analysis by setting up a measurement system. The key to measurement is to correct the right price.

Govern Programs (Making Reviews)

A proper governance structure can help maintain the momentum of a program. Poor governance or excessive governance can cause vision to fall apart.

For example, setting up a Business Quality Council (BQC) can help remove any obstacles that can slow the project down, and allow the project to follow timelines.

Appropriate governance also helps practitioners create a best practice sharing forum, which helps to redesign plans and highlights common challenges.

Without regular scheduled, fruitful meetings or review meetings, the program can halt courses and employees may lack guidance.

Recognition with Contributions

Rewards and recognition play a vital role in ensuring team members are satisfied with their role. They can help create excitement from the top to bottom and from the bottom up.

Rewards and recognition can also help drive innovation across the organization. Proper rewards and recognition ensure consistency in achieving excellent performance. Let me present my personal example of reward and recognition at the grassroots level.

Chapter 46. Tools to Use with Six Sigma

There are many tools that you can use in order to make Six Sigma work for you. These tools are there to ensure that you are providing good quality management to your business and some of the tools are so successful that they can be used outside of a Six Sigma application as well. Some of the main methods that can be used include:

5 Why's

The 5 Why's is a technique that is there to explore the cause and effect relationship of a problem. Each answer is going to form the basis of the following question. The 5 in the name derives from the idea that it takes about five iterations in order to resolve the problem, but depending on your particular issue, you may need to use more.

Not all problems though are going to have one root cause. If you would like to figure out more than one root cause, this method is going to be repeated by asking a different sequence of this question each time that you use it.

In addition, the method is not going to provide any hard rules about what lines you should explore with the questions, or how long you need to continue your search to make sure you find the root cause. Thus, even if you follow this method closely, it may not give you the outcome that you want.

An example of the 5 Why's includes the following:

My vehicle is not starting:

- Why? The battery is not working.
- Why? Because the alternator is not functioning
- Why? The belt on the alternator has broken off.
- Why? The belt should have been replaced a long time ago, but was not.
- Why? The vehicle owner did not follow the required maintenance schedule for the vehicle.

This helps to show why there was an issue with the vehicle, and you can easily choose to take it further into some more why's until you find the solution that you are looking for.

Axiomatic Design

The axiomatic design is a systems design methodology that is going to analyze the transformation of the needs of the customer into design parameters, functional requirements, and process variables. The method is going to get its name because it is going to use the design principles that govern the analysis and decision-making process. The two types of axioms that are used with this process include:

Axiom 1: This is the independence axiom. It is going to help you to maintain the independence of your functional requirements.

Axiom 2: This is the information axiom. This is going to help you to minimize the informative content of the design.

Cost-Benefit Analysis

Cost-benefit analysis, or CBA, is an approach that is meant to estimate the strengths or weaknesses of varies alternatives. It can be used with project investments, processes, activities, and even transactions. It can be used to determine, out of several solutions, which options will provide the best approach to a business in order to achieve benefits while still saving the company money.

To keep it simple, the CBA method is going to come with two main purposes. These purposes are:

- To determine if a decision or an investment for a business is sound. This means that the benefits will outweigh the cost. You also want to look at how much this is. If the benefits do not outweigh the costs much, then it is probably not the best option to go with.
- To help provide a good way to compare projects. This can involve comparing the total amount that you expect each option to cost against the benefits you expect to get.

The benefits, as well as the costs, are going to be shown in monetary terms, which makes it work well for Six Sigma. Moreover, they can be adjusted in the formula for the time value of money. This ensures that all flows of costs and those from benefits over time are expressed with a common basis.

The simple steps that you will follow when you are working on a cost-benefit analysis include:

- You first have to define the goals and the objectives of the project or the activity.
- You can list the alternative programs or projects that you may be able to use.
- List the stakeholders
- You then select the measurements you want to use in order to measure all of the elements when it comes to benefits and costs.
- You can also work on predicting the outcome of the benefits and the cost of each alternative over a period of your choosing.
- You can then convert all of the benefits and costs into a common currency to help them compare better.
- Make sure to apply any discount rates
- Next, you can calculate the net present value of all project options.
- Perform a sensitivity analysis: This is going to be the study of how the uncertainty of the output from a mathematical system can be shared to different sources of uncertainty in its inputs.
- After you have all this information, you can then pick out the option that is the best.

Root Cause Analysis

A root cause analysis, or RCA, is going to be a method to help with solving problems and it focuses on finding the root causes of the problem. A factor will be considered the root cause if you can remove it and the problem does not recur. Essentially, there are going to be four principles that come with this type of method including:

- It is going to define and describe properly the problem or event.
- Establish a timeline from the normal situation until the final failure or crisis occurs
- Distinguishes between the casual factor or the root causes
- Once it is implemented, and the execution is constant, the RCA is transformed into a method of problem prediction.

The main use of the RCA is to identify and then correct the root causes of an event, rather than just trying to address a symptomatic result. An example of this is when some students receive a bad grade on a test. After a quick investigation, it was found that those who took the test at the end of the day ended up with the lower scores.

More investigation found that later in the day, these students had less ability to stay focused. In addition, this lack of focus is from them being hungry. So, after looking at the root cause and finding it was hunger, it was fixed by moving the testing time to right after lunch.

Notice that the root causes are often going to come in at many levels and that the level for the root is only going to be where the current investigator leaves it. Nevertheless, this is a good way to figure out why one particular process in the business is not working the way that you want and then finding the best solution to fix it.

SIPOC Analysis

If you are talking about process improvement, a SIPOC is there to be a tool that can summarize the inputs and then the outputs of at least one process and then shows it in table form. This acronym stands for suppliers, inputs, process, outputs, and customers and these will be used to form the columns on your table.

Sometimes the acronym is going to be turned around in order to put customers first, but either way, it is going to be used in the same way. SIPOC is presented at the beginning of a process improvement efforts or it can be used during what is known as the define phase of the DMAIC process. There are three typical uses of this depending on who is going to use it including:

- To help those who are not familiar with a particular process a high-level overview.
- To help those who had some familiarity with the process, but may be out of date with the changes in the process or those who haven't used it in a long time.
- To help those who are trying to define a new process.

There are also some aspects that come with this method that are not always apparent. These include:

- The customers and the suppliers are sometimes external or internal to the organization that is trying to perform the process.
- Outputs and inputs can include things such as information, services, and materials.
- The focus of this method is to capture the set of inputs as well as outputs, rather than worrying about all the individual steps that are in the process.

Value Stream Mapping

When it comes to value streaming mapping, we are talking about a method that is there to analyze the current state of a business and then designing a new state to use in the future. It is meant to take a service or product that a company offers from its very beginnings all the way through to when it reaches the customers. The hope is that the process is used to help reduce lean wastes, especially when compared to the process that the business is using right now.

The value stream is going to learn how to focus on any areas of a business that helps to add in value to the service or product. The purpose of this is to learn where the waste is in the business and then remove or at least reduce it. This can increase the efficiency of the business and can even increase productivity.

The main part of this process is to work on identifying waste in the business. Some of the most common types of waste include:

- Faster than necessary pace: This is when the company tries to produce too much of their product that it can damage the flow of production, the quality of the product, and the productivity of the workers.
- Waiting: This is a time when the goods are not being worked on or transported.
- Conveyance: This process is used to move the products around. It can look at things like excessive movement and double handling.
- Excess stock: This is when there is an overabundance of inventory. This can add on storage costs and can make it more difficult to identify problems.
- Unnecessary motion: These wastes mean employees are using too much energy to pick up and move items.
- Correction of mistakes: The cost that the business will have when they try to correct a defect.

This process is used often in lean environments to help look at and design flows for the system level. This is often something that is associated with manufacturing, but it can be used in many other industries including healthcare, product development, and even software development.

Business Process Mapping

The idea of business process mapping is going to be all activities that are involved when you try to define what a business does, who is the person or persons responsible, and at what standard a process in the business needs to be completed. It can also determine how the success of the process in the business can be measured.

Business process mapping is there to help a business become more effective. A clear business process map will allow even outside firms, such as consultants, to come in and look to see where improvements can be made, such as what can happen with Six Sigma, to help the business.

This mapping is going to take a specific objective of a business and they can measure and compare it to the objectives of the company. This makes sure that all processes that are done can align with what the company holds as its capabilities and values.

A good way to do business process mapping is with a flow chart. This can help you to see how the business does a certain process and can even include who is responsible for each part if that is important.

These are just a few of the options that you can choose from when it comes to working with Six Sigma. All of the options above can help you to make informed decisions while finding the process that is causing your business the most trouble at the time. Pick one of these options that go along with your biggest issue and find out how you can make smart decisions that will turn your business into something even better.

Chapter 47. Lean Six Sigma Certification

Lean Six Sigma improves quality control & different business forms more rapidly and more productively than standard Six Sigma. Along these lines, there are numerous individuals who are currently keen on getting their own Lean Six Sigma Certification so as to enhance their own organization or to enhance the eventual fate of their vocation.

Lean Six Sigma Certification is gotten when an individual finishes Lean Training. Lean standards are now and then observed as only an augmentation of the ordinary Six Sigma process. Hence, some data and examination utilized for the Lean Certification is fundamentally the same as customary Six Sigma Training and Certification. The thing that matters is in the genuine procedure and ultimate objectives.

To become familiar with the additional standards of Lean, you should know the Six Sigma Methodology, else you won't know the essential nuts and bolts. A representative with Lean Certification will have the option to help in squander decrease, disposing of procedures and sub-forms in the business that are never again required, squandered developments of numerous types, just as end of sat around idly. These individuals will be extraordinary for any organization and will find that they are truly necessary for some applications. Those with a Certification will have the option to spot overproduction, any unnecessary stock, and might have the option to help move workers who are not understanding their maximum capacity at their present situations in the organization to different positions where they will be better utilized.

Lean applications for a business will be centered around the speed of the procedures and their proficiency, however there is a contrast between this speed and the general timetable of the organization. Those with Lean Certification won't attempt to fit a bigger timetable into a littler time period, they will work to streamline the entirety of the procedures so more can be fit into a day. Lean Certification is an extraordinary thought for the individuals who as of now have their standard Six Sigma Certification, as it will be a legitimate augmentation of their insight base just as a resource for any organization they may decide to work for. Lean Six Sigma Training and Certification courses enable a person to work at their own pace, in spite of the fact that there is normally a set time limit inside which one should complete their Training. The online Lean Six Sigma Training and Certification courses are finished at assigned occasions and days that are foreordained by the Training supplier.

Lean utilizes the way of thinking of applying pressure for speed and quality in the assembling universe of business. This has advanced from a little to an enormous scale quality activity to dispose of deformities in business and creation by disposing of varieties in a procedure or administration. This was first utilized in the United States by GE. At that point came Caterpillar account, just as Lockheed Martin.

The Lean ways of thinking and apparatuses for administrations are utilized as a strategy for improving business, utilizing the best pieces of the Six Sigma ways of thinking. This gives investors more worth, yet in addition gives the organization a quick pace of progress with regards to speed, quality, cost, capital, and consumer loyalty. The contrast among Lean and customary Six Sigma is that the lean strategy acknowledges and encourages that you essentially can't just concentrate on speed or quality, however the general organization must be adjusted so as to enable the organization to be as well as can be expected be. Lean Six Sigma causes organizations to improve their administration quality, which clients consider as worthy.

Without clients, a business is basically a fantasy. The thought behind Lean Six Sigma Trainings &Certification in a business is to concentrate on what the client sees similar to item or administration, in general expenses, and working. In the event that an organization must pass on expenses to a client rather than assimilate them, the client may not utilize this organization or administration. Lean Six Sigma finds and trains methods for assisting with decrease of the utilization of significant cash-flow to help keep away from this circumstance. Lean can manage forms, improve speed and diminish capital required, just as lessen cost of intricacy for the business.

The six sigma accreditation is granted after a person's abilities required for the particular organization are confirmed. The organization has a progression of steps characterized by which the work intensity of an individual is estimated all through the work procedure. On the off chance that they are sufficient, an accreditation is granted by the concerned position.

The Lean Six Sigma can be seen as used for outline the administration approach towards estimating the business execution. Lean sigma and the six sigma join together to frame up the Lean Six Sigma. It is equipped for taking care of complex issues with the assistance of its administration strategies to improve the general execution of the association. It is a productive procedure with quick improved results. It is a procedure to create viable administrations and thoughts for the welfare of the clients and the association.

Preparing

Learning the six sigma requires broad preparing and endeavors. You can experience the preparation guides accessible for the tests of the American Society for Quality (ASQ) and the International Association for Six sigma (IASSC). The aides contain different connections from which you can access significant themes and necessities of the test. Completely perusing the guide will demonstrate productive for you to accomplish a superior outcome for the six sigma assessments.

Expenses

The cost for the accreditations change far and wide. The establishment truly matters from which you are getting the confirmation for which you will need to pick the best one among the others. You ought to know about the outcomes if there should be an occurrence of any loss of installment for giving erroneous individual subtleties to the foundation.

The International Six Sigma Institute causes you meet to the expert prerequisites by its broad preparing process. The procedure is directed by the Six Sigma standards and technique. The foundation has effectively granted in excess of 187,000 affirmations all around the globe with radiating the Green Belt, Black Belt and Master Belt grants to its clients. They help people and organizations to deal with their business just as expert needs. The enlistment technique is simple and very straightforward. You can enlist yourself for the accreditation online for the necessary program and an Exam access code will be sent to you. Lead the online test whenever and area which you like. After you breeze through the test, the affirmation is granted to you in a flash at the online entrance.

The organization offers a 100 percent unconditional promise on the off chance that you neglect to finish the six sigma affirmation test. The program is believable all around the world as the accreditation is given by the International Six Sigma foundation. You shouldn't go to the entirety of the study hall trainings and instructional exercises though the establishment centers around self-perusing of the expert without anyone else's input. The accreditation has a lifetime legitimacy with unlimited potential outcomes in the building procedure. Premium preparing can likewise be benefited free of cost through the online gateway of the establishment. This is a useful asset to finish out your Six Sigma test.

Lean Six Sigma Belt Online Training & Certification

Web has made some amazing progress in a matter of a brief timeframe. For the individuals who are needing Lean Six Sigma Black Belt Certification who can't discover an opportunity to get their preparation in a conventional setting, online courses are an extraordinary spot to turn. Getting on the web Lean Six Sigma Black Belt Certification manages numerous advantages and focal points to the individuals who pick it, including more comfort and decision in the projects that are taken. At the point when you are thinking about online courses, it is fundamental that you set aside the effort to look at all of your alternatives and ensure that you are getting a total Lean Six Sigma Black Belt Certification course from a legitimate organization and not only a 'program' from some organization who has no clue what they are instructing.

Online Lean Six Sigma Belt Certification will bear the cost of you the advantage of finishing the real task required for confirmation alongside the internet preparing in a similar measure of time. Contrasted with the common longer calendar of preparing offered by most workshops and on location courses, this can be an immense improvement. The data that you learn will all be equivalent to it would nearby when you pick a certified program to work with, and you'll have the option to do it on your time, whenever the timing is ideal, and without having the problem of voyaging or going to classes when you could be accomplishing different things.

Lean Six Sigma Black Belt Training can help an assortment of associations and businesses. A large number of them are looking for the Lean procedure due to its speed. In the event that the procedure offers a snappier goal, shouldn't preparing be less difficult and quicker, too? Online courses offer that speed, yet at the same time assist you with adapting about Lean squander decrease standards and procedure improvement methods that are made through the waste disposal as a rule. By taking Lean Six Sigma Black Belt Certification on the web, you'll have the option to speed up your prosperity and demonstrate to your manager that you are submitted and arranged to deal with a Six Sigma Project in a shorter measure of time.

In the event that by chance you're not a mechanically propelled individual or you aren't especially web insightful, don't stress! Web based Lean Six Sigma Black Belt Certification courses are very easy to use, and frequently accompany a help group you can email for help - regardless of whether it be inquiries concerning the Six Sigma course material itself, or what your secret word is in the event that you overlook it! Simply realize that when you're needing to prepare in Six Sigma, speed isn't simply all the while yet additionally in the preparation through the accessibility of online Lean Six Sigma Certificates.

Conventional Lean Six Sigma Certification Vs Lean Six Sigma Certification

Speed is the essential contrast between customary Six Sigma and Lean Six Sigma Certification. Lean Six Sigma confirmation is a speedier rendition of customary Six Sigma. Lean Six Sigma focuses on accelerating business forms so as to make an organization or association run better and smoother. The procedure isn't upgraded by basically turning up the dial and running the machine at a quicker speed. Lean strategies recognize issues in center forms and wipe out the hindrances backing them off.

Expanding speed additionally doesn't mean shortening your center procedures or pressing your conveyance plan just to get the item out of the entryway quicker. It is just about eliminating abandons in the framework, which hurt conveyance and quality. Lean Certification implies the individual has become equipped in searching for approaches to streamline the work procedure. Affirmed people have Six Sigma apparatuses that they use to concentrate on the center procedure by making it work all the more easily. It likewise implies the individual comprehends the fundamental orders required for accelerating forms, shortening learning cycles or information creation, just as postponing responsibility.

A lean Six Sigma Certification shows that the individual has aced the factual abilities and devices with which to achieve organization objectives for streamlining the center procedure.

Lean Six Sigma encourages that speed and quality come at whatever point there is more information creation as opposed to learning replication. Learning creation consistently brings about stream improvement, bringing about better assistance. Issues do emerge inconsistently when task chiefs mess up the works by front stacking a venture. As it were, making the task fit as opposed to giving the undertaking a chance to uncover how it functions all through the procedure. Front stacking is settling on all choices about the undertaking before it hits the gathering belt or machine. In a working lean Six Sigma venture run by a guaranteed lean Six Sigma individual, the procedure is contemplated as opposed to constrained. Considering the center procedure opens up more alternatives for taking care of business.

Lean Six Sigma accreditation empowers the laborer to successfully tinker with the center procedure empowering a smoother stream with less or no issues. Lean Six Sigma and Six Sigma affirmation contrast here too, in light of the fact that Six Sigma includes layers of technique that may not directly for your center procedure, some of the time making it increasingly slow. Lean, then again, empowers the person to perceive the issue, dissect it and use the accessible devices to expel the barricade in a sensible measure of time.

Speed is straightforwardly attached to greatness in process, as attested by Lean Six Sigma confirmation and preparing.

Improve the procedure stream by disposing of deviations or blunders, and you will naturally accelerate the procedure, conveying better quality, and improving your association with customers and clients. Having an accreditation in Lean Six Sigma implies that you can take a gander at the procedure and find the hindrances so as to turn out better items and administrations all the more quickly.

Speed doesn't mean truncating or crushing your conveyance plan for request to get the item out more rapidly. What it means is disposing of slip-ups that delayed down or stop the procedure, in this manner harming quality and conveyance. Utilizing Lean Six Sigma implies that you have gotten skillful in searching for chances to streamline your procedure. It implies you can recognize your center procedure, and you have the apparatuses expected to concentrate on making that center procedure run better and all the more easily. Having a Certification in Lean implies that you comprehend the two fundamental orders for accelerating the procedure; short continuous learning cycles or information creation, and deferred responsibility. Being Certified in Lean Six Sigma likewise implies that you have aced the measurable apparatuses and abilities with which to achieve your objectives just as those of your association.

At whatever point the task incorporates data creation rather than simply learning replication, speed and quality will start from improving the stream, and Lean procedures tell senior organization that you have the right stuff to achieve this objective. Some undertaking chiefs are now and then blameworthy of gumming up the procedure by constraining early decisions and lessening the quantity of conceivable outcomes, as opposed to tuning in to their Lean experts. As it were, the venture administrators are blameworthy of task front stacking, where they settle on all choices forthright as opposed to permitting those ensured to run the procedure to uncover what is correct and what's up in the application. Lean Six Sigma confirmation means having and understanding a huge number of choices essentially by taking a gander at the center procedure itself, which is the thing that Lean Six Sigma laborers have been affirmed to do.

Tweaking the procedure as you travel through it will limit the procedure into a smoother stream that normally accelerates in light of the fact that the issues have been killed. This is the distinction of Lean Six Sigma Affirmation Lean Six Sigma. Layering in Lean Six Sigma incorporates rehearses that are unmanageable, and not directly for your focal procedure, making it moderate, just as not tolerant to change.

Lean Six Sigma Certificates Using Lean Six Sigma Training

Lean Six Sigma confirmation courses likewise give a portrayal of the framework expected to get the best results just as stress the necessity of perceiving varieties from the plans that reason lower quality administrations. Lean six sigma preparing centers around benefiting as much as possible from process speeds, gives instruments for investigation of stream and times, focuses on esteem included and non-esteem included work, for example, squandered ability, surrenders, stock issues, holding up times, overproduction, and transportation costs. Lean six sigma preparing encourages the member to understand that individual segments don't make quality, however there must be a reasonable procedure set up to finish this.

Lean six sigma preparing/affirmation courses will cover the examine stage which incorporates such devices as stream graphs and conceptualizing, while the measure stages will cover FMEA. The characterize period of the courses will cover partner investigation's and arrangement decreases, techniques for disposing of blockage or postponements just as Kaizen.

Kaizen can be considered as continuous enhancements. The aftereffect of Kaizen is aggressiveness and achievement of organizations wherever that utilization it. Most organizations stress advancements to change business, yet Kaizen rotates around proceeding to turn out to be better and not depending just on new ideas to work. Kaizen pushes that HR are the most significant resource an organization has, and enhancements must be founded on a measurable assessment of execution.

An alum of the Lean Six Sigma preparing or accreditation will be a pioneer in their general vicinity.

Chapter 48. Lean Six Sigma Certification Levels

The Six Sigma is divided into different levels:

- White Belt
- Yellow Belt
- Green Belt
- Black Belt
- Master Black Belt

These certifications are obtainable by getting accreditation from a body like ASQ (American Society for Quality).

Six Sigma White Belt

The most basic or entry-level certification deals with basics of Six Sigma concepts. White belts are helpful for an organization's change management and involve with company's problem-solving teams who help with projects.

Six Sigma Yellow Belt

This level provides Six Sigma's specifics, how and where they are applicable. You will be able to help project teams with problem-solving.

Six Sigma Green Belt

This level of advanced analysis is understood and helps in resolving problems regarding quality. Green belts lead the projects and help black belts in gathering data and analyzing.

Six Sigma Black Belt

Black belts are the professionals and experts of change. They provide training along with leading the projects.

Six Sigma Master Black Belt

The highest level of Six Sigma achievement is the Master Black Belt. This level professionals design strategies, develop key performance indicators, coach green, and black belts, and act as a consultant.

Is Six Sigma really that important? The idea of this can be best understood from case studies of different who adopted Six Sigma which is given below. Six Sigma process helped General Electric to put $350 million in savings back in 1998. Motorola allocated its highest savings by 2005, of $17 billion. After a decade GE was able to increase that amount over $1 billion.

Six Sigma Certification Benefits for Individuals

The Six Sigma certification isn't just another addition to your resume the certification comes with a lot of advantages for companies and individuals.

Improve business processes and durable quantity improvement.

Once done with Six Sigma certification you will be investigating the manufacturing and business processes of a company and take actions to improve them. You will be able to do a complete evaluation of company's current procedures and assess how they affect the quality.

The certification displays that you are able to reach the durable quality that the firm is looking forward to. Keeping check of processes carefully to make sure that there isn't any deviation from the meanwhile taking right actions to bring projects back online which were deviating from path.

Having value in every industry

Being a highly demanded methodology in industries. Six Sigma techniques are useful in electronics, aerospace, telecom, financial services, IT, marketing, banking, HR and various industries.

Industries certified in Six Sigma have knowledge in many different methods which can be opted to streamline business processes, reduce costs, improve employee acceptance, and increase revenue, all these lead to an improved bottom line in any industry.

The Six Sigma certification earns an individual the title of a change agent in any organization. Working alongside teams further refines the leadership skills and adding more value to the individual.

Ensure Compliance

Six Sigma requires extremely high-quality standards. This is the reason a noteworthy number of procurers, vendors and oversight organizations use Six Sigma Standards when reviewing products. Individuals with Six Sigma certification can help their company with profitable contracts and working with international standards.

Rise to higher positions

Once done with Six Sigma certification an individual gets a clear picture of how to make maximum profit from any Six Sigma project. The certification helps individuals in getting financial management and risk assessment skills. These types of skills are always in demand for top-level and middle-level managerial positions.

Greater Salary

Six Sigma Certification is not easy to get, there are lot of studies, and the exams are tough. Furthermore, getting from one belt level to another requires years of actual work. For this reason, Six Sigma Certified individuals are the highest paid professionals in the world having pay bracket above $100,000.

Get practical experience in Quality Management

The Six Sigma training program provides individuals with practical experience on industrial projects and making use of theories in real-life workplace. Getting started with Six Sigma Certification gets an individual a valued knowledge even before working with a team. The professional acquiring such a certificate is refined to take strategic decisions and tackle the obstacles causing delays in processing.

Six Sigma Certification benefits for Organizations

In 1995, Jack Welch introduced Six Sigma as a key component to General Electric's Business Strategy. From that time, firms have put up Six Sigma to use with major success, the benefits can be seen below:

Higher Productivity

Engineered for the space industry for making new products, Allen medical implemented DMAIC methodology and lean tools for overall improvement to production of Arm boards. The new methodology allowed them to save 45 seconds per arm board production, hence increasing the arm boards produced per hour from 5.3 to a bit over 6.

Lower Costs

Decreasing defects reduced and minimized wastage resulting in overall lower production cost with greater profits. Failing to produce a quality product can get costly. Developing a poor service or product can greatly reduce the cost which is the true meaning of cost of quality.

Raising the client's confidence in one's business

Using Six Sigma can reduce processing steps and increase customer satisfaction. For example, through the use of cross-functional process mapping (CFPM) methodology, Citibank removed the unnecessary steps from their process which resulted in higher customer satisfaction.

Gaining reliability and shareholder's trust

Customers and shareholders trust a company where employees are relatively qualified. A company having a significant number of Six Sigma certified employees it means that quality is expected from that company. A company having quality is competitive in the market and inspires confidence in partners and investors.

Reduce training costs and employee turnover

The DMAIC methodology is applicable to be used in HR management. Research shows that in a multinational company losing millions of dollars because of employee turnover of 35% each year wanted to reduce the numbers to 25%.

After applying Six Sigma methodology, they came to know about few contributing factors which were: low compensation and poor career prospects. The solution was to make use of new hiring processes and training new employees. The outcomes were great reducing the turnover by 10% and saving $1.1 million as a result.

The Six Sigma Progress

The numerous cases of Six Sigma implementation success can be studied from all over the world. It is an internationally accepted standard that can be used in small to high profile organizations. The methodology is a logical and structured approach to develop a chain of continuous improvement.

Six Sigma isn't a destination that stops after accomplishing single milestone instead it is a journey of continuous improvement which doesn't end. The outcomes are excellence and higher customer loyalty with bottom line profits. Implementing Six Sigma is worthwhile for any organization in search of reaching near perfection.

Once the road of implementing Six Sigma has been taken by an organization it doesn't want to get off it. The company sees for itself the benefits of the process as it solves the complexity of the production processes and resolves issues arriving one after the other. The smoothness inflow of the production process is what inspires any company to opt the methodology in very first place.

Criticism of Six Sigma

There are multiple reasons why a business might not be adopting Lean Six Sigma. A few of the reasons can be stated to be valid, a lot can be stated as a misconception, while some stand as pure fictions. The ten common reasons observed over the years are:

Fear of the unknown or failing

The one reason which we can all agree to is the fear of the unknown. The effects of such fear can be paralyzing in the real world and in the business world it can also occur. The fear prevents a business from growing and making it stuck with the same old procedures and outcomes.

Not able to afford Six Sigma

The reason for not adopt the methodology is the fear of finance. It is not a process requiring large capital instead it should be looked as an investment which will give turn your results 5 to 10 times better in a year. A business can get started with Six Sigma after obtaining the Yellow belt certification. However, hiring an external black belt certified professional for training will be a good idea to grow. A business can also buy projects and statistical management software.

Never heard of Lean Six Sigma

This seems to be a valid criticism as Lean Six Sigma is growing in popularity but still, it isn't a part of the normal business language. Many small organizations mainly are unaware that it is present which keeps them behind.

Lean Six Sigma is a trend which will fade away

The presence of Lean Six Sigma can be found since the 19th century with business and quality leaders like Toyota's Shigeo Shingo, Henry Ford, Western Electric's Walter Shewhart, Edwards Deming, Taichi Ohno, and Joseph Juran. Six Sigma has grown over time and is different from other kaizen programs. People think that it might fade away with time, but the improvement techniques are something that an organization always want. The customer's choice is well focused on Lean Six Sigma techniques. So there's little to no chance that it may get lost in time any time sooner.

Lean Six Sigma is too much calculation and statistics

The truth is a lot of companies don't even need advanced mathematics and statistics to get benefitted from Lean Six Sigma. A lot of principles of Six Sigma can easily be applied in any business.

The most powerful amongst all tools is to know the wastes in the process and their types. Planning out a map to point out all the bottlenecks, and gaps in the process. If the employees can understand what the customer needs then arriving at a solution to solve the problem won't be that difficult.

The employees don't necessarily need to be engineers; they can be front line supervisors and trained to work and understand the needs of the customers. Proper training will play its role again and again till the perfection that is expected is reached by the employees.

Don't have time to dedicate to Lean Six Sigma

A company that is not being able to identify the cause of the problem will always be stuck to it. No matter what is done to solve the issue, when the root cause is not defined, the problem will appear again. The only solution to make things right is finding where the problem has been initiating from.

The biggest waste a business can make is of time. The businesses do it so often that they don't even regard it as a waste. They take it for granted.

Every material waste can be salvaged but no amount of time can ever be salvaged once it is gone it can never come back. The truth is Lean Six Sigma can help a business put the time to efficient use, so understanding the methodology is a smart choice for any business. The outcomes will be rewarding for any business making a business reach its maximum output with minimum wastage.

Our Business is not that big

The most common voice raise against Six Sigma by Mid and Small-sized businesses is that they consider that their organization is not a large corporation to implement Six Sigma. The solution here is that Six Sigma won't be applied in a day and show the results immediately. Following its principles will show benefits sooner and an improve infrastructure will come forward. Six Sigma will make it easier to understand customers' needs and work according to it.

Once the key wastages are identified in any business it becomes easy to use them in the DMAIC framework. Time management gets easier to handle tasks that were taking longer periods of time. It is to understand that Six Sigma methodologies are there to improve the overall processing of the company by utilizing every material and reducing waste. The size of the organization doesn't matter at all as it benefits all.

We aren't manufacturing anything

While the Six Sigma methodology was born in the manufacturing industry it has left a greater impact on services and transactions environment also. Many people think that its parent organization is a manufacturing company thus it can produce the results only in the manufacturing environment. This is a total misconception as the Lean Six Sigma methodologies can equally be used in the companies that offer services only.

The services industries need it more than anything as their product is intangible and the work done is in a repetitive process in a large volume. Delivering, invoicing, order processing, employee onboarding, accounts payable, all of this can become smooth to handle with the help of Six Sigma methodology.

We used Six Sigma in the past but the results weren't good enough

Defining success here is really important and finding the reasons for Six Sigma failure are more important.

- Were the processes tracked and shared properly?
- Was the communication between managers up to date?
- Were the employees were trained to use the tools?
- Were the leaders committed to the program?
- Was the program internally driven?
- Was it in the context of people or technology?

- Were the employees aware that you were launching such a program?
- Were the goals realistically set?
- How the projects were chosen?
- Were the projects managed carefully?

Before raising the question against Six Sigma, evaluating the reasons for adopting Six Sigma are more important. Six Sigma methodology will work efficiently according to the efforts of the people implementing it. It is a commitment amongst all the levels of a corporation including front line supervisors. Six Sigma is a culture that is adopted gradually by the whole organization. It is not something that should be the duty of one sector only. Failure to accept the change could be one reason of malfunctioning.

We find Lean more appropriate for our business than Six Sigma

Six Sigma and Lean production complement each other running side by side along with other concepts. Where lean simplifies business by eliminating waste and getting more from less, Six Sigma refines the process making it near perfect. The Lean can be stated as an efficient method, the Six Sigma can be stated as an effective method. Combining effectiveness and efficiency a company can get great results. With the use of Lean production only you are sacrificing the perfect quality while adopting Six Sigma only you reduce the chance of efficiency. Hence, both concepts run side to side complementing one another.

Chapter 49. Criticality of the Lean Six Sigma Method

Many people in the business world have been talking about Six Sigma and how great it has been for them. Many of the organizations who choose to implement this method have found that it can improve their processes, services, and products. Having the ability to reduce their defects has helped these companies to increase their profitability, customer satisfaction, and productivity.

However, there are going to be some obstacles that can show up, and these will often stand in the way of being able to implement Six Sigma properly. You need to make sure that you recognize some of these hurdles and that you know how to address them if you want to be able to make Six Sigma work for you. Here are some of the common issues that sometimes come up when you are implementing Six Sigma and how you are able to fix them.

Lack Of Commitment From Leadership

Six Sigma is not a methodology that you can read about once, hand off to the employees, and hope that it goes well. There needs to be a big effort among the whole company to make Six Sigma work, and getting commitment from everyone in management is one of the most important steps.

A true test to see if a company is truly committed to working with Six Sigma is going to come when the management decides which employees it is going to dedicate to the new Six Sigma project. It is always best to go with your top talent on a Six Sigma project, rather than just picking out whoever is available.

If you just choose to use some random people in the business who are available but do not have the right training, then you are already starting the project off on the wrong foot. Moreover, this can reduce how likely it is that the project will be a success. A successful Six Sigma project is going to require leaders who have the dedications to provide money, talent, time, and resources to this new endeavor.

You will find that taking your top performers and reassigning them from their current work so that they can work with the Six Sigma project is going to be the best bet. Sure, you may have to make some short-term sacrifices to make it work. However, in the end, you will end up getting the most benefits out of Six Sigma, which can greatly improve your business, when you choose to do this.

Not Understanding How Six Sigma Works

It is hard to get a methodology to work well if you do not have a complete understanding of how it works. Some organizations try to do it simply because they think they should. Some do it because they see that someone else was successful, and they want to be successful too. Others just rush into the project because they are so excited, but they do not have a firm grasp on what it requires to implement Six Sigma successfully.

The first thing to understand is that you should never implement the Six Sigma methodology just to keep up with the competition. You should also not waste your time on it if your only reason is to impress the shareholders. If you are only planning on using Six Sigma as a cosmetic change, or you implement it without giving it all the resources that it needs, then you are just inviting failure into the project from the start.

The best way to overcome this kind of obstacle is to commit to the process fully from the beginning. You can make sure that you employ and support the Six Sigma experts on your team to ensure that the new process starts working, rather than just bringing it on to use the terminology.

These experts, who may work for the company or not, are there to keep the project focused on the areas where they can make the biggest difference. Do not waste your time or the time of your team by using Six Sigma to help with simple changes that will not make that much of a difference. Six Sigma can do some amazing things for your business, but you have to be willing to take on the big tasks, the ones that really need to be changed, rather than the smaller options.

Poor Execution

Even if you have some expert guidance to help with this process, there are times when the project is not going to go well because it was not executed properly. This poor execution will happen when the improvements are not aligning with the goals of the organization. It can be an issue when the project is reactively solving problems, rather than meeting strategic objectives. Alternatively, it can be when the quality improvement project focuses too much on the outputs of the project rather than focusing on the inputs.

When companies that use Six Sigma are able to understand that these methodologies are not there to act inside a vacuum but are there to work while aligning to the objectives and goals of the organization, they will find that it is easier to stay on target.

If you are working on Six Sigma and find that you are not getting the gains in productivity that you were hoping for or the savings financially, then it may be time to look for a reason. The reason is not going to be that the methodology of Six Sigma is ineffective. Instead, it is going to most likely come from a lack of effective leadership and the fact that the project was not managed in the way that it should've been.

When the leadership learns how to be committed and completely on board with the methodology of Six Sigma, they work to assign the top talent to their teams. They put the project through all the right steps, including the formal selection and the review process, and it provides the required resources to all people in the process. The odds of seeing success with Six Sigma are then going to increase quite a bit.

If Six Sigma is used in the proper manner, you are going to see some amazing results. You will be able to cut out wastes, help your customers out better, and make more profits in the long term. However, there are times when a business will take considerable resources to work on Six Sigma, and they will not see the results they had hoped for. Making sure that these top issues are not a part of our project can increase your chances of seeing success.

Chapter 50. Why Companies Are Not Taking Advantage of Lean Six Sigma

Do you recall the mention that Lean Six Sigma helps companies reduce expenses and thus end up with increased revenues? Well, Praveen Gupta, a consultant who is also an author and who has had occasion to teach matters of business at Illinois Institute of Technology, says that no other methodology of management comes close to creating great savings for an organization like Six Sigma. He says that the amount of savings companies using Six Sigma are making is in the range of billions of dollars.

Of course, as you have already read here, Six Sigma is a management system whose main focus is on customer satisfaction in terms of the appropriateness of products and services that the customer receives. And you also strive to minimize variations in agreed specifications as well as defects. To achieve this, you must be looking at processes that are consistent, and as such, predictable.

Now, when you bring in the strength of Lean to complete the methodology that is Lean Six Sigma, you are bringing in a management arm that is also centrally targeting the customer – using data to determine objectively how close the organization is to meeting the customer's demand and hence to make necessary process adjustments. Here, you look at functions that you want added to your processes but use data to establish if they are worthwhile or not – how worthwhile being a measure of the customer's willingness to pay for that added bit of work. Likewise for the product or service – you check if it is worthwhile adding a certain feature by the willingness of the customer to pay for the extra expense. However, there are some cases when you will not look at the issue from a compensation point of view. Rather, you look at how much of a competitive edge your additional feature or function is likely to give you.

- Does the change result to shortened delivery times?
- Does it lead to decreased costs that allow for a drop in product price?
- Does the adjustment lead to decreased number of defects?

Just to recap then, when you are weighing whether to take up or not to take up Lean Six Sigma in your organization, you need to be aware of the main benefits at stake:

- Improving the quality of products or services
- Improving the customer experience
- Increasing your bottom line

Those were the principle targets of the pioneers of Lean Six Sigma as exemplified by Henry Ford of Ford Motor Company and Taiichi Ohno of Toyota; and they are the same principle targets that continue to guide this methodology as is evidently clear when you consider the case of General Motors and Volkswagen. In fact, Toyota has been consistently on the list of Fortune 500, and a number of times within the Top 10.

Why, then, are some companies still not applying Lean Six Sigma?

Lack Of Relevant Information

Well, for one, this methodology has not penetrated the general market. It is safe to say that it is still with the pace setters. So the reason some companies who would otherwise make huge strides in growth do not even talk about Lean Six Sigma is sheer lack of knowledge. In fact, apart from coming across the term when trying to Google something, or hearing it from word of mouth, there are few other sources of information on this cutting edge methodology.

Believing Lean Six Sigma To Be A Fad

There are many Doubting Thomases, so to speak, the reason some companies lead while others follow. Some companies that are yet to implement the Lean Six Sigma methodology have heard about it and its advantages. However, often you find CEOs who are close minded and not willing to do anything that seems to challenge the status quo. That is why you find sudden structural overhaul of a company's top management by the board when some forward looking member introduces the idea of change of management style. In short, there are those who dub the relatively new management style a fad simply because of the fear of implementing something new.

Time Management That Is Wanting

Have you ever taken into consideration the fact that time spent, no matter how well or poorly, cannot be salvaged? This, of course, as opposed to an exam failed – you can always do a re-sit. Even a product not well completed – final touches can usually be made later. Anyway, some executives who know about Lean Six Sigma keep it at bay citing lack of adequate time to implement it when really it is a shortcoming in time management.

What such people miss out is the essence of the methodology which is not to become an addition in the organization but rather a modification of the existing methodology; and if necessary, replacement. In any case, if the worry is on the issue of time to train your workforce, there are professionals who are already versed in these matters, as has been indicated before in this book, and they even bear relevant certification. If you hired one of those, they would help you out without the inconvenience of stopping any of your production lines for any significant duration.

The Expenses Involved In Lean Six Sigma Implementation

Do you think you need millions of dollars to begin implementing Lean Six Sigma? No way! In fact, some companies that are not heavily endowed but who happen to appreciate a good thing when they see one have delved into the process of implementing the methodology by giving their key personnel the Yellow Belt training. That is just two days at most. How big, really, is such a cost compared to the doubling and trembling of returns that you are looking at if you implement Lean Six Sigma in full?

Underrating The Size Of The Organization

This business of ours is too small for big methodologies! Do you think you could be too tiny for a fat bank account? If not, how then can you dismiss an improvement tool that does not come as a whole mass but as a combination of implementable principles? If you are small or just medium size but you acknowledge that reducing product defects is worthwhile and you are ready to use reliable data to improve your processes in a way that can be objectively assessed, then you are ready for Lean Six Sigma. In short, you could embrace Lean Six Sigma but implement it in phases. In fact, your most fundamental step no matter the size of your organization is to be able to pinpoint the specific needs of your customer.

Not Being Involved In Manufacturing

Birds fly – fine. Do airplanes fly? Yes, they do as they have what it takes to fly. That is the same case with Lean Six Sigma. Where was it that this methodology was first tried out? In the manufacturing sector – and this was with the likes of Motorola. Does that mean that only the manufacturing sector needs to cut down on losses? And are customers of manufactured products the only ones that need great products? Of course, not! If you want a service, you surely want the best and as per your specifications. And the business enterprise providing the service wants to make as much money as possible by cutting down on costs. In short, there is no business, irrespective of whether it is in the manufacturing sector, the service industry or even trade, that does not wish to be as profitable as it can and to please its customers.

The Massive Statistics And Advanced Math

Have you also misconstrued Lean Six Sigma to be all about big math; statistics and probability? Well, it is not. You can still make a big improvement in the success of your business entity without involving yourself with complex figures. Even a business that deals with customer care and not anything like engineering can do with reduction of waste. It can also do with happier customers. Can you identify obvious duplications and redundancies in your organization without holding a calculator or mathematical table? Yes, you can. Can you identify obvious wastage without doing number related calculations? If it is a yes to both questions, then you surely can apply Lean Six Sigma without having to employ a statistician and still reap higher revenues.

Planning To Embark On Six Sigma Or Lean Methodology First

Do you take the two – Six Sigma and Lean – to be mutually exclusive? Of course, they are not. Both Lean and Six Sigma have the customer's satisfaction as their main focus. So you need not delay your endeavor to transform your enterprise as you try to determine which of the two methodologies is best to begin with. That is the main reason you will be talking of Lean Six Sigma projects and not Lean and thereafter Six Sigma down the line or the other way round.

Having Tried Lean Six Sigma Before And Not Succeeded

Can you identify the reasons you failed? What, exactly, failed you? Was it the technology you used; the people handling the processes; or the processes themselves?

In short, wisdom lies in you learning from your experience even when that experience involves failure. You fail and then you try yet again – not quit because you once tried and did not make it. In fact, you have great role models in instances of turning failure around to become exemplary success. Think of Henry Ford, he of Ford Motors Company, and the number of times he failed before actually succeeding.

Chapter 51. How to Embark on Implementing Lean Six Sigma

Ever heard someone warn that saying the ram is fat is no proposition that it be slaughtered? If you have not, no worries – in any case, that saying is organically African. But here, you would not be exercising prudence if you let a good system go untried. You have seen that Lean Six Sigma cuts operation costs drastically; involves virtually every team member thus making everyone feel valued; makes revenue figures somersault eliciting wide smiles from shareholders; and basically makes everyone happy. Why then would anyone with this valuable information not embark on implementing it? Please say you are not too mesmerized to begin.

Identify A Champion

Champion…? Well, a champion leads, right? And here in Lean Six Sigma you are looking to building a team. You are also looking to soliciting resources. There is also the building of some kind of working structure – call it even your modus operandi (Let them know you know some Latin, why not? Or some legal jargon…). Anyway, all these fundamentals need someone to structure how they are going to happen. And hence the need for this Project Champion.

When To Bring In The Project Champion

The Project Champion is the one to take the project from the ground. So you need him or her like yesterday. In fact, even before you know what shape the Lean Six Sigma project is going to take, it is important that you have this guy. If there is anyone to pull hairs to baldness, it is the project champion – convincing top management that the project is worth the paper it is outlined on; and even laying its groundwork. In fact, do not lose sight of the grim reality that some organizations still have those old guards – wise alright – but still with the 18th century thinking. And without their signatures on the check you are not going to get any funds.

The Basic Role Of The Project Champion

Coming up with the project

You know if you come up with a project that gets stakeholders wondering if your organization has been bought out you will be digging your own grave. So the project champion needs to be able to come up with a project that is relevant to the operations of the organization. A project that draws attention to the organization's increased efficiency rather than superficial changes is what you want.

Gauging your project against your organization's strategic objectives

After all the good work of sourcing materials and engaging everyone in cost cutting is done, you need to emerge from the same end of the tunnel that the organization envisaged long before your project came to being. If, for instance, the organization looks forward to serving the region in 5yrs, you need to have that in the picture even as you improve efficiency. In short, you could be termed unsuccessful if you attained 98% efficiency but ended up serving only your country by that time.

Liaise with the very top

For every penny that gets out of the organization's bank account, the top leadership must give their blessings. That goes for other major decisions like altering employees' working schedules and so on. That is mainly why you need to have a project manager who does not freeze in the presence of the big guys and who also does not have a tendency to grow horns when given important responsibilities.

Pinpoint key project personnel

The Project Lead

Project Finance Certifier

I hope that tells you outright that the Project Champion is not the guy for the dirty work. Challenging, yes – bumping onto each other with regular team members on a day-to-day basis, no. And even the sensitive role of saying the team is justified to request this and to spend that the Champion delegates to someone else.

This underlines the importance of the Champion's role; being able to observe the overall picture of the Six Sigma project. For this reason, it is presumed that the Champion is capable and willing to appoint the two main officers for their competence and competence alone. Obviously, anything with the semblance of biases or prejudices being a factor would be jeopardizing the success of the project.

Analyzing Project Performance

Of course, you must remember reading that the project is assessed periodically. Now the person to give the project the green light to proceed to the next stage is the Project Champion. If, for any reason, he feels dissatisfied with your product at that stage, then the relevant parts would have to be redone. And if it is to do with provision of a service, even that would be reviewed and if farmhands have to be replaced, then that would happen.

Whereas the Project Champion may come across as the boss with both hands in the pocket, his is not such an easy job. To be a Project Champion comes with great responsibility because at the end of the project, the buck stops with him or her. However, seeing a Lean Six Sigma project to its successful completion is an additional feather to the Champion's hat; a real boost to the Champions resume.

Who Qualifies For The Position Of Six Sigma Project Champion?

Me! Me! Oh, no. This position is not filled in a haphazard manner. Just like the Champion is expected to be diligent when appointing a Finance Certifier, so is anyone in top management when it comes to supporting someone for the role of Project Champion. This is not one of those offices where you sit and rock the chair all day long waiting to append your signature onto something that nobody will ever inquire about. So, here are the criteria:

Be part of senior management

Do you know the reason?

It is unlikely that you left college and found yourself in a senior management position. So, naturally, you have gone through muck to get to where you are. You have, for example, witnessed firsthand the reality of employees being all smiles today and tomorrow they have placards with your name on it – and in negative light, for that matter. Having survived such challenges, you now know how to run a team.

Your time climbing up the ladder has given you great experience that is necessary for such changes that would be seen to be radical.

Being one with the top management puts you in good stead when it comes to lobbying for resources.

Having held a similar position before

Obviously, if you can truly say, been there and done that, you are very well placed. You know what challenges to anticipate, which means you can put measures in place to cushion your project and your team; you have an idea how resources become necessary along the way as incidental costs and hence you can provide for them; you are aware how tight employees schedules can become a handicap and so you can psyche the top management to expect requests for flexible working hours; and so on.

A bonus if you have been a Project Lead before

You see theory and practical are two different realities. Please... Isn't that really obvious? Maybe; but in some areas, once you know the theory the practical part is a smooth ride. But there are positions like this one of Project Lead that you may not exactly understand until you enter those shoes.

At times you may find yourself dealing with clients who like giving verbal specifications and you are not worried because you scribble down as they speak. But then the danger is that they have no qualms denying those specifications when the product is finally complete. And they make you look bad. Not to mention you have to face the reality of the organization losing resources on your watch. How can you empathize with your Project Lead unless you have been in such a situation yourself? How would you bring yourself to tone down criticism on your Project Lead when team members fail to attend meetings having been derailed by their department heads?

Yet for there to be a healthy working atmosphere, empathy and support are necessary amongst team members; between the Project Champion and the team; between the Lead and team members; between the team and the client; and even between the Project Champion and his appointed assistants – the Project Lead and the Finance Certifier. In fact, it can be very frustrating, for example, for the Project Champion to trash particular demands for funds just because of the timing, without understanding that it is very difficult to anticipate all expenses.

Be aware of the tools to measure quality

How else would one tell if the quality has been met unless with clear knowledge of the relevant tools of assessment?

Be alive to the strategic goals of your organization

Why is this, yet the Project Champion is not becoming the CEO's equal? Well, he or she is not getting any more senior than he or she already is, but then it would hurt the organization to have the Champion working towards divergent goals. Remember that everything happening under the organization should be geared towards achieving the ultimate goals of the organization.

In fact, it is in this light that the Champion will identify the Lean Sigma Project to undertake. The strategic goals will determine too how the Champion lays down the resource allocation structure.

Chapter 52. Why Use Lean Six Sigma Systems For Your Small Business?

The Lean Six Sigma revolution is systematically carrying more non-manufacturing businesses in small and medium-sized organizations. IT, telecommunications, banking, promotion, insurance, health, and construction organizations have looked into the advanced lean six sigma approaches to boost their own quality and standards in handling their clients, providers, and customers. A slender six sigma system enriches every location of your business with just one, only system. It eliminates and reduces value-added activities and waste in your enterprise. In general, it provides you with a competitive advantage by lowering operating expenses and improving productivity.

It defines a job route for many individuals, diminishing wasted labor and emphasizing specific elements of this project. It gives tools to enhance worker efficiency and boost their efficacy, quality of output signal, confidence and motivate them into enhancing performance degrees. It generates process improvements through the duration of the job flow procedure. You learn how to classify many items and expel the people not linked to the procedure. This permits you to concentrate on what ought to be executed on an everyday basis. On top of that, it elevates the career of one's business in the market. It's merely good sense. Why waste substances? Why spend time searching for funds? Why waste space saving surplus stock? Get outcomes. Employ lean-to your factory or administrative procedures.

Or create it an above-mentioned option and expand it into a supplier and sub-contractors.

The tiniest lean execution might impact your own workflow as well as your bottom-line. You want to compete. Your organization has gone going there at a worldwide market that's less money to pay off. Why should anybody choose your service or product? As you've made sure that your products or services are your very best. Lean six sigma may help reduce waste, in addition to expel the sources resulting in waste. It highlights a successive operating system which focuses solely on those degrees demanded and just once they're required. This method was developed particularly for small to midsize organizations that are attempting to boost their endurance throughout the operation. Expert advisers in thin six sigma can jumpstart your own business progress. Or you could possibly get training online or at live training classes.

Be mindful that there are a few gaps between the original six-sigma machine and the lean six sigma system: Generation I is targeted on defects, Generation III centers around value. Generation I puts focus on the provider, while Generation III puts concentration to the customer and the provider. Generation I experts are called Black Belts, Generation III pros are White Belts. They make results quicker because of thinner focus and also a thorough schedule. Rather than earning its principal attention on the decrease in prices, and Generation III is targeted on the invention of value. This really is a huge advancement in plan, specially for its small and medium-sized organizations.

The objective would be always to get a business provide services and goods of optimum price, at the ideal location, punctually, while in the ideal amount, and at the best possible price. This also boosts the view of consumers, analysts, investors and workers equally. Everyone else is on board working toward aims everyone plays a role in achieving! The actual beauty of thin six sigma is you may tailor the procedures to fit your company as they aren't adjusted methodologies which need to get utilized in a given purchase. Today, employers, irrespective of their size, will benefit from the advantages and potential offered by the lean six sigma procedure.

Challenges And Problem Of Lean Six Sigma Improvement Teams

Organizations which cannot supply because of consideration for the particular aspect, frequently don't exploit the entire potential of little implementations and thus begin whining that 'Lean Six Sigma doesn't work'. They don't appreciate that the issue isn't with little theories; their failures are the result of the inherent inability of their execution team to overcome the usual difficulties and challenges.

Pinpointing Implementation Issues and Challenges

For making sure the achievement of Lean Projects, the execution team should try to recognize the common difficulties and challenges that it may encounter throughout the execution period. For that, the team should use time tested Sigma tools and processes such as 'Procedure Records' that highlight every single event, functionality, and also sub-processes of this provided process selected for advancement.

But as it's not achievable to start looking into each and all aspects of this given business method, the team needs to concentrate on just those aspects which can be critical to the most important procedure. In consequence, the team needs to pay attention to pinpointing potential issues in mere people sub-processes which may be donating significantly more than 50 to 60 per cent to the delivery of the last outcome. That is essential because when issues occur in significant sub-processes throughout the execution period, the small business will lose its productive efficacy, something which is likely to produce a mockery of 'Lean' goals and targets which involve improved efficiencies that are sustainable.

For greater results, they ought to search Input from individuals like floor managers, managers, process managers, along with many others that may possibly be needing viable understanding in regards to the provided business procedure. When required, top and middle management may be asked to supply their valuable inputs and suggestions.

Overcoming Challenges

The project is stated to be 'half done' because soon while the difficulties have been identified, however, the execution team must not lose its attention at this point since it has to complete the rest of the half, i.e. beating the recognized challenges and problems. That is the toughest part, as not even the very experienced professionals like Black Belts will guarantee the achievement of initiatives required for beating execution issues and challenges.

The very best that the execution group certainly can do afterward would be to use Seven Sigma simulation software, that could create predictions that are very accurate. Simulations enable a whole lot since they have the ability for that team to make use of the 'hit and trial' system without fretting about real reductions, physical or monetary. Employing the 'hit and trial' procedure, they can then readily choose an initiative which most suits the requirement of beating implementation issues and challenges.

Besides placing their faith in Six Sigma tools and methods for overcoming challenges and problems, they ought to attempt to boost innovation and creativity as some times merely these skills may save a job from certain failure. Constant motivation, guidance, and comprehension are all good methods of promoting innovation and creativity on the list of Lean Six Sigma implementation team associates.

Keep Costs In Check With Six Sigma

While Six Sigma can maximize various other procedures as a way to squeeze more from these, a lean manufacturing procedure can pay attention to reducing the expenses specifically related to transporting and manufacturing, from raw material into finished product.

Here are some ways by which Six Sigma Contributes to lessen costs.

Implementing the Principles of Six Sigma

As Six Sigma is mainly geared toward Increasing the return on investment [ROI] and absolute client care; activities from Master Black Belts or Black Belts in specific areas could lead to cost-saving measures like process inventions and product upgrades.

This is done so as to catch a larger market combined side high degrees of consumer care. By executing Six Sigma, Black Belts could pull on a bigger yield from assorted endeavors by making certain every one of the tools are useful to the fullest.

Six Sigma may additionally identify different risk factors which empower businesses to produce counter-plans on how best to market them. It can offer necessary data to find out if certain projects will need to be left in favor of the others that may possess more potential.

Using Six Sigma in Numerous Procedures

After you employ Six Sigma to different procedures, like stabilizing manufacturing procedure and moving towards zero rejection, you can perform enormous savings as your cost of production has been paid off radically.

By paying heed to a clients' complaints concerning the accessibility and level of one's services and products, you're able to make certain you maintain your work and production centers at probably the most perfect levels.

Get Lean and Mean

From the production process, Lean Six Sigma may lead to lower transportation prices, faster processing of orders and material and preserving ideal stock amounts, averting over- or-under-processing of products and orders.

By making sure that workers are Producing at optimal levels, waste might be curtailed, which translates into reducing costs and high economies. By employing minimum resources like raw material, machines and labor - and - from getting the full process right first time round - associations may get minimal wastage of resources that are available.

While price cutting the substance Side is very predictable, finetuning the wave lengths of a high quantity of employees to execute cohesively is quite troublesome - which really is where adapting and embracing six-sigma can create effective outcomes.

Generally, employing a mix of Six Sigma and lean production procedures which are always monitored by Master Dark connectors could lead to substantial cost cutting edge and coast up the main point of their company, hence helping to survive and flourish in the face of demanding competition.

It'll take some time and Decision to make certain that all method merges effortlessly into a while decreasing wastage at precisely the exact same period - however, that the upshot of such efforts might be extremely rewarding.

Rightsizing Lean Six Sigma Teams

It's quite true that brains mean more processing power, the concept doesn't find prefer when choosing team size as what exactly is even more essential is communicating - a thing which becomes a massive problem when significantly more than the requisite amount of employees is invisible to the Lean Six Sigma implementation crew.

Therefore, rightsizing Lean Six Sigma Teams ought to really be the initial priority for most organizations that are looking sure to the victory of 'Lean' endeavors and realize the entire potential of such endeavors.

How Does a Small Business Make Means for Rightsizing?

Within their attempts to decrease the group size, most organizations frequently make the error of inducting 'top-rated' workers, so believing they will compensate for the size of their 'Lean' implementation crew. Organizations don't appreciate that a lot of 'top-rated' employees are respective actors and they could possibly not have the capacity to present their utmost when asked to behave like a team. In addition, since celebrities generally have enormous egos which could result in conflicts and maybe not cooperation, it seems sensible to not include them at the 'Lean' team.

The group size may vary depending on the complexity and vastness of this 'Lean' job, however, for an ordinary job, organizations should start looking for a group of three to four associates. When choosing associates, direction should start looking for employees who could have worked for no less than five to ten decades and demonstrated consistent operation through recent years.

Since keeping appropriate communications is among the major responsibility of 'Lean' execution teams, the direction must gauge the communication and social skills of possible applicants prior to inducting them at the team. Ability to consider this package, solve issues, view things in the ideal view, and also motivate the others are a few of the additional qualities which the direction should keep an eye out for when selecting 'Lean' execution team.

Great Things about Rightsizing Lean-six Sigma Teams

The real advantages of rightsizing might differ based on the sort of 'Lean' job and also the sort of company, however, a few basic benefits which each company could aspire to derive from rightsizing comprise the next.

Increased communications amongst implementers, direction officials and other things connected with all the 'Lean' task

Better liability on a part of the team members because actions and decisions taken by the group could be tracked right back to members

Reduced cost of operations since lower the amounts, the less are the number of tools employed for doing the exact jobs and responsibilities

Higher efficacy in solving complicated problems and problems since workers would know the Precise individual to contact should they experience difficulties throughout the execution stage

Less likelihood of self and conflicts issues because the size will stop the creation of subgroups within the crew

These advantages are sufficient to prove the significance of rightsizing and rightsizing is your thing to do for associations seeking to eventually become 'Lean' and then enhance their efficiency and endurance.

Chapter 53. The Six Sigma Infrastructure

One other Significant change initiative needs an obviously defined encouraging infrastructure to induce the application. Coding means the inherent base and basic frame of supporting and personnel systems necessary to guide Six Sigma installation tasks. Because every component of a provider engages in Six Sigma tasks, the infrastructure has to be clean, consistent, and comprehensive.

A successful infrastructure eases the maturation of the core competency that'll establish and connect Six Sigma project teams into (1) projects, (2) financial goals, and also (3) the tactical plan. These project teams will probably be multi-functional and certainly will be needing multi-functional aid to perform the projects. If six-sigma has any potential for achieving success, the infrastructure may interval from the CEO and his leadership team to both industry leaders and also to those executing the projects. Remember we heard early in the day that you of Kotter's eight stages of pioneer shift is "Produce a Guiding Coalition." Thus, there's the objective of the Six Sigma infrastructure.

The infrastructure makes a solid network on the list of the executive team, the Six Sigma Champions, the Belts, and also the serves and companies. This is logical since the CEO's leadership team holds the responsibility for executing the organization's strategic plan, and Six Sigma projects are instrumental in proceeding together with the tactical plan.

One learning obstacle of a Six Sigma Deployment entails training the Six Sigma project teams. The individual resources on such teams must discover what is a Six Sigma team. A fresh road map and also a brand new group of tools, and an even more different focus on job liability, enhance the fluctuations faced with a business when designing a Six Sigma environment.

Equally more significant and complicated is the learning barrier of these senior executives. Teaching the direction team to master to direct a home-based organization is imperative to tactical and long-term success. Because the execution of this plan is a very clear responsibility to the senior executives that are more liable, it follows becoming a lively team leader over the Six Sigma installation which will encourage the tactical efforts.

Implementing a fantastic strategic plan involves the manipulation of multi-functional internal pursuits. Mature executives must figure out how to take care of a multi-functional stadium as opposed to the conventional functions. A huge selection of Six Sigma teams started simultaneously could be that the results of an exceptional installation of Six Sigma. All those teams want at minimal

- Clear purpose for your Six Sigma team structure.
- Clear six-sigma app expectations.
- Six Sigma job charters.
- Six Sigma infrastructure monitoring the Number of clubs.
- Centralized repository for job results.
- Six Sigma team objectives.
- Six Sigma team monitoring mechanism.

- Recognition and reward orientation.
- Six Sigma development and training plan.
- Six Sigma team operation measures.
- Deployment management of Six Sigma teams.

To achieve all the previous requirements requires a thorough infrastructure together with encouraging systems. Preexisting tools are largely utilized to staff of that particular infrastructure. Deploying a Six Sigma application, but will not assume that a requirement to put in outside resources at lots of fresh places. The extra costs will normally need related to the outside consulting group you hire.

By way of example, the sole real resource that Larry Bossidy inserted when he started Six Sigma to Allied Signal had been a corporate application pioneer. Larry Earned Richard Schroeder out of ABB to push the app. The rest of the tools for AlliedSignal's Six Sigma program existed within the provider. Even a few additional tools were inserted with the organizations as needed. Because liability reflects the sign of successful Six Sigma deployments, specifying the Six Sigma staffing and infrastructure and training that the infrastructure players should come about early at the Six Sigma setup. Training is vital as you need to "understand the courage of this initiative" In addition, he adds that key members of the leadership staff should know the courage of this initiative. Historical leadership training is a standard area of Six Sigma deployments to permit the app leaders to know that the courage of six-sigma until the app becomes too far over.

Assessing the Six Sigma infrastructure is just somewhat catchy. There ought to be a tiny centralized unit to guarantee consistency and cost-efficacy of Six Sigma tasks round the functions and businesses. There should likewise become a decentralized procedure which makes it possible for each small business and be capable of tailoring the Six Sigma installation for its special wants. There's a difference in deploying Six Sigma into the hour work when comparing to deploying product development and R&D. Thus, our advocated infrastructure includes both centralized and decentralized elements in it.

Initialization and Developing an Infrastructure with Lean Six Sigma

Infrastructure preparation could be learned in a Six Sigma training curriculum in less than a day or two having some work help with. You are going to discover to process launches of endeavors, maintain and assess the accomplishment of performance improvement programs, and initialize or supply the outcome of their company vision to some solid action program. Once you walk off from a slender Six Sigma class you may truly have a good base of how you can work a whole operation improvement program and you'll have the ability to reach Six Sigma results.

When someone goes throughout the Initialization and development part of the Lean Six Sigma app, they are going to discover to roll out and convey the particulars of a job's installation to every one of the personnel. You are going to discover just how to successfully gather a realistic deadline

428

for the whole job, for example training and proceed live customs. You may see about the significance of a Six Sigma green belt, yellow belt, black belt, and also other degrees of Six Sigma expertise.

All instruction inquiries will probably be replied here because this really is actually the initialization and installation period. After you undergo Six Sigma training, then you are going to have the ability to answer questions regarding how training will happen. It's crucial that you be aware of the form of training that'll function as the most reliable for staff. Can be an off-site classroom that is the ideal option or even on the web may be your very best means for your own category to master.

Prioritizing tasks for your organization is just another component of lean Six Sigma you are going to see. It's vital in order to recognize projects which may forge the business into a success, maybe not bogged down a wealth of productive employees while hardly making a profit. Once you finish a Six Sigma black belt certificate, you're going to learn precisely how to spot and find the worthy projects which are going to soon be successful for that provider.

The Lean Six Sigma app or the Six Sigma classes are intended to assist you to know about initialization and installation for a personal infrastructure. Become familiar with about building an infrastructure in the vertical building, deploying an eyesight during a business, discovering successful jobs and training, plus even more.

Six-sigma As A method to Develop People

Some of the numerous benefits of Six Sigma is the way that it will help to build people. This cultivate excellence in not only product quality and also benefits but also from the data, confidence, and caliber of the men and women in your own organization. Individuals are, after all, your businesses' most valuable assets. To preserve and always improve, a business should develop its own people. Six Sigma helps develop your visitors in 2 different areas: it grows leaders plus it enables people to become more knowledgeable and valuable contributors to this company's success. Every company needs people with leadership qualities. Leadership skills are necessary at each level of the company. Ongoing Six Sigma training and execution from the executive degree online supervisors can help grow leadership in your own organization. With Six Sigma, you can find various chances to build leadership abilities and leadership qualities at all levels from the company. Six Sigma certificate training and also the hands-on real-world training of leading Six Sigma projects cultivate direction abilities.

Six-sigma attempts to mature leaders at a company through its training programs. Individuals who've completed Six Sigma practice develop a Belt name. It denotes their amount of wisdom and responsibility. A greenbelt is someone that has completed fourteen days of training over the Six Sigma road map and fundamental elements of statistical methods encouraging Six Sigma projects and who's part of a Six Sigma process improvement crew. A Black Belt is someone that has completed four weeks of practice concentrating in the Six Sigma road map and extensive statistical methods and also can be experienced at directing cross-functional process improvement teams. Black tutors become pioneers of Six Sigma project teams plus they mentor other employees to help them grow. Six-sigma values direction, however in addition, it protects participation in employees at all levels of this company. In case everyone could possibly access the origin of an issue and help solve that, then it isn't important where the concept comes out of. Six Sigma needs to own absolute commitment and support from all levels of this company. Six Sigma requires purchase from everybody involved with the commercial procedures which can be quantified. This condition actually will help develop a better company.

Involvement from all degrees of employees comes around by the Six Sigma plan of construction project types. Continuous improvement procedures, such as Six Sigma, means, for example, people, gaining their participation, after which encouraging what they have been attempting to achieve. Six-sigma requests input improvement solutions from all employees since it acknowledges that the worth of creative methods to issues in all sources. The easy reality is that workers know some matters the higherups do not. Frontline employees know the customer better than anybody. Businesses that solicit thoughts from line workers can discover innovative methods to conditions which may never be discovered by detached investigation. Involving people through six-sigma additionally results in enabling people. Six-sigma's data-driven methodology supplies people appropriate feedback regarding the procedure and quantities of advancement that they have been achieving- exactly what they did well and exactly what they needed poorly. Throughout Six Sigma, the folks receive real methods to get rid of the actual root causes of issues. Plus, it provides the comprehension of the data, where, and whys as the info is not there. So, Six Sigma helps develop the awareness, confidence, and caliber of individuals in your own organization.

Further, the Six Sigma helps encourage a civilization of confidence that everybody else's energies will be led to favorable and constructive work. This kind of civilization contains including people, providing them with the tools that they will need to ensure success, a proper amount of control and influence, and being offered together. As confidence builds, people begin to receive are more involved, become committed, accept greater empowerment, and more profound levels of confidence grow. Teamwork, coordination of tasks and also hoping that one of the teams get the method to attempt of Sigma successful.

The end result of doing so well is Professional growth, improved morale and favorable attitudes toward combined efforts. Six Sigma will turn into one of those facets which perhaps not merely fuels stunning excellent advancement on your employees but also creates a workplace that is exceptional.

How To Use Lean Six Sigma In Your Business

Businesses competing at a complicated international market place face enormous pressure to keep up functional excellence. Applying Lean Six Sigma, the standard control technique utilized to decrease waste, eliminate product defects and enhance client care, involves focusing on customer desires and in-depth data analysis to be able to meet that challenge. Shifting your own company to work with better procedures is dependent upon executive livelihood and trained employees. Employ Lean Six Sigma methods not simply on your manufacturing processes but also your ceremony and also other business purposes.

- Teach your employees on Lean Six Sigma Theories in order that most employees can notice that Six Sigma methods improve customer care levels by reducing flaws to no further than 3.4 per thousand. Lean manufacturing methods reduce ineffective actions as a way to boost product progress. Together, they allow you to conduct a far more efficient and profitable company. The Motorola internet site offers complimentary courses on six-sigma topics. The American Society for Quality offers a certificate to qualified applicants because of a blackbelt, an average of accountable for job management or greenbelt, frequently accountable for team donations.
- Identify procedures requiring improvement Predicated on non-performing usable metrics. By way of instance, if customer satisfaction levels for a specific product always fall, inspect the support logs to isolate

the issue, for example as raw material employed in fabricating or even a defect at the original layout. Conduct focus groups or interviews with clients, production specialists along with also other employees to collect information.

- Utilize resources, like a Fish-bone Diagram, to demonstrate the reason and effect of all people, techniques, equipment, substances, data and also the surroundings on the creation of one's service or product. To earn a fishbone diagram, then draw an arrow from the left on the best in the middle of a webpage. On left end, draw lines above and below the point, such as fish scales, also list the complexities. On the best, clarify the issue or effect. Add extra lines to list sub-causes. Use this advice to work out just how to successfully cover the issues.

- Concentrate on reducing prices by optimizing your own processes. Get a grip on process inputs and that means that you may expel flaws. Monitor and track your own progress achieving those aims. By way of instance, to apply Lean Six Sigma processes to human resources activities, correct your procedures to decrease the time that it will take to recruit, and orient a new employee by standardizing your procedures and training employees effortlessly. Employ Lean Sigma for a fund company through the elimination of unnecessary approval workflows, reducing the time that it requires to accomplish trades, like paying vendors or calculating your own payroll.

- Give attention to reducing mistakes by Streamlining and simplifying the procedures of completing work. By way of instance, centralize your database surgeries to ensure if your earning team goes in order, strains pre-populate with existing customer info, available inventory and also the purchaser's credit line. Catch awareness for debugging client service calls into a database accessible with service employees therefore that your service teams can lower the time that it requires to fix customer issues.
- Inspect and audit procedures frequently, for example, in a yearly basis to keep a high amount of quality on your own systems.

Conclusions

Now that you understand what the Lean Six Sigma method of management is, you can start living it every day. Start with implementing the various aspects of waste reduction. As you get all the respective aspects of process improvement working, you will see a definite change for the better on the overall performance of your organization. Wastage will be a thing of the past; or it will, at least, be reduced to negligible levels. And since waste constitutes a big part that eats into revenues, your bottom line will automatically shoot to impressive levels.

There is also the aspect of problem solving that you have learnt in the form of DMAIC. As you embark on practicing those systematic steps of problem solving, your processes will be improving and your revenues will be increasing as a consequence. That will show you that, evidently, cutting waste and solving problems in the way prescribed by the Lean Six Sigma approach gives fast and progressive results. And you will also see the benefit of having more of your people trained in matters relevant to Lean Six Sigma.

The next step is to go back over the book as needed. At the same time, observe the systems existing in your organization and see where they require modifying. Once you take those initial baby steps leading to more efficient processes, you can easily change your employees' old mindset and help them adopt a new one where they feel in-charge and accountable for their actions. That, in turn, means that they will revel at the success of the organization. What this effectively does is give you a motivated workforce that is eager to save costs for the organization while doing everything to make the organization succeed and beat competitors.

With this powerful knowledge, the ball is now in your court. Work towards helping your organization reach its potential and do not hesitate to congratulate yourself for a job well done when you are finally the leading light in your industry!

CPSIA information can be obtained
at www.ICGtesting.com
Printed in the USA
LVHW011938050121
675671LV00007B/389